Rascuache Lawyer

Rascuache Lawyer

Toward a Theory of Ordinary Litigation

Alfredo Mirandé

The University of Arizona Press
Tucson

The University of Arizona Press
© 2011 The Arizona Board of Regents
All rights reserved

www.uapress.arizona.edu

Library of Congress Cataloging-in-Publication Data
Mirandé, Alfredo.
Rascuache lawyer : toward a theory of ordinary litigation / Alfredo Mirandé.
    p. cm.
Includes bibliographical references and index.
ISBN 978-0-8165-2983-4 (pbk. : alk. paper)
1. Mirandé, Alfredo. 2. Cause lawyers—California—Biography.
3. Sociology teachers—California—Biography. 4. Hispanic Americans—
Legal status, laws, etc.—California. 5. Legal assistance to the poor—
California. 6. Critical legal studies—United States. 7. Race discrimination—
Law and legislation—United States. I. Title.
KF373.M534A3 2011
340.092–dc22 [B] 2011007961

Manufactured in the United States of America on
acid-free, archival-quality paper and processed chlorine free.

16 15 14 13 12 11   6 5 4 3 2 1

Contents

Acknowledgments   vii

Introduction: The Return of the Brown Buffalo and the Rise of the Rascuache Lawyer   1

Crimes against the Person

1. Attempted Murder: "My Brother's Keeper"   21
2. Child Abuse: María y José   54
3. Domestic Violence: Xavier, the Painter   73

Denial of Due Process

4. Concealed Weapon: Carlito's Güey (Way)   91
5. Trespassing: Benny, the Homeless Man   104
6. Speedy Trial: Rodrigo Torres   125

Morals Charges

7. Indecent Exposure: The Story of Bud Black   143
8. DUI: A Bag Full of Tricks   165

Wrongful Termination

9. Age Discrimination: Big John   207
10. Toward a Theory of Rascuache Lawyering   228

Notes   243

Index   255

⁖ ⁖ ⁖
Acknowledgments

Many people have contributed directly or indirectly to the completion of this book. I would like to first thank the students in the Lawyering for Social Change (LSC) curriculum at Stanford Law School and Gerald P. López, who taught me much about rebellious lawyering and has served as a colleague, mentor, and friend. I took a directed-readings course on critical race theory (CRT) from Professor Thomas C. Grey during my second year of law school, and he guided me through the readings, introducing me to the writings of Richard Delgado and *The Rodrigo Chronicles*. Professor Kim Taylor taught a valuable criminal law trial practice class, while Gerald López and Shauna Marshall provided input and direction in the community law trial practice class. Bill Hing and Eric Cohen served as important teachers and mentors in the immigration law clinic where I represented my very first client in a political asylum case.

David López, a former student of mine and now a successful attorney, not only was a friend and confidant but assumed the role of informal mentor and taught me a great deal about lawyering and law practice. Walter Martínez and Enrique López, also former students, supported me in various tasks associated with the practice. The Academic Senate of the University of California, Riverside, gave me seed money that supported my writing and research. Janice Searle and other staff at the Riverside County Law Library were extremely helpful and assisted me in conducting legal research that supported my practice. I would like to thank the three anonymous reviewers who commented and made valuable recommendations for revising the book.

My daughter, Lucía, read and made helpful suggestions on earlier versions of the manuscript for this book and encouraged me to complete it. Ingrid Carolina Parra served as my research assistant and provided valuable support by reading and commenting on the entire manuscript and assisting in the organization and formatting of the book. I would also like to thank all of my clients who trusted me, let me into their lives, and provided the stories that made this book possible. The names, locations, backgrounds, and all identifying information for the people in this book have been changed to protect their privacy and maintain their anonymity. A final thanks goes out to Fermina, my fictional friend, who always challenged me, pointed out my mistakes, and inspired me to become a better lawyer and person.

Rascuache Lawyer

⁂ ⁂ ⁂

Introduction

*The Return of the Brown Buffalo and the
Rise of the Rascuache Lawyer*

Since its inception in the 1980s, critical race theory (CRT) has challenged the basic assumptions underlying traditional legal scholarship and law practice.[1] Francisco Váldes, Jerome McCristal Culp, and Angela P. Harris note that CRT challenges three popular beliefs about racial injustice in the United States.[2] The first and most resistant belief challenged by CRT is that "race blindness" will eliminate racism.[3] The second belief challenged is that race is a matter of individual prejudice, rather than of systemic racism.[4] Finally, CRT challenges the popular belief that one can fight racism while ignoring sexism, homophobia, class exploitation, and other forms of oppression.[5]

An additional distinguishing characteristic of CRT is that it has sought to incorporate the voices and narratives of previously excluded groups into law. Following in the tradition of CRT, since it emerged more than a decade ago, Latino critical race theory (LatCrit) has similarly challenged liberal law theory and practice by incorporating the experiences and voices of Latinos into law and law scholarship and articulating an antisubordination theory and praxis.[6]

Derrick Bell and Richard Delgado have been two of the pioneers in the use of narrative and storytelling techniques to advance law scholarship. Bell blazed the trail in his classic *And We Are Not Saved: The Elusive Quest for Racial Justice* by first introducing a fictional figure, Geneva Crenshaw, the heroine of his book.[7] A brilliant civil rights litigator, Geneva was participating in a voter-registration drive in 1964 when she was severely injured after her car was run off the road in an attempted murder. Emerging from a coma after some twenty years, Geneva presents Bell's alter ego, a law professor, with the fictional text *The Civil Rights Chronicles*, a fresh and innovative look at race and law in contemporary society.[8] Bell pioneered the use of fictional stories, fables, parables, and tales in law. Kimberlé Crenshaw, a well-known critical race theorist, notes, "Allegory offers a method of discourse that allows us to critique legal norms in an ironically contextualized way. Through the allegory, we can discuss legal doctrine in a way that does not replicate the abstractions of legal discourse. It provides therefore a more rich, engaging, and suggestive way of reaching the truth."[9]

More than a decade after the publication of Bell's book, Richard Delgado introduced Geneva's half-brother, Rodrigo Crenshaw, a brilliant young law-student-turned-law-professor. Born in the United States and raised in Italy, Rodrigo attempts to return to his native country to help it deal with its current racial crisis, engaging a law professor, Delgado's alter ego, in a series of chronicles focusing on topics such as law, racism, civil rights, and affirmative action.[10] Rodrigo's father was apparently in the military and stationed in Italy, allowing Rodrigo to have graduated from the University of Bologna, one of the oldest law schools in the world. In his first chronicle, Rodrigo seeks out the professor for advice on how to pursue a career in law teaching.

Despite the significance and impact of these and subsequent works, in the end critical race theory (CRT) and LatCrit have done little to advance our understanding of law practice. This book seeks to continue the tradition and style introduced by Bell, Delgado, Patricia Williams, and other critical race theorists by using narrative and storytelling as a technique to address current issues not only in CRT and LatCrit but also in law practice.

While teaching a sociology graduate seminar on gender several years ago, I "created" and introduced a fictional *mujer* and my alter ego, Fermina Gabriel, in letters that I wrote and shared with my students. Like Geneva and Rodrigo Crenshaw, Fermina Gabriel is imaginary, but in this book—like Bell and Delgado—I seek to use narrative and storytelling to address theoretical, practical, and ethical questions and issues that arise within law and law practice.

Although substantially influenced by Bell and Delgado, my *cartas*, or fictional letters to Fermina, differ from those authors' works in several important respects. First, while Fermina is fictional, and the names I use have been altered or disguised to protect the privacy of the parties, the events described in the ensuing pages are not fictional. Second, Fermina has not been in a coma, nor was she raised abroad—she is a Chicana and firmly anchored in her community, culture, and language. Third, rather than using allegory, fables, or tales, I attempt to incorporate biography and personal narratives into my letters. Ironically, while we learn much about Geneva and Rodrigo and the fictional law-professor alter egos created by Bell and Delgado respectively, from these brilliant essays one learns precious little about the authors' personal biographies—other than the fact that Bell was a civil-rights-litigator-turned-law-professor and constitutional law scholar, and Delgado was an attorney-turned-law-professor. In short, my letters to Fermina are not fictional, although Fermina herself is. Rather, my *cartas* are "field reports" or journals that I have incorporated into my pedagogy in teaching law and law-related classes.[11] Here, I use the letters in an effort to elucidate law practice.

Fermina Gabriel: My Alter Ego

Like others who have migrated to the United States in search of work, most *mexicanos* can recall writing or receiving letters from distant relatives who were left behind. I came to the United States with my father and brothers at the age of nine. My oldest brother, Alejandro ("Alex"), was fourteen, and my middle brother, Hector Xavier ("Gordo"), was thirteen. I have vivid recollections of the countless letters I exchanged over the years with my mother, my paternal grandmother, my *tías*, and other relatives in Mexico. When my mother passed away several years ago in Mexico, we discovered many of the letters that my brothers had written to her over the courses of their lifetimes, neatly arranged in shoe boxes in her bedroom closet.

But enough about me. Let me tell you a little more about my friend and alter ego, Fermina. First, although I made her up, Fermina is a composite of a number of very real women I have known. With her brilliance and years of formal education, at her core she remains a lot like my mother and her sisters (Margara and Licho); my sister and my daughters; my colleagues, Chicana staff at the University of California, Riverside; my students; my friends; and my acquaintances. An extremely accomplished lawyer, author, and singer—a "super-Chicana"—Fermina nevertheless remains rooted in her community and culture. She was born and raised on Washington Lane in the barrio of South Colton, California. Her father was a *bracero* who first worked for the Southern Pacific Railroad, then became an orange picker and migrant farm worker. Don Manuel, as he was called, eventually got a permanent job (or *jale*, as he called it) at the

Colton Portland cement plant. It was hard work lifting hundred-pound bags of cement, but the position offered job security and since it was a union job, it provided health insurance for him, his wife Doña Rosauro ("Chayo"), and his nine daughters and one son.

Most of the Gabriel children were very hard workers and high achievers. Fermina, the oldest, graduated second in her class from Colton High School; attended Valley Community College and the University of California, Santa Cruz; and subsequently received joint doctorate and juris doctor degrees from Stanford. After graduation, Fermina considered going into law teaching and had several attractive job offers at elite law schools, but she decided instead to pursue public interest law, teaching and writing on the side. Fermina went to work for the United Farmworkers of America for a while and is now a staff attorney at the MILAGRO Immigration Clinic in Watsonville. She has taught as an adjunct at several institutions, including the University of California, Santa Cruz; California State University, Monterey Bay; and the University of Santa Clara College of Law. She has by now published two novels and a collection of poems and short stories, as well as several law-review articles based on her practice. On the weekends, Fermina participates in a *folklórico* dance group and occasionally sings at El Sombrero Restaurant and Night Club in Watsonville.

Although born on this side of the border, Fermina is uncompromisingly *mexicana* and is extremely proud of her heritage. She religiously follows El Tri, the mexicano national soccer team (or as she calls it, "La Seleccíon"), and on game day, she always wears the Mexican colors. Her mother is from Aguascalientes and her dad is from Jalostotitlán ("Jalos"), a little town in Los Altos de Jalisco (the Highlands of Jalisco), so she is also an avid fan of Mexico's most popular soccer team, Las Chivas de Guadalajara. Fermina recently became a dual mexicano/a and United States citizen; she was once a member of the Mexican Olympic Equestrian Team and also has a black belt in karate. Nonetheless, she is proudly "Brown," identifies closely with her Indian heritage, and is in no way racially indeterminate, or Mediterranean-looking, like her counterpart Rodrigo Crenshaw.

Over the past few years, I have used my cartas as a vehicle for addressing a variety of theoretical and practical legal issues. The narratives in this book differ from Bell and Delgado's work and most CRT and LatCrit scholarship in that they are real cases from my law practice.

Although I am a full-time teacher and researcher at the University of California, Riverside, over the past decade I have managed to develop a small, largely pro bono law practice. My practice has been anything but traditional, since I do not have a law office, a business phone, a paralegal, or clerical support staff. I also separate my teaching from my law practice and work largely out of my home or on the streets. I meet with clients at coffee shops, taco stands, or restaurants. My telephone number is unlisted and I have never advertised or sought out clients. Yet clients always seem to have a way of finding me. I do not make any money in my practice. My clients are not all poor, but most are low-income persons, or what sociologists call the "working poor," who lack access to law or to lawyers. I normally charge little or nothing for my services and sometimes exchange services by having clients do work, like painting, home repairs, or mechanical work on my cars, in quid pro quo fashion. Unfortunately, I spend much more on my practice than I take in and have even lent or given money to some clients.

One of the major obstacles in my practice has been that I lack the vital resources that facilitate carrying out effective law work. For example, rather than subscribing to electronic legal services like Westlaw or Lexis, I spend a lot of my weekends and spare hours at the local Riverside County Law Library doing legal research. I also lack the resources to hire private investigators or expert witnesses. On the other hand, because I do not bill my clients, I am able to devote much more time and energy to my cases than I could if I was billing them for my services—much more than traditional lawyers devote.

Despite the obstacles, I have had some success and have found law practice to be at once frustrating and extremely exciting and rewarding. As I am a part-time practitioner, my practice has been limited in many ways, but in other ways it has been broad—and what I initially lacked in experience I tried to make up for through dedication, perseverance, and hard work. In law school, I remember interviewing for a job as a public defender and closely identifying with the slogan used by one of the legal-services offices that interviewed me, which characterized its services as "the best representation that money can't buy." I am not a fancy lawyer, but I would like to think that I have been able to provide the kind of legal representation that money literally cannot buy—not necessarily because of my unique skills, talent, or experience but because of the time, effort, and care that I put into my practice.

Most books written about law and law practice have focused on high-profile cases brought by fancy lawyers like William Bella representing celebrity cases, or on highly publicized crimes such as those involved in the O. J. Simpson, Robert Blake, and Phil Spector trials. But very little work describes the experiences of ordinary people and ordinary cases and problems.[12] This book is not about celebrity crimes or high-profile cases. It is about routine cases and regular folks with ordinary problems. It is about the gardener, mechanic, secretary, student, cafeteria worker, friend, neighbor, or relative who encountered a problem or problems with the law.

In this book, I draw not only on CRT and LatCrit but also on a substantial body of work focusing on community law practice and grassroots community organizing and empowerment among the poor. Much of this work challenges the traditional hierarchical view of law, lawyers, and lawyering and attempts to develop a theoretical framework and a vision of lawyers as working for social justice and social change with, and on behalf of, subordinated communities. Unfortunately, as with CRT and LatCrit, little of it attempts to link the work of CRT and LatCrit scholars with that of practitioners. Work on community law practice and rebellious lawyering is the overarching goal of this book.

Rebellious Lawyering

Gerald ("Jerry") Pablo López is undoubtedly the most notable scholar writing about community law practice. In his book *Rebellious Lawyering*,[13] as well as in dozens of law-review articles and countless speeches he has authored and given, López has sought to articulate an alternative vision of progressive law work that challenges the traditional "regnant" conception of law and law practice and seeks to develop a theory of practice grounded in the everyday experiences and worldviews of subordinated groups.

In seeking to supplant the prevailing regnant approach—which is hierarchical and sees the lawyer as all powerful and all knowing and the client as subordinate, passive, and dependent—López adopts a client-centered approach that aims to bring about community empowerment and uses lay-lawyering and teaching self-help to organize and empower clients. This vision of law practice sees lawyers as working not only "on behalf of" but also "with" and in solidarity with subordinated communities in the struggle for social justice and social change, with the aim of teaching clients to continue their struggles on their own. Kevin R. Johnson notes that "political, as opposed to strictly legal, strategies are the most likely to bear fruit"[14] for Latino communities. Drawing on López and other progressive advocates, Johnson adds that lawyers need to collaborate with subordinated communities and that "strategies that allow Latinos to control their lives when the lawyers are gone are the ones most likely to result in lasting change."[15]

Bill Ong Hing, a noted progressive law practitioner and successful immigration lawyer, similarly rejects the top-down, hierarchical, and condescending conception of law and law practice, reminding us of the mutual benefits of progressive work.

> Those of us who engage in progressive legal work need to be constantly reminded that we do not know everything—that we are not knights in shining armor swooping in to save subordinated communities. We should be collaborating: working with rather than simply on behalf of clients and allies from whom we have much to learn. Though lawyering for social change is arduous work, there is much to gain in these battles against subordination, not simply from the potential outcome but from the collaborative process itself: as our clients gain strength and confidence, we too are renewed.[16]

Hing describes the organizing work of Y. C. James Yen,[17] a remarkable man largely unknown to lawyers who carried out a literacy campaign with Chinese coolies working in France during World War I, helping empower these homesick workers by teaching them how to read and write and having them write letters home. Hing contends that although Yen was not a lawyer, his approach was consistent with the progressive lawyering theoretical frameworks proposed by Jerry López, Lucie White, and Ascanio Pomelli,[18] scholars whose work is grounded in a "bottom-up" approach to organizing and who champion "a collaborative approach that respects clients' decision-making capacities, seeks allies in the pursuit of social justice, and is open to learning from clients and community partners."[19]

In law school, I was immersed in the local community law clinic and public interest law. I participated in numerous clinics and workshops and was fortunate to have been exposed to many of the writings and theories of progressive lawyers like Gerald P. López, Lucie White, and

Bill O. Hing. It was also in law school that I was first exposed to the rich and compelling narratives of CRT scholars Derrick Bell, Patricia Williams, Angela Harris, Harold Dalton, Mari Matsuda, Chuck Lawrence, Richard Delgado, and Margaret Montoya.[20] One of the questions that has intrigued me since my law school days is: Why, despite obvious points of commonality between CRT and progressive law practice, does a huge gap yawn between critical race theorists and progressive lawyers?

In a classic commentary and critique of critical legal studies (CLS), a movement led largely by progressive White men teaching at elite law schools,[21] Bob Gordon notes a split between theorists and practitioners attending CLS conferences.[22] While theorists generally eschew and devalue practice, practitioners hunger for theory. Gordon notes that despite differences among members of the CLS movement, an amazing amount of convergence characterizes their work, since the prototypical CLS scholar was a progressive who first started thinking about law as a student in the late 1960s, or a progressive lawyer who tried to use the system against the system. Gordon notes that the lawyers who participated in CLS came from diverse but converging backgrounds, as "some of us [were] law teachers with humanist intellectual concerns and left-liberal (civil rights and anti–Vietnam war) political involvement . . . others radical activists who identified with neo-Marxist versions of socialism or feminism or both; still others primarily practitioners . . . who worked in collective law practices, legal services offices, law school clinics, or a variety of other progressive jobs."[23]

Harlon Dalton adds that people of Color[24] hold the potential for bridging the schism between theorists and practitioners because they are "practitioners" almost by definition, in the sense that the consequences of racism have direct, practical, inescapable, and immediate relevance for them.[25] In other words, even if we are not practitioners in the technical sense of the word, we cannot simply "walk away" from race issues the way White progressives can. Dalton relates the example of an exchange that he had with Morty Hortwitz, a prominent legal historian and noted CLS theorist, to illustrate the difference between the prototypical critical legal studies theorist (CRIT) and critical race theorists.

> It was, in fact, a quite pleasant encounter, during the course of which Morty quite gently asked me, in essence, whether I, in my earlier incarnation as a public interest lawyer, minded serving to legitimate

The System and providing a palliative for the underclass.... Eventually I got up the courage to ask Morty whether he truly believed that "the revolution" would begin at Harvard Law School.... He said, "I guess I really do, but the truth is that I was a four-eyed kid who read books and that was about all that I could do.[26]

Dalton would thus add to the biographical description of the prototypical CRIT that he was a "four-eyed kid," or nerd, alienated and distanced from his immediate environment, leading us to conclude that differences in biography and experience may aid in understanding why the CRIT leadership has not developed a positive program, whereas people of Color tend to hunger for praxis.

I propose that the current gap between CRT and LatCrit, on the one hand, and rebellious lawyers, on the other, calls into question Dalton's basic assertion that people of Color and law scholars of Color are practitioners by virtue of their pigmentation, whereas White progressives are not. The people who were in law school in the late 1960s were predominantly White men, according to Dalton, not only because of their pigmentation and chromosomal structure but also because they were part of the privileged race for "whose benefit patriarchy exists."[27]

Despite the schism that currently divides critical legal studies and CRT, the two movements exhibit inevitable parallels and points of overlap. Both movements espouse an antisubordination ideology that challenges traditional conceptions of law and lawyering. Both reject the ideology of "race blindness" and the belief that it will eliminate racism. Both challenge the belief that race is a matter of individual prejudice, rather than of systemic racism, as well as the prevailing belief that one can fight racism while ignoring sexism, homophobia, class exploitation, and other forms of oppression.[28]

An additional goal of both the CRT/LatCrit and rebellious law practice movements is that both use storytelling and narrative to incorporate into law the voices and stories of previously excluded groups. In the foreword to Delgado's *The Rodrigo Chronicles*, indigenous legal historian Robert A. Williams describes Delgado as a great indigenous American storyteller, pointing to the importance of stories for indigenous peoples. In the Native American tradition, being a storyteller is a heavy responsibility. "To be a Storyteller, then, is to assume the awesome burden of remembering for a people, and to perform this paramount role with laughter and tears, joy and sadness, melancholy and passion, as the occasion demands. . . . The Storyteller is the one who sacrifices everything in the tellings and retellings of the stories belonging to the tribe."²⁹ However, in the Native American tradition, the great storyteller never tells people what they expect to hear and "a Storyteller, in this sense, is always a prophet."³⁰ While not focusing on the role of the storyteller per se, Gerald P. López also sees storytelling as a generally unstated, useful problem-solving technique used by people to address and resolve everyday problems.³¹ López observes, for example, that lawyers working with subordinated groups are inevitably "bicultural" and "bilingual" in the sense that to represent well, they must know and be able to think like an insider in both the lay and legal worlds and to simultaneously translate, interpret, and make sense of both worlds. "A professional lawyer's practical knowledge of the legal culture demands a studied appreciation for the uses and limits of the story/argument strategies available in that culture," he writes. "Lawyers . . . must translate in two directions, creating both a meaning for the legal culture out of the situations that people are living and a meaning for people's practices out of the legal culture."³²

The Brown Buffalo and Rebellious Lawyering

Unfortunately, the writings of one of the most colorful figures in the Chicano movement, Oscar "Zeta" Acosta—a self-described "Brown Buffalo"—have been largely ignored both by critical race theorists and by rebellious lawyers. Acosta is undoubtedly better known as a creative writer and prominent Chicano movement figure than as a lawyer, but he was unquestionably an influential Chicano lawyer whose work has important though largely unexplored implications for rebellious lawyering. One of the only law scholars to seriously consider Acosta's work as a lawyer independent of his political activism was Ian F. Haney López.³³

Acosta was born in El Paso in 1935, and because his parents could not make a living there during the Depression, they moved to California to work as migrant farm laborers.³⁴ He grew up in Riverbank, an agricultural town in the Modesto area, which he described as being composed of three groups: "the Mexicans, the Okies, and middle-class Whites, with no Jews or Blacks."³⁵

An accomplished jazz musician and clarinet player, as well as a mathematics major, Acosta abandoned the Catholic Church and became a charismatic Baptist Evangelist preacher in Panama. Although best known for his two fictionalized autobiographical novels, *The Autobiography of a Brown Buffalo* and *The Revolt of the Cockroach People*,[36] after working as a copy boy for *The San Francisco Examiner* he went to night school to study law, graduating from the San Francisco Law School. He was also part of the San Francisco drug scene of the 1960s. Acosta served as a legal aid lawyer in Oakland for a year and "hated it with a passion," because "all we'd do was sit and listen to complaints. We didn't have a direction, skills, or tools."[37]

Acosta was uncompromisingly irreverent toward the legal and judicial system, describing himself as "the only Chicano lawyer here [in Los Angeles]. By that I mean I am the only one that has taken on a militant posture, to my knowledge in the whole country."[38] He saw the courtroom as an organizing tool, noting that he took no case "unless it is or can become a Chicano Movement case."[39] Although unorthodox, Acosta was a rebellious lawyer who worked on behalf of and with Chicano clients, and he certainly had a bottom-up view of law.

After moving to Los Angeles and representing the defendants involved in the Chicano School Walkouts and the Chicano movement, Acosta decided, "If I was going to become anything 'legal' I couldn't use the profession as it was. Lawyers were basically peddlers of flesh. They live off people's misery."[40] He declared, "I would never charge a client a penny. As a matter of fact, I ended up supporting some of my clients."[41]

My goal in this book—to link Delgado's rich *Rodrigo Chronicles*, Acosta's autobiographical Chicano movement narratives, and López's fictional vision of progressive law practice—is perhaps ambitious. In pursuing this goal, I draw on my own experiences as a pro bono attorney in Southern California and present case studies based on actual cases and real people. A related goal is to inform our understanding of critical race theory and law practice.

Although López focuses on practice on behalf of and in solidarity with subordinated groups, as with the chronicles of Geneva and Rodrigo Crenshaw, the characters and stories in his *Rebellious Lawyering*, too, are fictional. López remarked that some observers might question the wisdom of creating fictional case studies, but he points to the value of using ideal types or prototypes that enable us to manipulate reality. Although obviously drawing from his own observations and experience, he is not limited by them.

> Everything I describe is fictional. But I do draw on my observations of and my work with a wide range of people. Yet I don't limit myself only to what I have seen and heard. Instead, by using imagined characters and storylines, I try to extend the boundaries of, nearly as much as I try to report, all that I so much admire. . . . I'd like to believe what I have to say challenges even the best activists about what they do and don't do in practice.[42]

Like the Indian storyteller, then, López does not tell us what we expect to hear but rather what we need to hear, and in this sense he is not only a brilliant and creative law theorist and storyteller like Delgado but also a prophet, who reports on and at the same time seeks to extend the boundaries of progressive law practice. Many of our oral traditions as organizers and activist lawyers are seldom recognized or reported because the accounts rarely report activist work as well as they might. Most oral stories seldom circulate outside small, local circles. "And when they do, they either lose detail and spirit along the way or gain so much that they get treated as make-believe."[43]

Rascuache Lawyering: Toward a Theory of Ordinary Litigation

In this final section, I want to lay out the preliminary framework for a theory of ordinary litigation, or what I call (for lack of a better term) "*rascuache* lawyering." I must admit that I was reluctant to write this section because I realized all too well that setting out a theory of ordinary litigation is an ambitious undertaking and that it may be premature to propose a full-blown theory at this time. I am also aware that my career as a practitioner is far from ideal or exemplary, since the truth is that I have only been a part-time lawyer for a little more than a decade, with limited resources and practice experience.

I wish to clarify at the outset, then, that what I am proposing is not really a carefully developed or fully articulated theory, but a set of tentative guidelines or basic tenets, or paradigms, for carrying out litigation for and on behalf of subordinated people. Perhaps the best way to see this is not as a formal theory but as a set of preliminary guidelines based on my admittedly limited experience—guidelines that are flexible and can be freely modified and/or altered at a future date.

I should first explain the concept of rascuache lawyering a bit more, since "rascuache" is a vernacular term with uniquely mexicano meanings and connotations. The *Collins Spanish Dictionary* defines rascuache[44] as: "1 (=*pobre*) poor, penniless; 2 (=*desgraciado*) wretched; 3 (=*ridículo*) ridiculous, in bad taste; 4 (=*grosero*) coarse, vulgar; and 5 (=*tacaño*) mean, tightfisted.[45]

Ilan Stavans notes that "rascuache is a Mexican colloquialism" ignored by the venerated *Diccionario de la Real Academia Española*, which has no English cognate and "is used in Mexico to describe a cultural item of inferior quality and proletarian origin," such as "the Pachuco fashion style in Los Angeles"[46] or Cantinflas's uniquely Mexican and proletariat comedic style.

The theory of rascuache lawyering I propose, then—like the work of Richard Delgado, Derrick Bell, Gerald P. López, Lucie White, and Bill O. Hing—is a bottom-up view of law, lawyering, and law practice. It is a conception of law and lawyering, in other words, for and on behalf of *los de abajo*—people either at the bottom of the social hierarchy or on the margins of society and outside the parameters of the legal establishment. Perhaps what is mostly needed is the development not of a singular theory but of a tentative paradigm of ordinary rascuache law practice that might subsume exiting theories in CRT, LatCrit, and the rebellious idea of law practice first articulated by López and developed by others.

George Ritzer maintains that paradigms are "the broadest units of consensus"[47] within a field and notes, for example, that within sociology we can identify three distinct paradigms: Durkheim's social facts; Weber's social definition, *Verstehen*, or sympathetic understanding; and Skinner's social behavior. A paradigm "subsumes, defines, and interrelates the exemplars, theories, methods, and instruments that exist within it."[48]

While Derrick Bell, Richard Delgado, Gerald P. López, and Oscar Zeta Acosta are obviously key practitioners and theorists of rascuache lawyering theory, perhaps the most prominent exemplar of the proposed paradigm of everyday law, ironically, is the distinguished jurist and Supreme Court Justice Oliver Wendell Holmes. It was Holmes who first endorsed one of the founding principles of rascuache law practice: that legal theories should be derived from experience. In an often-quoted section of *The Common Law*, Holmes declared, "The life of the law has not been logic: it has been experience. The felt necessities of the time, the prevalent moral and political theories, intuitions of public policy, avowed or unconscious, even the prejudices which judges share with their fellow-men, have had a good deal more to do than the syllogism in determining the rules by which men should be governed."[49]

A second tenant of rascuache lawyering, which borrows from Holmes, is that the theory of practice, too, is ultimately inductively derived from experience. The proposed paradigm of rascuache lawyering differs from Holmes, however, in its bottom-up view of law and law practice *based on* experience.

Many years ago, I proposed a paradigm for a Chicano social science[50] that rejected the basic tenets of scientism and challenged the idea that social science can or should seek to be objective, value-neutral, and universal. As in anthropology and sociology, all too often academic accounts of law and lawyering are presented as detached, objective, neutral and impersonal, universal descriptions of reality, devoid of feeling and emotion.

This book is a decidedly personal account of law practice, and its observations and conclusions are not presented as being universally true, objective, or value free. They are instead personal, passionate accounts of my cases, clients, and, most importantly, of my responses to the issues, questions, problems, and dilemmas that have arisen during the course of my law practice. I have certainly not been a detached, impersonal observer who neutrally recorded my experiences and observations but an active, imperfect participant who responded and reacted to the things I experienced. A third tenet of rascuache law practice, then, is that it is personal, subjective, and particularistic.

As noted, rascuache lawyering necessarily draws from the rich narratives found in the fictionalized accounts of critical race theorists like Derrick Bell and Richard Delgado, as well as the creative scenarios described by rebellious lawyer and theorist Gerald P. López. Despite the significance and creative genius of these works, they share an important limitation—the very fact that the works are fictional.

Despite the power of fiction to transcend ordinary reality and present an emancipatory vision of society and law, one of the problems with fictional accounts of law and law practice is that because they are idealized views of reality, the characters are often depicted as ideal types, rather than as real people with human foibles, imperfections, contradictions, and limitations. Bell, for example, describes Geneva Crenshaw as a brilliant litigator who has been in a coma for twenty years after her car was driven off an isolated rural Mississippi road by a pickup truck in the summer of 1964. "Strikingly tall, well over six feet, Geneva, as I soon learned, was able to display an impressive intelligence honed by hard work."[51] Prior to the tragic incident, Geneva had been a civil rights litigator in the South and was about to embark on what undoubtedly would have been a distinguished law-teaching career at Howard Law School. In his introduction, Bell notes, "In order to appraise the contradictions and inconsistencies that pervade the all too real world of racial oppression, I have chosen in this book the tools not only of reason but also of unreason, of fantasy."[52] In the book, Bell uses fairy tale and science fiction in the form of ten metaphorical tales, or chronicles, that as Professor Linda Green notes will follow the ancient tradition "in using fantasy and dialogue to uncover enduring truths."[53]

Delgado, in turn, borrowed Geneva's persona from Bell and developed her "family tree" a bit more by creating her fictional half-brother, Rodrigo,[54] who was born in the United States and raised in Italy, and like his African American super-lawyer sister, seeks to come to the United States to pursue a career in law teaching. In the introduction to *The Rodrigo Chronicles*, Delgado thanks Bell, noting, "Bell's book and this one are parts of the legal storytelling movement which sprang up a few years ago and which, in turn, builds on a legacy of storytelling by outsiders going back to slave narratives and even before. These early tellers of tales used stories to test and challenge reality . . . to reconstruct the dominant tale of narrative."[55] Delgado's alter ego, like Rodrigo's brilliant sister, is ultimately a superhero of gigantic proportions; he is described as a "tall, rangy man" and "of indeterminate age, somewhere between 20 and 40, and ethnicity," so that "his tightly curled hair and olive complexion suggested that he might be African-American. But he could also be Latino, perhaps Mexican, Puerto Rican, or any of one of the many Central American nationalities."[56]

Rodrigo was raised in Italy; graduated from one of the oldest law schools in the world; did well on the LSAT, finding it "easier than expected";[57] displays technical virtuosity on the computer; and has returned to his native country to help it deal with its many contradictions and crises. Although born in the United States, he was subjected to "denaturalization" after the immigration authorities learned that he had spent six months in the Italian Army in order to comply with his military service and repay his adopted country.[58]

As noted, the characters in Gerald P. López's *Rebellious Lawyering* are also fictional. López rejects the reigning regnant idea of law practice and uses two characters, Amos and Sophie, to articulate a rebellious vision of progressive law practice that is client centered and seeks to work with subordinated clients.[59] In this idea of lawyers working against subordination, "lawyers must know how to work with (not just on behalf of) women, low-income people, people of color, gays and lesbians, the disabled, and the elderly. They must know how to work with other professional and lay allies.... [T]hey must open themselves up to being educated ... particularly about the life and experiences of life at the bottom and at the margins."[60]

The rascuache vision of lawyering proposed here seeks to incorporate and expand on López's vision of progressive law practice. This vision, too, seeks to work with—and not just on behalf of—subordinated people. Although the names have been changed to protect the anonymity of the parties, the people, the cases, and the issues included in this book were all not only incredibly real, but, like the author, also flawed and imperfect.

Oscar Zeta Acosta is perhaps the prototype of the rascuache lawyer, although he is more well known for his visibility in the Chicano movement and, along with Hunter S. Thompson, for helping create and popularize "gonzo journalism."[61] Acosta's work as a rebellious lawyer is difficult to evaluate because his two books are autobiographical fictionalized accounts of real events in the Chicano movement, as well as because he was more interested in chronicling his life and search for identity and the development of the Chicano movement than in writing about law practice, clients, and cases.

Acosta himself identified more as a writer and a Chicano political leader than as a Chicano lawyer. His two major works were autobiographical novels, and his primary concern was "identity, individual and collective, and in that he foresaw the climate to flourish a decade after his disappearance."[62] Although Acosta said he hated working as a legal aid lawyer in a half-Black and half-Chicano section of Oakland—dropping out of law practice after a year and doing most of his writing under the influence of alcohol and drugs—his work as a Chicano lawyer in East Los Angeles, beginning in 1968, marks him as an important figure in the development of a paradigm of rascuache law practice. While Acosta hated the entire legal system with a passion, he certainly worked with—and not simply for—his clients. Largely because he never charged clients for his services, he worked in a small, dingy office in the middle of skid row in downtown Los Angeles. Acosta declared that psychedelic drugs "had been important for the development of [his] consciousness,"[63] adding, "Most of the big ideas I've gotten for my lawyer work have virtually come when I am stoned."[64]

Shortly after the High School Blowouts occurred in East Los Angeles in 1968, Acosta agreed to take on a few misdemeanor cases. Two months later, he represented thirteen of the organizers of the walkouts, who were charged with sixteen counts of conspiracy—which could have resulted in a forty-five-year prison term for each defendant.[65] This was his first criminal case. He also represented Corky González, founder of the Crusade for Justice in Denver, who was on trial on a weapons charge related to the East Los Angeles police riots on August 29, 1970, in which the police killed several people, including noted Chicano journalist Rubén Salazar.[66]

One of Acosta's most daring and creative ideas came in the trial of the Biltmore Six, who were accused of attempting to burn down California's Biltmore Hotel when Governor Ronald Reagan was giving a speech there. In an attempt to quash the indictments of the Biltmore defendants, Acosta subpoenaed all 109 Superior Court judges to show "that all Grand Juries are racist since the grand jurors have to be recommended by Superior Court judges and that the whole thing reeks of 'subconscious, institutional racism.'"[67]

I want to note that I see Acosta as an exemplar of rascuache lawyering in spite of, and not because of, his claim that he "got most of his big ideas for his law work" while stoned. In reading Acosta and evaluating his work as a lawyer, one has to remember that he was at heart a journalist and a creative writer who came to Los Angeles to write an article about the Chicano movement. It is important to note that Acosta ultimately fictionalized his experiences as a lawyer—and it is hard to imagine how Acosta could have been the effective, formidable, and zealous advocate that he was if he was always stoned or under the influence of alcohol or drugs. In an autobiographical essay, he notes that when he first came to Los Angeles in January 1968 to work for the *La Raza* newspaper in east L.A., he rediscovered his Mexican identity and came to identify closely with the Chicano movement and the ideology of Chicanismo.[68] In fact, he claims to have been sober for nine months when he first came to Los Angeles and to have gotten rid of his blubber, noting,

"For months now I had been without booze and dope. No whiskey, no wine, no beer. No more acid, or grass or hash."[69] Once in Los Angeles, however, he started drinking again as he began relearning Spanish—in his words, "partly because I decided it was my personal heritage and partly because nobody can learn Spanish sober. It is just too sensual a language, too rolling and flowing to want your tongue stiff and dry.... Booze helped my writing some, but as yet nothing worth writing about turned up. I still lay away from the dope."[70] Acosta maintained that he related to the court system "first as a Chicano and only seldom as a lawyer in the traditional sense."[71] Like Acosta, I feel that I have never identified strongly as a lawyer, but I would like to believe that I have taken my lawyering responsibilities very seriously and have always been a zealous advocate for the people I have represented.

Crimes against the Person

❖ 1 ❖
Attempted Murder
"My Brother's Keeper"

Querido Alfredo,

How wonderful it was to receive your last letter! It's been a long time. I hope this letter finds you in good health and in excellent spirits. I am well, although singing at El Sombrero last weekend has taken a toll and added a lot of strain on my voice. By the way, there is a great vegetarian restaurant that I would love to take you to when you come to the Bay Area. I am working on a new song from Los Panchos, "Sin ti," and I am hoping to have it ready to perform soon. The Gutiérrez family has given me the honor of asking me to sing at their parents' thirtieth-anniversary celebration, and as you may remember, Señor Gutiérrez was a *bracero* and worked on the railroad with my father in Colton.

I was very excited, too, when I received your manuscript! From the onset, I've had some reservations about the title: *Rascuache Lawyer*. Don't get me wrong—it is very creative and intriguing, but I worry that many people might not understand the concept, since it is a uniquely Mexican expression, so that even some of my South American friends don't know what it is. I am not suggesting that you change the title, because it's perfect, but that you make sure to discuss and illustrate rascuache lawyering thoroughly so that those unfamiliar with the term will understand the concept through its use.

I hope you won't be offended, but I also wanted to comment on your grammar and punctuation. There are a few typos in the manuscript, so you need to give it a last, careful edit. Make sure that you pay close attention to terms so as to not confuse them—for example, you confused "discretely" (i.e., separately) with "discreetly" (carried out privately and with discretion) and "sloped" (as in slanted) with "slopped" (as in messy or overflowing). Although the terms are very similar and one can see how they can be easily confused, as you know, they have completely different meanings and connotations. This could radically change what you are attempting to relate to the reader. Also—and this would be caught in copy editing—you have a tendency to overcapitalize what you see as important, and you love commas! Lastly, your descriptions of your clients seem a bit limited and restricted. You tend to overuse "nice" when describing people, and as a reader, I would prefer that you use other terms. How about "warm," "engaging," "obliging," or "cordial," for example? Better yet, you could *show* me (through words) that they're nice rather than tell me.

It was interesting that you commented on Oscar Zeta Acosta, "the Brown Buffalo," as the prototype for rascuache lawyering. Your description of Acosta mentioned Acosta's struggle with alcohol and drugs, but you failed to mention Acosta's sexism and misogyny. I hope that you take my criticism to heart and see it as constructive and well intentioned. I am looking forward to receiving your next letter and continuing to discuss your book. Best wishes to you and your family. Wish me luck!

Saludos,
Fermina

✧ ✧ ✧ ✧ ✧

Querida Fermina,

Gracias for your recent letter. I am glad you are in good health and that everything is going well with your work, writing, and the weekends at El Sombrero. I hope you take it easy and rest your voice. I am hoping that I can make it up to the Bay Area and catch one of your shows in the next few weeks, and as you know, I love the music of Los Panchos and other trios. I want to focus this carta on one of my current cases, but I first want to thank you for your comments on the first chapter and earlier drafts of the manuscript. I am glad that you like the concept for the rascuache lawyering book. I agree that a lot of people may not know what "rascuache" means. It is, as you note, a uniquely mexicano expression, and I can't think of an equivalent term in English. Can you think of an English translation? I guess you could say "low brow"—or, as some people in the art world describe unpretentious, bottom-up Chicano art, "low Brown"—but these terms are not quite as appropriate as "rascuache."

While I appreciate your taking the time to read the chapter and your comments, I admit that your criticism is hard on the ego. By the way, I don't remember using "sloped" *or* "slopped" in the manuscript. You also suggested that I use fewer commas and avoid capitalizing everything that I deem important. You are correct. I do tend to overcapitalize, and I certainly overuse commas. I will try to take your comments into account when I edit before finalizing the chapters. I especially like your suggestion of showing, rather than telling, when I describe someone.

The case I wanted to share with you is an interesting and important gang-related attempted murder case. One of the things that is frustrating about the case, though, is that there are multiple defendants and five lawyers, which makes it difficult to coordinate our various schedules. As a result, we have had an inordinate number of delays and continuances. I've tried to schedule the trial so that it is in the summer or during a vacation period, but it is very difficult to coordinate the calendars for five defense attorneys, the DA, and the judge.

I should begin by telling you a little bit about my client. Marcos is a twin, so it is hard for me to talk about him without also talking about his identical twin, Mario, and it is hard for me to talk about the twins without also talking about their cousin Junior, because they are all virtually inseparable. I therefore usually refer to them as "the twins" or "the boys," the latter term including Junior.

"The Boys"

I first got involved in this case through a fellow attorney, Clemente Coronado, an experienced criminal defense lawyer who has an office in Pomona and handles a lot of Los Angeles County cases. Several years ago, Clemente had represented one of my close friends, a very popular Chicano teacher in Los Angeles who was accused of interfering with a police officer and inciting a riot during a student protest at the campus where he taught.

Our association worked out well because Clemente needed help and support with his cases and I needed experience. An added benefit is that I could use his office as my official mailing address and as a place where I could meet with clients, if I needed to. Clemente usually brought me into cases where there were two defendants; it would be a conflict of interest for him to represent more than one defendant on the same case, so he would ask me to represent the secondary defendant in the case. It was a way for him to "have his cake and eat it, too," in the sense that he was able to remain involved in both cases while eliminating at least the appearance of a conflict of interest. You know how it has been said that lawyers are more interested in appearances than in the reality, so what mattered for him was not so much eliminating the conflict as eliminating its "appearance." I soon learned that Clemente was very good at doing this, but I often felt that the conflict remained, nonetheless.

As I worked with Clemente, I soon found that—for me, at least—there was often a potential conflict. I generally represented the secondary defendant, who was ostensibly less culpable than the primary defendant always represented by Clemente, so there was sometimes pressure on me to have my client plead guilty, even if my client was not guilty. Clemente and I generally negotiated joint offers, and his clients would usually get the better deal, relatively speaking, because they were the primary defendants.

We had a case involving a young couple, for example, in which Clemente's client, the wife, had worked as an accountant for a small business and was charged with embezzling about sixty thousand dollars from her employer. I represented the husband, who was charged with a misdemeanor because the wife had apparently commingled the embezzled funds with the money in the couple's personal bank account, so it was alleged that the husband either knew or reasonably should have known of the embezzlement. I really do not believe that my client knew of or was involved in the embezzlement, since his wife handled the couple's finances. Even though I believe he was not involved at all in the embezzlement, he ended up pleading guilty to the misdemeanor, and in exchange, his wife was able to avoid doing jail time. Clemente was able to negotiate a joint deal with the district attorney in which his client was simply placed on "house arrest" and was allowed to wear an ankle bracelet at home, instead of going to jail. Clemente also asked me to make a lot of special appearances in which I would go to court and continue various cases for him.

The three primary defendants in the case I'd like to tell you about were accused of being members of an organized criminal street gang and of attempted murder. The girlfriends of the boys were charged as secondary defendants. Two of the primary defendants were the Mercado twins, Marcos and Mario; the other primary defendant was their younger cousin, Junior Díaz. Junior was not an ordinary cousin. He was a *primo hermano*, or first cousin, and in Mexican culture a primo/a hermano/a is thought of as being more like a brother or sister than an ordinary cousin. The twins and Junior lived in the same household, without a father in the home. Junior's mother Jennie was a single parent and raised Junior while their maternal grandmother, la Señora Mercado, raised the twins.

I first met Marcos at the Los Angeles County Juvenile Court facility in Los Angeles. The boys were juveniles at the time of the arrest, but the district attorney was seeking to charge them as adults under Proposition

21[1] and California's anti-gang statute (Penal Code § 186.22). Marcos was a good-looking seventeen-year-old who was about five-foot-nine and a hundred and sixty pounds. He had short hair and a ready smile. The boys were identical twins, but I never had trouble telling them apart. Marcos was the less serious of the two and was usually smiling or joking around. His brother Mario wore his hair longer and was much more serious and intense. I was able to bond with my client Marcos because he reminded me a lot of my son, Alejandro, and the twins were only one or two months younger than him. Marcos not only resembled Alejandro in age and looks—he also reminded me of my son because he wore his hair short, was artistic, was involved in graffiti, and was sociable and charming. His brother Mario looked and acted less like my son.

Clemente prepared me for the juvenile hearing, discussing the law and explaining how in juvenile court the judge had the discretion or power to have the boys charged as adults. The juvenile hearing was more informal than a trial and something like a sentencing hearing in a murder case, in the sense that in deciding whether to transfer the case to adult court, the judge had to weigh and consider all of the aggravating and mitigating factors in the case.

Under Welfare and Institutions Code § 707, in any case in which a minor is alleged to have committed a crime for which he or she should be tried as an adult, a hearing is held to determine if the person is amenable to juvenile court. The court asks the probation office to investigate and submit a report on the behavioral patterns and social history of the minor being considered for a determination of unfitness. Following submission and consideration of the report and any other relevant evidence, the court may find that the minor is not a fit and proper subject to be dealt with under the juvenile court if the court finds that the minor would not be amenable to the care, treatment, and training program available through the juvenile court. The court bases its finding upon evaluation of the following criteria:

(A) The degree of criminal sophistication exhibited by the minor.
(B) Whether the minor can be rehabilitated prior to the expiration of the juvenile court's jurisdiction.
(C) The minor's previous delinquent history.
(D) Success of previous attempts by the juvenile court to rehabilitate the minor.
(E) The circumstances and gravity of the offense alleged in the petition to have been committed by the minor.

A determination that the minor is not a fit and proper subject to be dealt with under the juvenile court law may be based on any one or a combination of the factors.

The transfer of this case to the adult court was almost a forgone conclusion, and at the conclusion of the hearing, the judge determined that the boys were members of a criminal street gang and serious offenders who were not fit and proper subjects to be dealt with under the juvenile court. Before going into the case and discussing the charges and the police report, I should provide some background on Penal Code § 186.22.

Penal Code § 186.22: The STEP Act

The Street Terrorism Enforcement and Prevention Act (STEP Act)[2] is an aggressive piece of legislation drafted by prosecutors and law enforcement personnel that make "active participation" in a criminal street gang a separate criminal offense punishable independently of the underlying felony. Specifically, Penal Code § 186.22(a) provides that:

> Any person who actively participates in any criminal street gang with knowledge that its members engage in or have engaged in a pattern of criminal gang activity, and who willfully promotes, furthers, or assists in any felonious criminal conduct by members of that gang, shall be punished by imprisonment in a county jail for a period not to exceed one year, or by imprisonment in the state prison for 16 months, or two or three years.

If the felony is a serious felony, as defined in subdivision (c) of § 1192.7, the person shall be punished by an additional term of five years. And if the felony is a violent felony, as defined in subdivision (c) of § 667.5, the person shall be punished by an additional term of ten years. It should also be noted that many of these felonies carry a minimum of ten or fifteen years to life sentences.

The basic elements of the crime, then, are that a person (1) actively participated in a criminal street gang; (2) did so with knowledge that its members engage in a pattern of criminal gang activity; and (3) willfully promotes, furthers, or assists in any felonious criminal conduct by members of that gang. The section defines "criminal street gang" broadly and vaguely as an "ongoing organization, association, or group of three or more persons, whether formal or informal, having as one of its primary activities the commission of one or more of the [specified] criminal acts,

... having a common name or common identifying sign or symbol, and whose members individually or collectively engage in or have engaged in a pattern of criminal gang activity" (subd. [f]). The Act does not criminalize membership in a gang because that would be unconstitutional, but it does criminalize "active participation."

Although the statute fails to define exactly what "active participation" entails, "actively participating" in a criminal street gang is punished by "imprisonment in a county jail for a period not to exceed one year, or by imprisonment in the state prison for 16 months, or two or three years."

> In addition and consecutive to the punishment prescribed for the felony or attempted felony of which he or she has been convicted, a person convicted under the section shall be punished with an additional enhancement as follows:
>
> (A) Except as provided in subparagraphs (B) and (C), the person shall be punished by an additional term of two, three, or four years at the court's discretion.

"Serious" felonies, as defined in subdivision (c) of § 1192.7, are punishable by an additional term of five years, while "violent" felonies, as defined in subdivision (c) of Section 667.5, are punished by an additional term of ten years. In addition, if the underlying felony is committed on the grounds of, or within one thousand feet of, a public or private elementary, vocational, or junior high school, it is a factor in aggravation of the crime and in imposing a term. Moreover, under the Act, the court is ordered to impose the middle term of the sentence enhancement unless there are circumstances in aggravation or mitigation, and during sentencing it is required to state the reasons for its choice of sentencing enhancements on the record.

The STEP Act also provides enhancements for specified serious and violent felonies, mandating variable "minimum-to-life" sentences. Under paragraph 4, "Any person who is convicted of an enumerated felony committed for the benefit of, at the direction of, or in association with any criminal street gang, with the specific intent to promote, further, or assist in any criminal conduct by gang members, shall be sentenced to an indeterminate term of life imprisonment with a minimum term of the indeterminate sentence calculated depending on the offense."[3] Finally, under paragraph 5, any person sentenced to state prison for life under this subdivision shall not be paroled until a minimum of fifteen calendar years have been served.

Circumstances of the Offense

According to the police report, on January 27 at approximately 2 p.m., officers responded to a shooting that had reportedly just occurred in the vicinity of Melrose and Center in the city of Pomona. As a result of the investigation and information provided by the victim and witnesses, the suspects in the shooting were identified as Junior Díaz, Marcos Mercado, and Mario Mercado, and the shooting was reported to have been gang related, as the three suspects were members of the "Fourth Street" gang and the victim was associated with "Twenty-second Street," a nearby rival gang. The three juvenile suspects were arrested on a police warrant on March 4 and lodged in Juvenile Hall.

When the police arrived on the scene, the victim was found lying in the street and bleeding from his left leg as a result of a gunshot wound. Additional units were called to the scene, as a large crowd had gathered, and the people in the crowd were becoming irate. Initially, most of the individuals present were very hesitant to talk for fear of retaliation. The police observed that the words "Calle Cuatro" (meaning "Fourth Street") were spray-painted on a stucco wall on the south side of the street where the shooting occurred. A witness reported that the suspects—who were driving a blue Honda Civic with tinted windows—had spray-painted the wall.

The victim explained that a friend who drove him to the area so that he could attend a wake to pay his final respects to the family of another friend had picked him up from his home. He admitted to Twenty-second Street gang involvement, stating that he had been standing outside of a friend's home in the street drinking a forty-ounce beer, and that he had been accompanied by numerous family members who had attended the wake, as well as his girlfriend, when he saw three Hispanic males spray-painting the words "Calle Cuatro" on an adjacent wall of a residence. The victim reportedly walked over to them and said, "What the fuck are you doing? Why are you disrespecting us?" The male suspects, later identified as Marcos and Mario Mercado and Junior Díaz, whom the victim had never seen before, began to argue with him and tell him to "fuck off"; they then started to walk toward a parked vehicle. They got into the vehicle and as they drove away, they yelled, "Calle Cuatro, Calle Cuatro!" The victim stated he became angry and threw a beer can he was holding at the victim's vehicle, and the can struck the side of the car and angered the occupants of the Honda Civic. The victim stated, "The piece of shit leaned out the window and shot me!" He stated that the shooter was "riding shotgun," meaning he was seated in the right front passenger seat. He said the shooter leaned out the right front passenger window and fired approximately five rounds at him and that he was standing approximately ten to fifteen feet away from the vehicle when the suspects fired at him.

The victim stated initially that he did not know he was shot until he felt the pain and fell to the ground. He described the weapon as a black automatic weapon and stated that he was unwilling to prosecute anyone involved in the crime and did not want to testify in court. But he was very cooperative with police who questioned him at the East End Medical Center Hospital, where he had been transported by ambulance. A neighbor at the scene had initially applied a tourniquet to the victim's leg, using a belt in order to control the bleeding until paramedics arrived and administered first aid to the victim. When the police questioned the victim, he was obviously in pain and discomfort and was being treated and prepared for surgery. The bullet had entered his leg and caused a compound fracture to his left femoral bone immediately above the knee. Reportedly, the victim was unable to move his leg and needed a walker to get around. In addition, amputation had been considered, but the victim's leg was saved. It was also learned that a friend of the victim had been fired on but was not struck.

Further investigation revealed two additional suspects, both adults named Robert Pérez and Tina Marina, and the suspect vehicle was identified as belonging to Tina Marina's mother. It was further learned that Tina Marina was the girlfriend of Mario Mercado. Marina was identified as being at Town Square, a strip mall less than a mile from the scene of the shooting, just minutes prior to the shooting. And suspect Junior Díaz was identified by witnesses as having entered the suspect vehicle at Town Square during the time period when Marina was also there.

Witnesses questioned by police stated that the primary suspects were identified as "the twins from Calle Cuatro," referring to Marcos and Mario Mercado, and that they were in the suspect vehicle at the time of the shooting. The driver of the suspect vehicle was identified as a female, and the front seat passenger was also identified as Robert Pérez, a known Fourth Street gang member. The initial confrontation took place at Town Square, a Pomona gang area. Junior Díaz, also known as "Baby Bull" and an identified Fourth Street gang member, was seen in the right rear passenger seat of the suspect vehicle. He was also seen spray-painting the wall adjacent to the shooting location. The other two subjects identified as being in the company of Díaz were Marcos and Mario Mercado, and all three were heard to call out, "Calle Cuatro!" prior to leaving the scene.

Additional witnesses who had been attending a wake in the area had approached the Mercado twins and Díaz when they allegedly began spray-painting on a wall and asked them to leave the area. They were also observed getting into the car that fled the scene, and from which the right passenger shot at the victim, striking him in the leg. Witnesses identified either Díaz or Pérez as the right front passenger, who was also the shooter, while the Mercado twins were seen in the back of the suspect vehicle.

On January 27, further investigation revealed that school security from Ganesha High School had advised that a student there had been "hit up" by a former Ganesha High School student, Junior Díaz, approximately five minutes before the shooting. Specifically, Díaz had been identified as approaching this student at Rosita's Restaurant in Town Square and asking him where he was from. The student allegedly told security that Díaz had a gun and that the student escaped being shot by running through the restaurant and out a back door. At least one witness at the scene of the shooting identified Díaz as having exited the suspect vehicle at the scene. Additional information was also received that the driver of the suspect vehicle had possibly been in the Super Duper Video Store immediately before the shooting. This is located to the right of Rosita's Restaurant. Police contacted the owner of the video store, who was able to identify the suspect vehicle as belonging to a customer and having been driven by the customer's daughter, who frequented the store. It was through that information that the involvement of Tina Marina was pursued. On February 18, as a result of further investigation, police arrested the boys and Mario's girlfriend, Tina Marina, who was allegedly the driver of the suspect vehicle.

Overview of the Preliminary Hearing

As noted, the case was complicated by the fact that we had multiple defendants and that each defendant was represented by a different lawyer. The twins' cousin, Junior Díaz, was represented by my associate Clemente Coronado and retained by the boys' grandmother. I represented Marcos, and the other twin, Mario, was represented by Johnny Sanders, an experienced African American attorney. William Costello, another experienced attorney, represented Tina Marina, Mario's girlfriend and the alleged driver of the suspect vehicle. Michael James, a well-known defense lawyer, represented Dora Martínez, Marcos's ex-girlfriend, who was charged in a separate incident but was eventually released after she agreed to serve as a witness in this case. Deputy District Attorney Berta García appeared for the people. The Honorable Elizabeth Madsen was the presiding judge.

After the attorneys made their appearances on the record, the judge noted, regarding Mr. Marcos Mercado, "I have a new misdemeanor, 243(h) (Assault on Peace Officer), 148(a) (Resisting, Delaying, or Obstructing a Police Officer, which probably occurred in this building)." I told the judge we would like to enter a plea of not guilty and set it for pre-trial, and the judge said that we would deal with this matter at the conclusion of the proceedings that day. She told me to remind her to set a date after we finished with the testimony.

Before going into the details of the "prelim," I want to say something about preliminary hearings in general. The preliminary hearing is not a full-blown trial but a preliminary inquiry, which is held to determine whether there is sufficient evidence to establish probable cause in a felony case as to whether the defendant will be held to answer to the charges in the complaint in a regular trial. Obviously, the evidentiary threshold is much lower than it is in a trial, where the standard is proof beyond a reasonable doubt. Another change subsequent to Proposition 115 is that hearsay evidence is now admissible in the preliminary hearing, whereas it is generally not admissible in a trial, unless it fits within one or more of the recognized hearsay exceptions, so that potential witnesses in effect testify through the arresting officer. Unless there is little or no evidence, defendants are normally bound over for trial after the preliminary hearing.

District Attorney García was a young woman in her mid- to late thirties who worked in the gang unit. García was a Chicana raised in Los Angeles who showed little sympathy or compassion for gangs or gang members. She was a tough adversary and a zealous advocate for the people who worked closely with law enforcement. The defense lawyers described her as being like a pit bull who was constantly on the attack and relentless in her pursuit of gangs.

The courtroom was small and had a seating capacity of about only thirty to forty people. The defendants came into the room in chains and shackles and were guarded by two armed bailiffs. The boys were dressed in LA County–issued orange jumpsuits, while Tina Marina was dressed in an oversized, dark blue jumpsuit. Normally, the defendant is allowed to sit next to his or her attorney so that the defendant can readily confer with the attorney and ask questions of the attorney. However, because there were four defendants, the judge said that the defendants would not be allowed to sit by their respective attorneys and she ordered them to remain inside the iron cage, or holding cell, where defendants normally sit during arraignments and sentencing.

The seating arrangement bothered me a great deal, not only because it precluded me from conferring with my client but because it reinforced the impression that the boys were in fact gang members and criminals who were guilty of the crimes that they were accused of committing. Although there was no jury, everything done by the judge, district attorney, and detectives who testified further reinforced the impression that they were in fact criminals.

One of the reasons attorneys prefer that their clients dress up for court is that if a defendant is well dressed and in civilian clothes or is able to wear a suit and tie during court proceedings, for example, it reinforces the idea that he or she is to be presumed to be innocent until their guilt is proven beyond a reasonable doubt. Also, because the four defendants were sitting in close proximity to each other, the judge was continually admonishing them not to communicate with anyone in the audience or with one another. The seating arrangement reminded me a great deal of the famous Sleepy Lagoon case.

The Sleepy Lagoon Defendants

Sleepy Lagoon was a famous case in the 1940s in which seventeen young, innocent men were convicted of conspiracy to commit the murder of José Díaz, a murder that was never confirmed.[4] The young men were accused and later convicted of conspiracy to murder Díaz on the night of August 2, 1942. Díaz had apparently attended and left a drinking party on the Williams Ranch, near a reservoir and popular "lover's lane" called the Sleepy Lagoon, which was close to the defendants and other youth in the area. The reservoir was a popular hangout for Mexican youth because at the time, they were not allowed to swim in public swimming pools in the city. A fight was said to have erupted after members of the Thirty-eighth Street gang crashed the party. The conviction was obtained even though the prosecution failed to show that the boys had beaten Díaz or that he had in fact been beaten and murdered. Díaz had been drinking heavily, and his body was found on a dirt road near the house, after he was probably struck by a hit-and-run driver. Incredibly, each defendant was charged with the murder of Díaz, despite the lack of evidence establishing either that a murder had occurred or that the boys were responsible for the alleged murder.

One of the most outrageous aspects of the case is that the Sleepy Lagoon defendants were in jail for three months without being allowed to get haircuts or a change of clothing, because the prosecution maintained that the "appearance of the defendants is distinctive" and that "their style of haircut, the thick heavy heads of hair, the duck tail comb, the *pachuco* pants and things of that kind" were important "evidence" used in proving their guilt.[5] Also, despite repeated defense objections, the prosecution went out of its way to point to the ethnic origin of the young defendants. In fact, Judge Fricke was so confused as to the identity of the boys that each defendant was asked to stand up as he was discussed during a particular phase of the trial: "The boys were seated in a special section across the room from the jury and as their names came up, they kept popping up and then sitting down.... The effect was not only ludicrous, it was incriminating. For when you are made to stand up when you are being accused of this and that, the effect on the jury must be that you had acknowledged your guilt."[6]

The defense of the Sleepy Lagoon defendants was further hampered by Judge Fricke, who ruled among other things that the defendants were not allowed to sit next to or have access to their lawyers. Even during breaks in the trial, the boys were transported to a holding cell and were still not allowed to confer with their attorneys, despite strenuous protests from the defense attorney, Shibley:

> MR. SHIBLEY: If your Honor please, I object on the grounds that this is a denial of the rights guaranteed all defendants, and each one of them, both by the Federal and State Constitution. I think their right to counsel and to be represented by counsel at all stages of the proceedings demands that they have the right to come to their counsel and speak to them during the proceedings.[7]

The Sleepy Lagoon defendants were convicted. Two years after their conviction, the case was reversed on appeal.

Although the mistreatment in the twins' case was less extreme than in the Sleepy Lagoon case, one cannot escape the similarities in the treatment of the defendants. Like the members of the Thirty-eighth Street gang, members of the Fourth Street gang had to sit in a special holding cell. Although they were allowed to bathe and get haircuts, the fact that they were dressed in prison-issued jumpsuits reinforced the image of them as members of a violent and dangerous criminal street gang.

A Gang by Any Other Word Is Still a Gang

As noted, although the STEP Act does not make membership in a gang a crime, "actively participating" in a criminal street gang is a separate offense punishable by "imprisonment in a county jail for a period not to exceed one year, or by imprisonment in the state prison for 16 months, or two or three years." Unfortunately, the statute fails to adequately and independently define a criminal street gang.

The statute defines a criminal street gang as an "ongoing organization, association, or group of three or more persons, whether formal or informal, having as one of its primary activities the commission of one or more of the [specified] criminal acts... having a common name or common identifying sign or symbol, and whose members individually or collectively engage in or have engaged in a pattern of criminal gang activity" (subd. [f]).

Alice Greenfield, executive director of the Sleepy Lagoon Defense Committee, and romantically linked to one of the principal defendants, Henry Leybas, maintained that the Thirty-eighth Street defendants were not a "gang" in the traditional sense of the word.

> I would strongly disagree with anybody who would call them a gang. ... Groups, you know, were referred to as "gangs," even if they sort of hung out on the same corner, and that didn't mean anything. Our gang was our group, and prior to this period, and after, you would hear people talking about our gang goes to this or our gang goes to that. They don't mean gangsters at all. They simply mean a group of people who hang out. ... The kids who live on 38th street were said to belong to the 38th St. gang ... but it didn't mean at all, anything like what was inferred by people and was implied in the newspaper. The implication was that it was a group of marauding people who always went around together.[8]

As the Sleepy Lagoon trial progressed, the press ran sensationalized stories of crazed "zoot-suit gangsters" and "pachuco killers" who were running amuck, terrorizing innocent people.

While the twins' particular case was not widely publicized, there has been increased concern with criminal gang activity in Los Angeles and Southern California. Like the Thirty-eighth Street boys, the boys in this case were not an organized criminal street gang. The name "Fourth Street" or "Calle Cuatro" simply referred to the neighborhood where the boys lived, and the membership consisted of the twins, their cousin Junior, and their friends, girlfriends, and other acquaintances. The boys liked to hang out at the local strip mall, which included Rosa's Mexican Restaurant, Chico's Market, and the local video store where they would rent videos. The boys rode bicycles, rather than driving cars, and were usually transported over longer distances by their girlfriends, who were a few years older and did have access to cars. Also, although the boys had been in trouble with the police in the past and had been in juvenile hall, it was never established that one of the "primary activities" of the group was the commission of one or more of the specified felonies or that its members, individually or collectively, had engaged in a "pattern of criminal activity." Ultimately, the gang was identified and defined by police detectives who were brought in to testify, and did testify, as "experts" on criminal street gangs.

The Preliminary Hearing

The first day of the preliminary hearing began with the testimony of Detective Mike Hyatt, the principal detective assigned to the case two weeks prior, and it had been continued to December 11 because the detective had not finished testifying. District Attorney García began the second day of the preliminary hearing by asking:

MS. GARCÍA: Your Honor, before we begin, can we have the court ask the gentleman in the back row with the shaved head to identify himself, please?
THE COURT: Sir, who are you?
MR. DÍAZ: Joe Díaz.
THE COURT: Do you have any relationship to this case?
MR. DÍAZ: My brother. Junior Díaz.
MS. GARCÍA: Your Honor, we've checked; Mr. Díaz is on gang terms and a condition of his gang terms is he's not to be in any court proceeding where he is not a party or witness to the court proceeding. Can we ask him if he's either a party or witness to this proceeding?

THE COURT: Mr. Díaz, are you a party to this proceeding or are you a witness?
MR. DÍAZ: No.
THE COURT: May I ask you to step out or else you will be arrested for being in violation of your gang terms, so you probably want to leave.
MR. DÍAZ: Oh, fuck, all right.
THE COURT: Thank you.

This move clearly gave the district attorney the upper hand because even before anyone took the stand, she had excluded Junior's brother and the twins' cousin because he was a gang member who was on probation. More importantly, Joe Díaz's presence and quick exit from the court proceedings did not help the boys or their case because by association they, too, were directly linked to a known gang member.

The district attorney then asked to take another witness out of turn, Dora Martínez, because her attorney, Michael James, was unavailable in the afternoon. Dora, Marcos's ex-girlfriend, had initially been charged along with Marcos in connection with a second shooting incident that allegedly took place on January 19, but she had negotiated a plea for time served after she agreed to testify against the boys.

Testimony of Dora Martínez

After Dora Martínez took the stand, the district attorney asked her whether she was driving a white Honda Civic, license number 4POD431, on the evening of January 19. She admitted that she was driving the vehicle in the area of the Twenty-second Street gang neighborhood. All the initial questions by the district attorney were clearly leading, and although the other defense attorneys objected, the judge allowed the questions, ostensibly because this was a preliminary hearing in which there was more latitude in the questioning allowed. The district attorney said, for example, "And so let's just pretend I don't know anything about Twenty-second. Can you tell me how you would know that a gang called 'Twenty-second' controls that neighborhood? What is it about that that you are aware of?" I objected that the question was misleading, and Mario's attorney, Johnny Sanders, added that the question "misstates the evidence. No evidence [was introduced that] they controlled the neighborhood." The court sustained the objections, but only as to the word "control," and asked the district attorney to rephrase her question to become the question, "How do you know that's a Twenty-second Street neighborhood—can you tell me some details about that?" Dora responded that it was "the streets, the people who live there. I mean the graffiti on the wall and stuff." The district attorney also asked her if she knew what a moniker is and Dora answered, "A nickname?" and the district attorney said, "Yes."

The witness further testified that on the evening of January 19, she had driven Marcos and Mario Mercado and another person named Robert to the Twenty-second Street neighborhood. The district attorney asked her if she could identify Marcos in court, and she identified him. She added that she had known Mario for two or three years through school and had only recently met Marcos. She said that she could tell Marcos and Mario apart and proceeded to also identify Mario. The district attorney asked the witness whether she had ever seen Marcos and Mario making gang signs, and she answered that she had. She was then asked for the various monikers that the boys had used, and she said that Marcos was called "Dreamer," while Mario was "Sneaky" and Robert was called "Sleepy." She also admitted that the boys responded either to their first names or to their respective monikers.

Dora testified that on the evening of January 19, she arrived at the strip mall about 7:30 p.m. She had gone to Chico's Market, just to check out "who was out." In response to a question about whether Chico's Market was a place where Fourth Street gang members hung out, she stated yes, but that she was not a gang member, although she knew and associated both with members of the Fourth Street and the Twenty-second Street gang.

She was then asked to describe the streets that were included in the Fourth Street area that the gang claimed to control. She added that one could see graffiti throughout the neighborhood, but she had never seen Marcos or Mario Mercado write graffiti on walls or on anyone's property. In response to what she had ever seen Marcos and Mario write, Dora said she had seen them write "4th Street" on paper or their monikers on paper when they hung out, but nothing else, and she added that they normally threw the papers away when they finished.

On the evening in question, she said, Mario had asked her to give them a ride to the Twenty-second Street neighborhood near the freeway. She said that she did not want to drive around; Mario asked again, and when she said no, he said, "Okay, we'll take our bikes." She finally agreed to take them and they got into her car. Marcos was seated in the back seat behind the front passenger, Mario was sitting in the front next to the driver, and Robert was in the back seat, directly behind Dora, the driver.

She said that Mario gave her directions, like, "make a right here or a left there," without naming the streets, and that it took them just five to ten minutes to get to their destination—if that—and that she stopped and parked the car when Mario asked her to stop. When she pulled over to the curb, Marcos and Robert got out of the vehicle. She said that she had seen about five people standing together and that although she did not recognize any of them, they looked like "gangsters" from Twenty-second Street by their style and the clothes they were wearing, which she went on to describe as "big jackets, big pants, and bald heads."

After they got out of the car, Marcos and Robert allegedly started walking toward the five people. Upon further questioning, Dora added that Robert had a baggy jacket, like a Dickies brand jacket, and that she saw him pull out a gun. She said that she watched them for a while but then started listening to the radio. She admitted that she could not see very well because she did not have her glasses, and that after a few minutes she heard two or three gunshots. Dora said that as the boys ran back to the car she saw two guns, with Robert carrying a shotgun about three feet long and Marcos carrying a handgun, adding that she heard someone say something about "someone screaming like a bitch," but she could not remember who said it. She said that Mario instructed her to leave and that they drove back to Chico's Market. When they returned to Chico's, Dora said that Marcos and Robert got out of the car and started talking to other Fourth Street gang members, but that she never heard them talking about the incident and that they never spoke about the incident again after that. When asked whether she felt concerned about what the boys had just done, Dora responded, "I did but I didn't," and then she went on to explain, "Well, I wanted to know what had just happened because obviously I was involved, but I didn't want to know because the less you know the better."

Dora admitted that Marcos had been her boyfriend until recently and that she had corresponded with him since the boys were arrested. When the district attorney asked whether he had said anything about testifying, Dora said he told her "not to go against him," and added that she took that to mean "for me not to say anything."

My Cross-Examination

I was the first to cross-examine the witness, since Dora had seriously implicated my client. All of the defense attorneys took turns briefly cross-examining the witness, each in their own way trying as best they could to impeach or discredit her in some way. I began by asking her about my client, Marcos.

MIRANDÉ: Is Marcos your boyfriend?
DORA: He was my boyfriend.
M: He was your boyfriend, okay.
D: Was.
M: He no longer is your boyfriend?
D: No, my boyfriend.
M: Yeah, he's not your boyfriend?
D: No.
M: So what happened, why is he not your boyfriend?
D: Because he's in jail and I am not.
M: And because you are testifying?
D: Well, obviously.
M: Okay. Are you aware that Marcos has another girlfriend?
D: Yes.
M: You were in court, in fact here, a few weeks ago, were you not, and you saw his other girlfriend?
D: Yes.
M: So would it be fair to say that Marcos dumped you?
D: Or I dumped him.
M: You are his ex-girlfriend?
D: Yes.
M: How old are you?
D: Twenty—I just turned twenty-one.
M: You are twenty-one?
D: Yes.
M: How old were you at the time on January—January 19?
D: I had just turned twenty.
M: How old was he?
D: He was seventeen.
M: He was a minor?

D: Yes.
M: And you were an adult?
D: Yes.
M: And you drove a car?
D: Yes.
M: He didn't have a car, did he?
D: No.
M: Okay, and on the day in question, January 19, you saw them at Chico's Market?
D: Yes.
M: You were in control of your vehicle at that point, were you not?
D: Yes.
M: During that evening? No one pulled a gun and forced you to drive anywhere, did they?
D: No.
M: So you drove wherever you drove out of your own volition, right?
D: Yes.
M: You were in control, you were the one that decided, you weren't forced?
D: Yes.
M: When you went to Twenty-second Street, when you got to the Twenty-second Street area, you testified that you saw Twenty-second Street gang members there?
D: Yes.
M: And given the fact that you were aware of the conflict between Fourth Street and Twenty-second Street, were you scared?
D: Yes.
M: Why didn't you leave the area?
D: I don't know.
M: So you continued to drive even though you were aware of the problems, right?
M: When you go from Fourth Street to Twenty-second Street, do you expect trouble?
D: Yes, if I am with other people, yes.
M: You did that?
D: Yes.

M: You indicated that it's obvious that you wear glasses?
D: Yes.
M: And you indicated that you didn't have your glasses that night?
D: No.
M: But you did testify that you couldn't see because you didn't have your glasses, did you not?
D: Because it was at night; I can't see very good without any glasses at night.
M: You have difficulty seeing at night; is that what you testified?
D: Without my glasses.
M: You made a deal with the district attorney here; is that right?
D: Yes.
M: In exchange for your testimony?
D: Yes.
M: And so you are testifying here so that you don't have to go to jail; is that right?
D: Yes.

I was trying to show through her testimony that she was an adult, that she was in control of her vehicle, that she knew of the conflicts between the two neighborhoods, that no one forced her to drive her car to the Twenty-second Street neighborhood, and that she continued to drive after she saw the rival gang members even though she was scared. My intent was to show that she voluntarily and knowingly drove to the rival gang area even though she knew there was likely to be, as she put it, "trouble."

I also got Dora to admit that she had initially lied when she first met with detective Hyatt and his partner on March 4 when she told them she didn't know anything about the January 19 incident. I then asked her whether she was lying now and she naturally said, "No." She also admitted that when she goes from Fourth Street to Twenty-second Street, she expects trouble.

Finally, I questioned Dora on the fact that she testified that she didn't have her glasses that night and that she can't see without her glasses. She answered, "I could see. I just couldn't see very good." The final question was designed to get Dora to admit that she was testifying "so that [she wouldn't] have to go to jail."

Coronado's Cross-Examination

Clemente Coronado began his cross-examination by saying to Dora, "Tell us what your understanding is of the agreement that you have with the district attorney. In other words, what are you getting in return?"

> DORA: Um, I'm getting three years probation and I'm being charged with discharging of the firearm.
>
> CORONADO: So have you pled guilty already to that charge?
>
> D: Yes, I did.
>
> C: And you pled guilty to discharging a firearm, you said—anything else?
>
> D: I believe that's it.
>
> C: And so that night that we've been talking about, did you discharge a firearm?
>
> D: Personally, no.
>
> C: So you pled guilty to assisting others to do that; is that what you pled guilty to?
>
> D: Yes.
>
> C: And you got three years probation, did you get any jail time as a result of that?
>
> D: What I served. I think it was—I don't think—it is something like fifty-eight days that I had credit.
>
> C: Now, so you got three years probation, credit time served for the fifty-some days that you had in; any other terms or punishment?
>
> D: Yes.
>
> C: What?
>
> D: I am living in a recovery home.
>
> C: Is that a condition of—is that part of the agreement?
>
> D: That was part of the agreement when I got out of jail.
>
> C: And is the recovery home for some type of addiction?
>
> D: Yes.
>
> C: So are you addicted to something?
>
> D: Yes, I am.

Dora admitted that she had been using speed for more than two years and that on the night that this event occurred, she was an abuser of methamphetamine. She did not recall whether she had used methamphetamine on the night of the incident, but she admitted that she had been a daily or almost daily user and would have used it that day or the day before. Her practice was to use the methamphetamine when she got home from work at around 4:45 p.m. and to consume what she referred to as "a twenty" or twenty dollars' worth.

Mario's attorney, Johnny Sanders, asked Dora once again how long she had known Mario, and she said she had known him for about two or three years and that she had met him at Poly High School and was pretty sure it was three years ago. Although Mario left school, she continued to see him at parties, walking around, or whenever they felt like seeing each other. She denied being one of the "Fourth Street girls" and said, "I just hung around with some Fourth Street people." She also denied that another Fourth Street boy, Larry Trujillo, had been her boyfriend before Marcos and said she just partied with him. When asked what "partying" entailed, she said, "Meaning drugs, music, dancing, whatever."

She said she stopped hanging out with people from Fourth Street after she got out of jail and that she does not go into that neighborhood anymore. Upon further questioning from Mario's attorney, she admitted that she never saw Mario with a gun that night and did not see him directing the other guys to do anything. She also admitted that when they got back to Chico's Market, she never heard Mario say, "I ordered these guys to blast somebody" or, "We did it"; and she did not hear anyone say, "Yeah, we got that guy."

The last attorney to cross-examine the witness was Mr. Costello. Costello began by asking Dora if she had ever considered the pros and cons of testifying, and she said that she had. Some of the bad things about testifying, in her mind, were that she didn't want to be "a rat" and that she was scared for her personal safety, but the thought of going to jail and facing the repercussions of a serious felony helped her in making the decision to testify.

Costello then got her to admit that hanging out with people from the neighborhood did not make one a gang member. She admitted that because she hung around with people from Fourth Street, she could throw their signs and might see them committing their crimes but that she was not one of them. She admitted that when they got into the car, she didn't notice that one of the boys had a shotgun under his long jean jacket or that Marcos had a pistol underneath his shirt. She also admitted that once she decided to give the boys a ride to Twenty-second Street, "nothing good could happen."

Dora testified that when they got to the rival gang neighborhood and one of the boys asked her to park the car, they were about a block or a block and a half from the Twenty-second Street gang members, and that when someone asked her to pull the car over, she knew that something bad was about to happen. She also admitted that when they got out, she was curious as to what was about to happen and she was watching in the rearview mirror but did not see anything. Costello then asked why, after the shooting, she had not simply told them to get out of there, and she said, "Because I couldn't just leave them there ... because they would have gotten shot and it would have been on me." Dora reiterated that one of the boys had said someone had "screamed like a bitch," but that she could not remember who it was.

Dora said that she and Marcos were not boyfriend and girlfriend at the time of the incident but that she had accelerated her relationship with him after the boys were arrested. She also said that except for her attorney, she had not talked to anyone about her testimony, including the district attorney.

Testimony of Lead Detective Hyatt

After Dora finished her testimony, Detective Hyatt—the lead detective on the case—took the stand. Upon direct examination, he said he had responded to the January 27 incident in response to several 9-1-1 calls received by the local police department, and that the calls came in between 7:46 p.m. and 7:51 p.m., but he never testified that anyone was shot during that incident.

He said he also spoke with a person named Rosita Alvirez, who denied having witnessed the shooting. However, upon further questioning, Hyatt said that when he spoke to the victim on February 11, the victim told him that he had spoken with Ms. Alvirez and that she had told the victim that she saw the shooting, and that she said she had seen Marcos and Mario Mercado and, he said, "I believe Mario's girlfriend."

Detective Hyatt went on to testify that he also spoke to Rosita Alvirez's father and that her father also told him that his daughter had said "that she had witnessed the shooting and two of the suspects were the twins from Fourth Street, Mario and Marcos Mercado."

Hyatt further testified that he had gone to the crime scene on January 27 and that people at the scene were generally uncooperative and that this was typical in gang-related shootings. He added that as he was standing looking around and assessing the situation, another gang member named Rick Ortiz "walked past me at my side and he said something—'Look at the twins from Fourth Street,' or something to that effect." He added that it was clear that he did not want anyone to see him talking to the detective because "it was a soft voice to where only I could hear."

When I cross-examined Detective Hyatt, I asked whether Mr. Ortiz was a credible witness, and he responded that when he asked if he was a gang member, he said he was an ex–gang member. Hyatt also admitted that Rosita Alvirez had identified another person, Ron Vera, as being involved with this crime. He said that Vera was initially charged with the crime but that the charges had been dismissed, so he was no longer a defendant in the case.

Testimony of Detective Robert Gordon

The next witness was Detective Robert Gordon, who was assisting Detective Hyatt on the case and was part of the Special Enforcement Gang Unit in the area. Detective Gordon testified that he was on duty on March 4 and that he interviewed defendant Tina Marina on that date. When asked if he saw Tina Marina in court that day, he said, "Looks like she's wearing a blue jumpsuit in the defense cell." That remark was almost humorous, since although the three male defendants were in orange jumpsuits and she was in a blue one, she was the only woman in the cell, so it wasn't hard to identify her—regardless of the color of her jumpsuit. He said that he had read Ms. Marina her Miranda rights and that she said that she understood her rights.

Detective Gordon said he told Tina that "during our investigation it had been determined that her vehicle was the vehicle used in the shooting (on January 27), and we placed her at the scene of the shooting by checking video-rental records from a video store where she had rented a video approximately six minutes before the shooting occurred." He added that prior to his telling Tina about the video she rented, she had denied she was at the scene of the shooting, but she stopped denying she was involved in the shooting once she was informed she was known to have rented a video immediately preceding it.

Detective Gordon testified that on the day of the shooting, she had gone over to her boyfriend Mario Mercado's house at about 2 p.m. He added that Mario's brother, Marcos, and his cousin lived at the same location. Detective Gordon further added that Tina told him that her boyfriend had admitted to being a Fourth Street gang member. Detective Gordon identified each of the twins and their cousin, Junior, as being in the courtroom.

Detective Gordon testified that Tina told him that she had wanted to rent a movie and that they all drove to the strip mall. Detective Gordon added that at first Tina was extremely hesitant and that she told him initially that she couldn't remember where everyone was sitting in the car, but that eventually she told him that her boyfriend, Mario, was sitting in the front passenger seat; that the cousin, Junior, was sitting behind her; and that the other twin, Marcos, was sitting behind the front passenger seat. The detective said Tina told him they then drove to the strip mall and went to the video store and that after that, Mario and Junior went into Rosa's Mexican Restaurant to get a soft drink.

After that, he said, Tina stated that they all got into the car and started driving south down Central Street and turned westbound on Mission Boulevard and continued westbound, turning on Painter and continuing to drive until she heard someone in the car ask her to stop the car. Detective Gordon said that Tina alleged she could not remember who told her to stop the car. Gordon said Tina told him she parked the car on the north side of the curve, just off Mission, and turned off the engine. The detective added that the area where the car was stopped is controlled by the Twenty-second Street gang.

According to Detective Gordon, Tina said that she remained in the car with Marcos while Junior exited the vehicle, and that Junior went over to a wall that was painted white at 301 S. Painter St. and started spray-painting the wall, while Marcos was standing somewhere in the vicinity of the wall. The detective said that based on his previous work in the area, he knew the Alvirezes live at that address and that they are members of the Twenty-second Street gang. Detective Gordon testified that the graffiti on the wall was Fourth Street graffiti, but that it was incomplete and he could not make out what it said.

Detective Gordon added that Tina said at that point a male approached them and that "a skinny female with dark hair started yelling at them to stop disrespecting the neighborhood or stop disrespecting the house." Gordon said that Tina told him at that point, Marcos had gotten out of the car and "she believed that one of them, I think she said it was Marcos, she believed apologized to the lady and said they would leave."

Tina said that they then all got into the car, with her boyfriend Mario sitting in the passenger seat next to her, and with Marcos sitting in the right rear seat while their cousin Junior sat in the left rear. The detective said that the male who approached them turned out to be the person who got shot, and that when they left, Tina had to swerve to avoid hitting him. "As she passed, she said she heard something hit the back of the passenger side of the car but she didn't know what it was." And then after that she said she heard gunshots.

Tina then stopped answering questions and started to cry, but she eventually admitted to Detective Gordon that the gun was fired by her boyfriend Mario Mercado and that she heard approximately two to three shots. The detective said that Tina alleged that when Mario got back down in his seat, someone in the backseat asked if he had hit anyone and Mario said that "he thought that he had."

Reflections on the Case

Fermina, I wanted to take a moment to share my thoughts on the case. First, I should tell you that none of the defense attorneys were surprised that at the conclusion of the preliminary hearing, the boys were indicted and held to answer the charges. Unfortunately, there were numerous continuances and it took about three years before the case finally went to trial. In the interim, I had to substitute out of the case because I accepted a law teaching position at the Western Plains College of Law, and I decided that I could no longer continue on the case because I would be moving out of state.

Although I loved teaching in a law school and got along well with my colleagues at Western Plains, I felt strangely out of place living in Plainview. I don't know how to explain it, except that I felt like "a fish out of water." I frankly missed California and the students at UC Riverside. One of the things I love about Riverside is the diversity of the student body, which is more than 40 percent Asian/Pacific Islander and more than 30 percent Latino. The Western Plains law school student body was not diverse at all, as we only had one Asian and about three African American students in a school with a total enrollment of approximately 450 students. Hispanics made up about 8 to 9 percent of the law school student body. Although the faculty was congenial and fairly progressive, the student body was not diverse and surprisingly conservative.

Upon my return to Riverside after a stint at Western Plains and a one-quarter sabbatical leave, I ran into Clemente at the County Law Library and was surprised and saddened to learn that the boys had been convicted and had each been sentenced to forty-five years to life for attempted murder. Now that I look back on the case and the circumstances surrounding it, however, I am actually surprised that I was surprised at the conviction because the conviction seems now to have been almost a foregone conclusion. I was on the case for approximately eighteen months, and it took another two years or so before the case went to trial.

In retrospect, I believe that the key to the conviction was California's anti-gang statute (Penal Code § 186.22), which I have told you is better known as the STEP Act. There were so many enhancements for committing a crime during the course of participating in or at the direction of a gang—and so many mandatory life sentences for serious and/or violent felonies—that the boys were destined to be sentenced to indeterminate life terms. A related factor was the gang culture and the intense loyalty and the code among gang members, which values loyalty to the group and strongly frowns upon snitching on members of your gang, or "homies." This code of loyalty was exacerbated in this case by the fact that the boys were not only members of the Fourth Street gang but family.

As noted, in mexicano culture, being a primo hermano or first cousin is like being a brother, so the twins and their cousin were very close, like brothers. A final and critical factor in ensuring their conviction was that prior to the trial, Mario's girlfriend and the driver of the suspect vehicle, Tina Marina, accepted a plea bargain offered by the district attorney and was released in exchange for agreeing to testify against the boys. Since the victim refused to cooperate with the prosecution or to testify in the case, the only way that the prosecution could obtain a conviction was through Tina Marina's testimony.

As I reflect back on the case, it is hard to believe that my client was sentenced to what amounts to a life sentence for the crime of essentially being in the back seat of the vehicle from which the shots were allegedly fired, wounding the victim in the leg. Not only was my client not directly involved in the shooting or even in spray-painting the wall, but according to the testimony offered by the lead detective in the preliminary hearing, he apologized to the owners of the house and told them that the boys would be leaving the area shortly.

Do not get me wrong. I am not condoning going into rival neighborhoods or shooting people in the leg, but again, according to the lead detective at the preliminary hearing, Tina Marina told him that she heard a loud bang and felt something hitting the car prior to the shots being fired by the passenger in her vehicle, and the victim said that he threw a forty-ounce beer can at the suspect vehicle, so a case could have been made for the shooting being an act of self-defense. The boys, after all, were in a rival, hostile neighborhood and surrounded by members of the Twenty-second Street gang, who were attending a wake at the time, and when they heard a loud bang it would have been reasonable for them to think that someone was shooting at their vehicle. Finally, in the big scheme of things, the sentences certainly seem excessive, especially for my client and his cousin, who were in the back seat and did not directly fire the gun *or* drive the vehicle.

It was difficult for me not only to leave the case but to eventually learn that the boys were convicted. I take some solace in the fact that a very competent criminal defense attorney replaced me, and that all the criminal defense lawyers involved in the case were seasoned attorneys. I also take solace in thinking that the outcome would have been the same whether I stayed on the case or not, given the injustices and biases inherent in the criminal justice system, particularly against Latino gang members in Southern California.

In the eighteen months or so that I was involved in the case, I really got to know the boys and the family. I met the twins' grandmother, the person who retained us on the first day of court at juvenile hall. Doña Julia Delgado was a successful professional in her fifties who had a good job working as a social worker for the county of Los Angeles. She lived with her common-law husband, her daughter Jennie (Junior's mom), and the boys in a modest home in the Fourth Street neighborhood. The twins were raised by the grandmother because their mother was a heroin addict who spent most of her adult life going in and out of prison for various drug-related offenses. The boys saw and referred to Doña Julia as their mother because she was the only mother they had ever known. Junior's mother, Jennie or "La Güera," was an attractive ex-*chola* in her early thirties and extremely warm and engaging.

Jennie and her mother came to court dutifully throughout the course of the proceedings, since the boys had been arrested and placed in the County Juvenile Detention Center. They were always anxious to get updates on the case and would often give us messages to give to the boys or special insights into the case. The messages involved relatively simple matters like that the grandmother would be visiting them on such-and-such a date or relating some news from the neighborhood.

Since the case was delayed and continued a number of times, we had ample opportunity to interact with and really get to know the family. Doña Julia sometimes could not attend the proceedings because of her work, but La Güera attended just about every court date without fail, and she and other family members would sit and chat with the attorneys during breaks in the court proceedings, so that we began to feel like family. I do not know exactly how to explain it, but there was a certain bonding that took place between the attorneys, the family, and the boys during the course of the proceedings that was very special. We were like a team.

La Güera, Doña Julia, and other family members were also an excellent source of information on the case. They told us, for example, that the victim in this case had reportedly been convicted in a gang shooting and was doing time in the state prison up north, and that he would not testify against the boys, or they would say things like the word was out on the streets that someone else was bragging in the neighborhood about being the shooter in the case.

Marcos would ask me to visit him in the county jail and so I tried to go out on Sunday afternoons whenever possible. Even though Marcos was a gang member who was charged with attempted murder, he impressed me as a fairly typical eighteen-year-old who was not really that different from my son, Alejandro.

Our meetings were fairly formal at first, focusing mostly on the case, but our relationship soon evolved and became more like a friendship. I would talk about miscellaneous things like my son, things I was doing, my background, or how one becomes a lawyer, and Marcos would tell me about his art, his girlfriends, and how things were inside the county jail. He told me about an incident where another inmate was severely beaten by another inmate, while the guards just watched, and how the guards were always harassing him, as well as other inmates. He also gave me notes and questions to ask during the preliminary hearing.

Before closing, I wanted to talk briefly about the policy implications of the STEP Act. As noted, the STEP Act was crafted by law enforcement and is designed to wage a war against gangs. Los Angeles and other Southern California communities have gone so far as to use injunctions in the war against gangs, in order to declare them a public nuisance as specified in Penal Code § 186.22.

In Riverside, California, for example, the Riverside County district attorney held a press conference announcing an injunction filed by the county's district attorney and granted by the Riverside Superior Court. A story appearing in the Riverside *Press-Enterprise* described the injunction, modeled after similar injunctions in Los Angeles and San Bernardino:

> The Riverside County district attorney and Riverside police chief stood in the heart of East Side Riva territory Friday and laid out a new legal strategy to cripple the county's largest and most violent street gang. . . . More than 100 members of the gang will no longer be free to congregate on street corners, wear gang colors or carry weapons in a zone on the city's east side under a court order filed Wednesday by Riverside County prosecutors and the Riverside Police Department.[9]

According to the injunction, the district attorney was going against 114 gang members named in the injunction as a public nuisance, with the aim of putting the gangs out of business. The 114 named persons allegedly had 333 misdemeanor and felony convictions, as well as 46 outstanding cases. Seven of these outstanding cases were said to be for charges of murder and eight for attempted murder.

> Effects on the 114 East Side Rivas members and its 10 factions:
> No associating with any East Side Riva member
> No blocking access to any vehicle, building, walkway, 10 p.m. curfew
> Not allowed to act as a police lookout
> No reckless driving
> No giving false information to police
> No intimidation, including displaying East Side Riva tattoos
> No public consumption of alcohol
> No loitering
> No gang signs
> No use of police scanners
> No use of two-way radios
> No breaking the law[10]

The STEP Act has a number of important implications and raises constitutional concerns. First, there is concern that the Act may significantly impair the First Amendment right to freedom of association. Second, there is concern with the fact that the Act severely limits the discretionary authority of judges by providing fixed enhancements of five years for serious felonies (Penal Code § 1192.7) and ten years for violent felonies (Penal Code § 667.5) and stipulating that judges must normally impose the intermediate sentences, unless there are factors in aggravation or mitigation that justify otherwise, as well as that a judge who does not impose the intermediate sentence must state the reasons on the record. A third concern is that the Act provides an indeterminate sentence to life if the felony was committed for the benefit of, at the direction of, or in association with a criminal street gang. The last and final concern, as noted, is that the Act does not adequately define a criminal street gang, nor is it even necessary for the prosecution to prove that the person is a member of a criminal street gang or devotes all, or a substantial part, of his or her time or efforts to the criminal street gang. Active participation in the criminal street gang is all that is required. Despite these concerns, the STEP Act has successfully withstood constitutional challenges and it remains the major controlling statute governing street gangs in California.

The STEP Act places an especially heavy burden on family members who participate in gangs, especially family members in groups like mexicanos who strongly value familism. Although Mario and Marcos were unique in being twins, it is certainly not uncommon for siblings to participate in the same gang. Unfortunately, very little has been written on the impact of the STEP Act or gang injunctions on Latino families. For the twins and their cousin, Junior, it would have been virtually impossible to comply with a gang injunction that would have prohibited them from associating with any member of the Fourth Street gang, since they lived and associated with one another 24/7.

Although I can justify withdrawing from the case, I would be lying to you if I told you that it did not bother me to withdraw. The decision to withdraw was very difficult, in fact. I had gotten to know Marcos and his family, and I felt a strong sense of obligation and loyalty to the family and pressure to do all I could do to get an acquittal. I also knew that the case had been continued many times, and that with five defense attorneys and with the courts being backed up, it was likely to be continued again and again. Finally, I knew that it would have been very difficult for me to stay on top of the case or to make numerous trips to California once I moved out of state and started teaching at Western Plains. In the summer before I withdrew, the case was actually scheduled for trial in June, continued until August, and then continued once again until December.

When I informed the court that I would be moving out of state and requested to be removed from the case, Judge Macias joked with me in open court about moving to Plainview, then wished me the best of luck and said that he would appoint someone from the defense panel to replace me as the attorney of record for Marcos Mercado. I was relieved when Clemente informed me that the person who replaced me was a very experienced attorney.

Although I hated to leave the case and frankly felt like I was somehow letting my client down, as I look back with the benefit of hindsight, I now realize that it may have been a blessing in disguise, since it would have been extremely difficult and painful for me to see the boys convicted and sentenced to life sentences. I would have felt like I had somehow not done enough to save my client.

⁖ 2 ⁖
Child Abuse
María y José

Querida Fermina,

I want to talk about death, a topic most people would rather avoid, but I first want to thank you for your recent letter and for your comments on the first couple of chapters. I have tried to spell-check carefully, to use fewer commas, and to limit capitalization as per your suggestion.

One of my first and most interesting cases involved a young couple. María and José were typical hard-working Mexican immigrants who were not rich but appeared to be doing well in the United States. You could say, in fact, that they were living the American dream until the untimely death of their baby son, Jesús, turned the dream into a horrible reality and nightmare. On the surface, the case appeared to be another instance of sudden infant death syndrome (SIDS)—but then an autopsy revealed that the infant had cracked ribs and a possible fracture to his right leg, and the parents were charged with murder.

José Martínez was about thirty-two years old and was born in the historic town of La Barca, which is near the Jalisco-Michoacan border, and migrated to the United State at age twenty. María, thirty, was born in Xaripu, a small village on the outskirts of Morelia, and came to the United States at the age of sixteen. María graduated from El Rancho Grande High School in Ontario. At the time of the incident, José worked in a warehouse in Pomona, California, and María was cleaning industrial buildings in the evenings in Rancho Cucamonga, California.

The young couple had been married for about five years and had two children—Victor, nearly three, and little Jesús, who was six months old at the time of his tragic death. While Victor was a very active, healthy, normal toddler, little Jesús had suffered a number of physical ailments and had been sickly since birth. Before going into the details of the case, I should state that I served as María's attorney, and that her husband,

José, was represented by an older, experienced lawyer—Patricia O'Brien, a defense-panel attorney appointed by the court.

The Parents' Story

According to María, she and José worked different shifts in their respective jobs so that they could take turns caring for the children and save money on childcare. José had recently been laid off from his regular job and was now working the night shift at a local warehouse, and he got home early in the morning. María generally went to work around four in the afternoon and worked until about 11 p.m. The couple only had one car, and José usually drove María to and from work. It was also not uncommon for José to take lunch or dinner to María or for the couple and the children to eat together at her job.

Prior to their son's death, José and María appeared to be an ideal couple. They were hard-working immigrants who by all appearances had a happy marriage and were proud parents of two young and very active little boys. Little Victor was the "apple of his grandparents' eye." In fact, neighbors described the Martínezes as a close-knit, almost idyllic family. There was certainly no history of alcoholism or domestic violence, and neither José nor María had ever been arrested or charged with a crime.

The neighbors in the small apartment complex where they lived spoke highly of the Martínez family. I spoke to a young Anglo couple that lived directly behind the Martínez house and shared a wall with them. Jake and Lisa Adams had developed a close friendship with José and María and described them as a very loving couple and a warm and happy family, noting that José would spend a lot of time playing with and watching the children. Lisa would often keep an eye on the children for a short period of time when José had to run an errand or went to pick up María from work. The Adamses reported that they never saw any domestic abuse problems or José and María fighting or hitting the children. Another neighbor, Rosa López, also watched the children on several occasions and interacted extensively with the family. Rosa indicated that she never saw either parent abusing or mistreating the children and that they were an ideal couple.

On the night of the death, José told the detectives that he had taken María to work and returned to the apartment. He then fed the baby and put him down for a nap and went out into the cul-de-sac to play with little Victor. After about an hour, he said, he came back into the apartment to check on the baby and was shocked to discover that the baby was not breathing. The neighbors called 9-1-1. The paramedics tried unsuccessfully to resuscitate the baby, and he was pronounced dead on arrival at La Loma University Hospital.

María said that little José had appeared to be fine when she went to work that day, although he had been sick in the past few weeks and they had taken him to the doctor in Tijuana just a few days before he died. On April 13, days before the death, María had noticed that the baby was fussy and that his right leg was swollen and red. The parents took the baby to an orthopedic surgeon in Tijuana, Dr. Jaime Ibáñez-Ortiz, who took x-rays and reported an inflammation of the arms and leg. The Tijuana doctor also noted that the baby was wearing a brace on his right leg, indicating that he had obtained treatment for the swelling. He diagnosed the baby as having osteomyelitis, a rare disease associated with brittle bones that causes infection and inflammation of the bones. In his medical report, Dr. Ibáñez-Ortiz wrote that the baby appeared to be "well cared for" and that there was absolutely no sign of child abuse. The doctor said the x-rays showed no broken bones, but he noted "separation" in the bones caused by the infection. Since birth, little Jesús had suffered various physical ailments and had a history of apnea, viral meningitis, and respiratory infections. He was hospitalized for ten days when he was only approximately three weeks old because of poor feeding, fussiness, and difficulty in breathing. He also had a spinal tap at that time because the doctors suspected that he had meningitis.

The Tijuana doctor had prescribed some medication for Jesús, which the parents had given the baby. María said that José would not have done anything to harm the baby. None of the neighbors said that they saw or heard anything that was unusual until José came out of his residence screaming that the baby was not breathing and they called 9-1-1. About a week elapsed between the baby's death and the arrest of José and María.

An arrest warrant was issued by the superior court on April 24 and the couple was arrested. María, whose bail was set at fifty thousand dollars, was bailed out by her parents. José's bail was set at five hundred thousand dollars, and he remained in custody throughout the proceedings. José was arraigned on April 25 and María on April 28.

José was charged with violation of Penal Code § 273d(a), inflicting injury upon a child, and María with violation of Penal Code § 273(a), willful cruelty to a child, resulting in possible injury or death. According to Penal Code § 273d(a): "Any person who willfully inflicts upon a child any cruel or inhuman corporal punishment or an injury resulting in a traumatic condition is guilty of a felony and shall be punished by imprisonment in the state prison for two, four, or six years, or in a county jail for not more than one year, by a fine of up to six thousand dollars ($6,000), or by both imprisonment and fine."

A Zealous Advocate

One of the basic truisms in law is that a lawyer is supposed to always be a "zealous" advocate for his or her client. Some of the common synonyms for "zealous" are keen, eager, enthusiastic, fervent, ardent, passionate, obsessive, fanatical, and extreme. Being a zealous advocate means simply that you have to believe in people that no one else believes in. For example, it is hard to be sympathetic with a person accused of killing his or her own baby.

When I took on this case, no one had to tell me that I was supposed to be a zealous advocate for María. In a sense, it was easy to be a zealous advocate because I never questioned her innocence. Before elaborating on the case, I want to talk a little about what it feels like to be put in the position of being a zealous advocate for someone accused of committing a heinous crime, like child abuse or child molestation.

As I interacted with my client, it was not hard for me to believe that I was representing a mother who had been wronged and was being falsely accused by the criminal and judicial system. It was easy, in other words, to see María and her husband not as perpetrators of a crime but as victims themselves. They were victims not only in the sense that they had lost their infant son but also in that they had been wrongly accused of killing him. An additional problem the young couple faced, which will be discussed at length later, is that the inexplicable death of their infant alerted the California Department of Child Protective Services (CPS) to immediately challenge their fitness to care for their three-year-old son. In fact, in a very real sense, the problems José and María faced with the criminal justice system paled in comparison to the problems that they would encounter with the CPS and the Juvenile Dependency Court relative to the contested custody of their older son.

It was difficult for me to see the young couple as child abusers because, as I have made clear, there was nothing in their behavior or background to suggest child abuse. Their neighbors were unanimous in their praise and support of María and José, reporting that the two were excellent parents and that they never saw anything to suggest they would abuse their children or mistreat them in any way. María's parents and siblings were also extremely supportive and swore that María and José would never do anything to harm or injure the children. Finally, there was very little in the medical record to suggest child abuse. The doctor who conducted the baby's autopsy, Lawrence Turk, noted, "People who abuse their children don't routinely take them for medical care, as the Martínez family did." People who abuse their children either seek no medical care or do so only by going to different emergency rooms or anonymous clinics, rather than by pursuing regular health care.

In the course of a year or so after my client's arraignment on April 28, there were many court appearances and continuances in this case, both in the criminal trial and in child dependency court, and I felt that my loyalty to my client was questioned every time I appeared on her behalf. From the day I made my first appearance at the arraignment and said, "Good morning, Your Honor—Alfredo Mirandé representing María Luz Martínez, who is present and not in custody," I was made to feel like I was representing a deranged criminal who had committed a heinous crime and a child abuser—even though there is supposed to be a "presumption of innocence" in our legal and judicial system. Perhaps what is most ironic about this is that it was precisely the court personnel (the district attorneys, clerks, bailiffs, court reporters, interpreters, and other court staff) who made me feel like this. (Judges tended to be less overtly negative.) Nothing was said directly to me, but through the gestures and actions of the various players in the legal and judicial system, they conveyed a negative and condescending, if not hateful, attitude toward my client, her husband, her family, and—indirectly—me. It is hard to put one's finger on something like this, but the way people would look at my client and me did convey the message that I was representing someone who was reprehensible.

The problem was exacerbated by the fact that José's bail was set at five hundred thousand dollars and he remained in custody throughout the duration of the criminal proceedings. He made each and every court appearance dressed in an orange jumpsuit and wearing shackles. This was especially problematic in the child dependency proceedings because José frankly began to look like a criminal, increasingly so as time elapsed and he started to get more "buff" from working out with weights in the prison yard.

I should mention that this is a problem in all criminal defense work, but it was exacerbated in this case by the nature of the charges. I was, after all, representing a woman accused of directly or indirectly causing the death of her infant son. Even if one assumed that it was José who had been responsible for the baby's death—since the baby was in José's custody at the time of his death—María's charge was that she knew or reasonably should have known that her husband had killed her son, and that she had failed to protect the baby.

While I certainly would like to believe that I generally treat all of my clients with dignity and respect, the circumstances surrounding this case may have made me even more self-conscious not only about being respectful toward my client but about being her zealous advocate. I do not know exactly how to explain this, since it is not something I did knowingly and it is not something taught in law school, but in retrospect I believe that I instinctively became keenly aware of the way that my client was being judged and disrespected, and this made me that much more compassionate and respectful toward her. I somehow felt like everyone was watching me to see how I would relate with such a "despicable" human being.

I want to give you an example from the preliminary hearing to illustrate the point. Before delving into the example, though, I should tell you that I had a student intern working with me on a couple of my cases during the summer. That intern, Alma García, was a stellar student who was going into her senior year in college at UC Riverside, was poised to apply to elite law schools, and participated in a Graduate Division mentor program that paired undergraduates with faculty mentors in order to give the students hands-on experience doing research, so that they would be better prepared to eventually pursue graduate study.[1] I asked Alma to keep a journal during her internship, and this is what she wrote in it about her first day in court at the preliminary hearing on July 7:

> In spite of all of the backlash hoopla, as I walked into the court, observing the officers of the court, police officers, DA, public defender, court staff, and the judge, I was reminded of how White the legal justice system *still* is. The desperation and fear and anger came bubbling to the surface. [María] leaned toward me and whispered, "Pray for us." Alfredo wasn't kidding about how the case would break my heart.[2]

After describing how there was lots of waiting before the start of the preliminary hearing, Alma made the following observation:

> The [bailiff] made María leave her crucifix behind. Alfredo offered his chair to María after the DA instructed him to have her sit on the bench behind [the attorneys] because he needed a chair for one of the officers.[3]

Alma's journal entries indirectly illustrate the pervasive disrespect that was directed at my client and how I unknowingly sought to demonstrate my zealous advocacy in subtle yet important ways, like giving up my chair in order to have my client sit at counsel table. By the way, I should mention that I was never comfortable with the court practice of allowing the DA to have the lead officer sit at counsel table during preliminary hearings, ostensibly because the lead investigating officer would assist the DA in various ways as the case progressed. This seemed to me to create a pro-prosecution bias, giving the lead detective priority over my client. You will recall that Proposition 115 permits hearsay testimony during a preliminary hearing from experienced law enforcement officers who conducted an investigation.

The Preliminary Hearing

A preliminary hearing, as I have noted, is an evidentiary hearing held after a complaint has been filed by the prosecution in order for a court to determine whether criminal charges will be heard by the court and what evidence will be admitted. Specifically, the court must find the following at the preliminary hearing, or "prelim," to be true before holding a person to answer the charges: (1) a crime has been committed, (2) the crime occurred within the jurisdiction of the court, and (3) there is probable cause to believe the crime was committed by the accused. In most jurisdictions, because the prelim represents the initiation of "adversarial judicial proceedings," the indigent suspect's right to appointed counsel attaches at this point.[4]

The conduct and rules surrounding the admissibility of evidence at a preliminary hearing vary from jurisdiction to jurisdiction, but if the court decides that there is probable cause to hold the defendant to answer, a formal charging instrument, or information, will be issued, and the prosecution will move forward. If there is no probable cause, which is highly unlikely, the charges will be dismissed, although the prosecution has the option to refile.

As the day of the preliminary hearing approached, we had still not yet received the autopsy results. I, therefore, went into the prelim prepared to make an oral motion to postpone the prelim until such time as the autopsy results were available. The prelim was set for 8:30 a.m. on July 7, but we only received the results of the autopsy at around 8:20 that day. Despite my loud objections and request for a continuance, we continued with the hearing after the motion was denied. Alma, my assistant, captured the defense's mood when she commented in her notes:

> Getting autopsy report at last second possible—like cramming before a test! One does not get the impression of justice served, but of something to get over with. The backlog is a reality but in the interest of people's lives and reputations, it should be taken a little more seriously.[5]

María had brought a change of clothes for José, so his attorney, Patricia O'Brien, asked the judge, "When is the defendant allowed to change out of his prison uniform into civilian clothes?"[6] The judge answered that the defendant was allowed to change into civilian clothes only for the actual trial, when the jury would be present—not during the preliminary hearing. The implication was that, unlike the jury, the judge would not be biased by the fact that the defendant was wearing an orange prison uniform and certainly looked like a criminal.

The first witness for the prosecution was Dr. Lawrence Turk, who had conducted the autopsy on Jesús Martínez. The doctor reported that Jesús was six months old and weighed only 13.1 pounds, which put him in the fifth percentile for children his age.[7] Full body x-rays revealed healing fractures of two bones in the right lower leg (the tibia and fibula), a recent fracture of the proximal portion of the humerus, near the shoulder, and a recent fracture of the right radius.[8] Dr. Turk further testified that he saw older x-rays a few weeks after he had done the autopsy, from Mexico and La Loma Hospital. The La Loma chest x-rays showed that the acute fractures of the ribs were there on December 7 but not noted, ostensibly because the doctor treating him at the time was not specifically looking for fractures. The December 28 chest x-rays showed fractures of some anterior ribs on the right side near the breast bone.[9]

There was nothing in the autopsy suggesting that the child had been shaken, nor were there injuries to evidence strangulation. The injuries to the right leg showed a healing fracture of the proximal portion of the bones as well as new growth, which caused the bone to appear enlarged. There was no fresh hemorrhaging, so the injury was not recent. Dr. Turk testified that the April 6 x-ray showed fractures, which were healing on

April 13. He estimated that the injury occurred in the first few days of April but could not pinpoint the exact date.[10]

Dr. Turk testified that there were injuries to the right humerus and a spiral fracture–proximal part axis down the length of bone. The injury appeared on the April 13 x-rays and appeared to be recent. The doctor did not know when the injury occurred but he estimated April 10, give or take a few days. It appeared to have been caused by a twisting motion and would have required adult or adolescent force, so would not have been caused by another child.[11] Dr. Turk described the injuries sustained by Jesús as inconsistent with accidental injuries and likely the result of child abuse.[12] However, there was no external trauma to the body or other indicators that are normally associated with child abuse.[13] Dr. Turk also testified that people who abuse children do not routinely take them for medical treatment, as the Martínezes did on a regular basis.[14]

When Dr. Turk had first seen the baby, he described him as "well developed" and "well nourished"[15] and he indicated that he did not suspect child abuse. Significantly, during the preliminary hearing, neither Dr. Turk nor anyone else presented any evidence that José Martínez had inflicted great bodily harm or injury on the baby, or that María Martínez knew or reasonably should have known that her husband was inflicting corporal punishment on the child. And although the autopsy report revealed that the cause of death could not be determined,[16] at the conclusion of the preliminary hearing José and María Martínez were each held to answer for the crime of which they had been accused.

The 995 Motion to Set Aside the Information

After my client was held to answer, I prepared what is termed a "995 motion to set aside the information" because I was convinced that the prosecution had failed to show that a crime had been committed or that there was probable cause showing that my client had committed a crime.

A 995 motion is a procedural mechanism in California through which a defendant can challenge the judge's probable-cause ruling at the preliminary hearing and move to set aside the information under § 995 of the Penal Code on the grounds that the defendant was being held to answer without reasonable or probable cause.

The basis for the 995 motion, as noted, was that no evidence had been presented at the preliminary hearing that José Martínez had inflicted corporal injury on his son, or even if he had, that María knew or reasonably should have known that her husband was inflicting such injury and thereby failed to protect the child.

In fact, during questioning by police, both parents consistently denied any knowledge either of Jesús's broken bones or of how he might have sustained the breaks.[17] In separate interviews with detectives, the parents said that the baby had swelling in one of his legs and that they had taken him to an orthopedic specialist for treatment in Tijuana.[18] The parents indicated they had initially gone to Tijuana because Mr. Martínez's father was ill and they were on their way to Guadalajara to see him.[19] However, while in Tijuana, they received word that the father was feeling better and cancelled the Guadalajara trip.[20] The couple also said that they sought treatment in Tijuana because Mr. Martínez had recently lost his job and they did not have health insurance or money to afford treatment in the United States.[21]

When asked by detectives to explain a bruise on the child's head, José reportedly said that the baby had accidentally fallen on April 17 when he took him out of a car seat or swing of some type and that this might have caused bruising.[22] José said that he had not told his wife about the incident and was afraid to tell detectives but that was the only incident he could recall where the baby might possibly have been injured.[23]

I argued in the 995 motion that (1) there was not sufficient evidence at the preliminary hearing to justify holding María Martínez to answer, and (2) multiple hearsay is inadmissible at the preliminary hearing even when offered by a qualified investigating officer.

There was not sufficient evidence to justify holding María to answer because she could not have been charged with failing to protect her baby from José unless it was first shown that José did, in fact, inflict corporal punishment on his son and that she knew, or reasonably should have known, that her child was endangered.

Commitment without reasonable or probable cause within the meaning of Penal Code § 995 occurs when there is insufficient evidence to establish a reasonable belief that an offense has been committed and that the defendant is guilty of the offense charged.[24] In this case, the evidence presented was not only insufficient, it was nonexistent. There was no evidence presented either that a crime had been committed or that the defendant was linked to that crime.

In order to prove the crime of child abuse, according to the California Jury Instruction for Criminal Cases (CALJIC) § 9.37, the prosecution must show that

> Every person who, under circumstances or conditions likely to produce great bodily harm or death has care or custody of a child, and (a) willfully causes or, as a result of criminal negligence, permits the child to be injured, [or] (b) willfully causes or, as a result of criminal negligence, permits the child to be placed in a situation that endangers the child's person or health, is guilty of section 273(a)(1) of the Penal Code.

The word "willfully," as used here, means "with knowledge of the consequences" or "purposely." Again, there was absolutely no evidence at the preliminary inquiry that María Martínez "willfully" or "purposely" permitted Jesús Martínez to be placed in a situation or circumstance that endangered the child's person or health. On the contrary, evidence showed that Mrs. Martínez was constantly seeking medical treatment for her son's injuries. A search of the Martínez residence had uncovered various medicines, prescriptions, x-rays, hospital admissions, and other indicators of this. The Tijuana doctor said that the baby had a brace on his leg and that their family doctor, Dr. Murillo, had referred the couple to him.[25] In summary, the evidence presented at the prelim was that María Martínez sought medical treatment for her son in the United States and Mexico, that she had x-rays taken of the baby on April 7 and April 13 when she noticed something wrong with the baby's leg and shoulder,[26] that she kept meticulous medical records,[27] and that she was concerned with the health and safety of her baby. Incredibly, the fact that María kept meticulous medical records and that she took the baby for treatment in Tijuana was somehow presented as incriminating rather than exculpatory evidence.

Hearsay testimony was offered that there were inconsistencies in what José told the police. Mr. Martínez reportedly told detectives that the baby had accidentally slipped out of his arms on April 17 and hit his head on the carpet. And according to one of the lead detectives, "He was afraid to tell his wife and afraid to tell us what had happened, and that's why he kept it a secret."[28] Assuming that this hearsay statement attributed by detectives to José meets the constitutional requirement of reliability and is admissible, the statement actually serves to exonerate María because her husband kept the accident "a secret." Moreover, even if María had known that the baby had fallen accidentally—and there is no evidence that she did—having a baby accidentally fall out of one's grasp is not willfully and unlawfully inflicting cruel and inhumane corporal punishment and injury resulting in a traumatic condition upon a child that is likely to produce great bodily harm or death.

I further argued in the 995 motion that the hearsay statements of a codefendant implicating a defendant are not sufficiently reliable so as to be admissible under Penal Code § 872(b).

This is more of a technical point, but I would like to note that in a number of decisions, the Supreme Court has consistently refused to admit evidence against a defendant comprised of an extrajudicial statement made by a codefendant that implicates the defendant in the commission of a crime. The court has repeatedly explained that such statements are presumed unreliable:

> Not only are the incriminations devastating to the defendant but their credibility is inevitably suspect. . . . The unreliability of such evidence is intolerably compounded when the alleged accomplice, as here, does not testify and cannot be tested by cross-examination.[29]

Accordingly, evidence from a codefendant confession that implicates the defendant is "presumptively unreliable," and a magistrate's finding of probable cause on the basis of such evidence would raise constitutional questions that should be avoided. Although José Martínez did not confess to willfully harming his child, the hearsay statement that the baby had accidentally fallen was used to implicate the defendant and to suggest that she knew or reasonably should have known that her husband had inflicted corporal punishment on the baby. Because José's statement is inherently unreliable, and because the codefendant did not take the stand, it should not have served as a basis for a finding of probable cause against the defendant.

The Plea

Despite the fact that there was no external trauma to Jesús Martínez and that the autopsy report was inconclusive as to the cause of his death, at the conclusion of the preliminary hearing the parents were held to answer; they were arraigned on July 21. After several continuances, my 995 motion was heard and denied by the court on November 14.

We were on the brink of trial and had appeared for a pretrial readiness conference in November, when the prosecution made a plea offer that was ultimately accepted by both defendants. As per the plea agreement, José had been in custody for approximately nine months and would have credit for one year served if he remained in custody for another month and plead guilty. The charges against María, in turn, would be dropped. Although José had proclaimed his innocence from the start and was extremely reluctant to plead guilty, the decision in the end was a "no-brainer," since the alternative was for José to remain in custody, to have a trial, and for both defendants to face the possibility of a substantial prison sentence.

A Mother's Nightmare

Fermina, I want to take a moment to reflect on death. According to a Mexican saying, there is nothing more difficult in life for a parent, especially a mother, than to have to bury a child. I thought about the anguish that my mother felt after my two older brothers passed away. My oldest brother Alex died many years ago at the age of thirty-eight in a tragic car accident that also killed two of his three children, Alejandro (fourteen) and Gabriela (ten). His middle son Armando (twelve), who was in the back seat behind the passenger seat, miraculously survived. Later, my middle brother Héctor (or "Gordo," as we nicknamed him)—an emergency room doctor in Chicago—died from a sudden and unexpected brain aneurysm. Héctor had been suffering from intense headaches and in desperation had checked himself into the hospital where he worked. The doctors had given him an angiogram to see if his arteries were blocked when he suddenly had a massive brain hemorrhage and went into a coma. The doctors said he was virtually brain-dead and recommended turning off the life support, to which we assented. I remember my mother saying that there was nothing more difficult in life for a mother than burying a son, and she had been forced to bury two sons and two grandchildren.

María Martínez's lot was perhaps even more difficult than my mother's because not only was she accused of killing her baby, but shortly after the baby's death, the state moved immediately to take away her second child. As I explained, unlike baby Jesús, Victor was a very normal, healthy three-year-old toddler.

The primary mission of California Child Protective Services and of the Juvenile Dependency Court is to intervene in cases of suspected child abuse to protect children from harm. According to the California Department of Social Services (CDSS) Web site,

The CPS is the major system of intervention of child abuse and neglect in California. Existing law provides for services to abused and neglected children and their families. The CPS goal is to keep the child in his/her own home when it is safe, and when the child is at risk, to develop an alternate plan as quickly as possible.

When a referral is received, the social service staff obtains facts from the person making the referral to determine if the referral alleges abuse, neglect, or exploitation. The Emergency Response staff determines if an in-person response is indicated.[30]

If CPS finds it necessary to remain involved with a family beyond ninety days, the CPS worker on the case must obtain either a court order or a voluntary service agreement with the family. CPS may provide in-home protective services to keep a child safely in the family home or provide temporary out-of-home care during assessment or reunification efforts. If risk warrants ongoing placements, dependencies must be established in court and cases are prepared for transfer to ongoing child welfare services.

While CPS normally intervenes to protect children who are suspected victims of child abuse, in this case there was no indication that Victor Martínez had been abused or neglected in any way. In fact, what triggered the intervention by CPS were the allegations that the parents had inflicted serious bodily harm resulting in death to Victor's little brother.

I represented the mother, María Martínez, in both the criminal and the California dependency court, and while the criminal representation was difficult, it was not nearly as demanding or challenging as the dependency court proceedings. The standard of proof in dependency proceedings is essentially the same as in a civil case, which is the preponderance of the evidence, or the "more likely to be true than not" standard. This is obviously a much lower threshold than the "beyond a reasonable doubt" standard employed in criminal proceedings or the clear and convincing proof standard. The "beyond a reasonable doubt" standard is used in criminal cases in order to reduce the likelihood of convicting an innocent person. An additional obstacle encountered by defense lawyers in dependency proceedings is that, unlike the criminal court, there is no presumption of innocence in the child dependency court because the primary concern is protecting the child from possible harm rather than protecting the due process rights of parents suspected of child abuse.

Although the dependency court utilizes a "preponderance of the evidence" standard in deciding whether to terminate the parental rights of parents, in investigating possible child abuse, CPS uses a much lower standard such as substantial evidence, credible evidence, or probable cause that abuse may have occurred. CPS is obviously willing to risk making a false positive identification in having an innocent person falsely accused, rather than risking that potential child abuse will go undetected and result in harm to the child.

The states and jurisdictions vary in the standard used to trigger intervention by CPS, with some utilizing the "preponderance of the evidence" standard and others using a less restrictive standard. However, a study by Murray Levine[31] found that there was little relation between the standard designated by the legislature and the decision by CPS to intervene. A lower rate of substantiation of child abuse should follow from a higher standard, but the study found no statistically significant relationship between the percentage of cases that were substantiated and the standard of proof used in a jurisdiction. This suggests that social workers in charge of investigating possible child abuse may not make a clear distinction between the various legal standards of proof. While standards of proof are important to courts,[32] particularly to appellate courts, they are not necessarily important to persons delegated with the responsibility of investigating allegations of child abuse, since such persons are more interested in preventing harm to the child than in protecting the due process rights of parents.

I represented María in child dependency court for a period that spanned more than two years, and one of the most frustrating facets of this representation was that all of the police reports and unsubstantiated evidence where assumed to be true by CPS and the child dependency court.

One of the problems that I faced as a defense lawyer was that once the parents were arrested for suspected child abuse, CPS took immediate custody of Victor after assuming that all of the allegations against the parents were true—or at a minimum, believing that they could not risk the possibility that they could be true. While María was allowed weekly visitations with the child, the visitations were supervised and she was not ever allowed to be alone with her son.

At the "order to show cause" (OSC) hearing as to why the child dependency court should not have jurisdiction over the child, I argued vigorously against the motion that the court assume jurisdiction over

Victor, but the outcome appeared to be inevitable. We were eventually successful, however, in at least winning María's parents the right to have temporary custody of Victor. I should also note that CPS and the child dependency court had assumed jurisdiction even before the death of Jesús—the previous December, after it was discovered that the baby had broken ribs.

One of the things that helped us in the child dependency proceedings was the fact that María's parents were an ideal couple who had done an excellent job of raising seven grown children and were very involved with their grandchildren. Florencio and Mercedes Mendoza were a warm and caring couple in their mid-fifties. Mr. Mendoza had worked first as a landscaper and then for a local nursery and had recently retired. His wife, Mercedes, had been a stay-at-home mom who was very involved in the lives of her children and a dozen or so grandchildren. The Mendozas lived in the high desert, had been very close to little Victor, and were eager to assume temporary custody of the child. Neither of María's parents had ever been arrested or charged with any crime and had no history of child abuse or neglect. This, along with the fact that the court prefers to place children in dependency court with relatives, made them the ideal couple for assuming temporary custody of Victor.

The termination of the criminal case further complicated the child dependency court proceedings. While the decision to enter the plea agreement was a no-brainer for the parents, since it meant that José would not face additional time beyond the time he had already served and the charges against María would be dropped, it created enormous problems for the couple in the dependency proceedings. José, after all, was now a convicted felon who had pled guilty to the child abuse charges. Although the charges against María had been dropped, she was now in a double bind in which she virtually had to choose between being with her husband and being with her child. The court, in other words, was not inclined to allow Victor to have unsupervised contact with a convicted child abuser. This meant that the only way the mother could regain custody of her son was by ensuring that he would not have contact with her husband. This obviously created a serious dilemma for María.

I will not go into the details of the child dependency court proceedings except to say that we sought to regain custody for the mother and had a hearing in which we opposed the termination of her parental rights. We brought several character witnesses to the hearing, including a couple of María's neighbors who testified that María and José were excellent parents and that they had never seen them abuse or mistreat their children. I also subpoenaed the doctor from Tijuana, Dr. Ibáñez-Ortiz, who was prepared to testify that he saw baby Jesús on April 7 and 13; that he did not suspect child abuse; and that his diagnosis was that the baby had been suffering from osteomyelitis, an infection that weakened the bones and made them more susceptible to breaks and fractures.

Near the conclusion of our case in chief—just as our medical expert witness was about to testify—the county counsel suddenly called for a recess in the proceedings and came up with an offer, which we considered and eventually accepted. The offer was that the maternal parents would assume permanent custody of the child and that María would have liberal visitation rights.

Reflections

Amiga, as I think back on this case, I can say not only that it was clearly one of my most difficult and frustrating cases, but one in which I learned a great deal about the legal and judicial system. I learned, for example, that there is actually no presumption of innocence in the legal and judicial system, particularly for suspected child abusers. I also learned that suspected child abusers are despised and treated with disdain not only by the public at large but also by the various players in the legal and judicial system, including law enforcement officers, bailiffs, clerks, court reporters, and district attorneys.

I also learned that there is a very low standard of proof in investigations of suspected child abuse by CPS and the child dependency court, and that all unfounded accusations and allegations against parents are presumed to be true. Finally, I learned that parents charged with child abuse are presumed guilty whether they are in fact guilty or not. In this case, regardless of the merits of the charges, José, whether guilty or not, was destined to be found guilty. Because his bail was set prohibitively high and because of the backlog in the courts, his case was delayed for nearly nine months while he was kept in custody. On the brink of trial, José was given the option of either pleading guilty—serving just one more month and having the charges against his wife dropped—or of having a jury trial and risk facing a long prison term. No reasonable person would have chosen the latter option.

Yet perhaps the most important lessons I learned were that race, national origin, language, culture, and immigration status play an important role in criminal proceedings and that there is definitely a strong bias against immigrant, Spanish-speaking defendants. As noted at the beginning of this letter, María and José were an ideal couple that were living the American dream prior to the tragic death of their infant son. What I then found strange, both during the course of the investigation and during the court proceedings, was that the things that José and María did as normal parents were skewed and made to appear deviant and pathological by law enforcement, the prosecution, CPS, and the courts.

During the preliminary hearing, for example, the fact that the police uncovered numerous prescriptions and carefully maintained medical records during a search of the Martínez apartment that were introduced as exhibits and as somehow being incriminating evidence by the prosecution. One Detective Pelado, for example, testified that María Martínez kept meticulous medical records and that there were numerous prescriptions and x-rays in the house, as well as medicines in the refrigerator. Thus, what would appear on the surface to be exculpatory evidence was treated as somehow being incriminating evidence. The detective also introduced an exhibit that appeared to be paperwork and forms for the WIC Program, a federally administered special supplemental nutrition program for women, infants, and children. This program helps safeguard the health of low-income women, infants, and children up to age five who are at nutritional risk by providing nutritious foods to supplement their diets, information on healthful eating, and referrals to health-care providers. The fact that the Martínezes participated in WIC—while it *should* have shown them to be a health-conscious, responsible family—was instead viewed as incriminating evidence because they had claimed that they did not have medical insurance and did not qualify for public assistance. This is one of the reasons that they went to Tijuana for medical treatment.

In the end, one of the most incriminating pieces of evidence offered against the Martínezes, both in the criminal and in the dependency proceedings, was the fact that the parents had taken the baby for treatment in Tijuana. As noted, most people who abuse children do not seek treatment for them, and if they do seek treatment, it is generally at various emergency rooms or urgent-care centers were they can remain relatively anonymous, rather than with private physicians or specialists. María and José had first taken the baby to their primary care doctor, Dr. Murillo, who had referred them to Dr. Ibáñez-Ortiz, an orthopedic surgeon in Tijuana.

From the standpoint of the dominant society and law enforcement, medical care in Tijuana was viewed with great suspicion and as somehow deviant, but from a Mexican perspective it was perfectly normal behavior and not at all pathological. From an economic perspective, bringing a sick child to Tijuana is a better choice than seeing a U.S. doctor, since both medical care and prescription drugs are much more reasonably priced and accessible in Tijuana. In addition, the medical care in Tijuana was provided in Spanish, the parents' native tongue, and in a culturally familiar and sensitive environment. However, in the context of the criminal charges and the child dependency court, Tijuana appears to have conjured up images of cheap, illicit, unsafe, unsanitary abortion clinics. It was assumed, in other words, that the Martínezes sought treatment in Tijuana because they had something to hide, rather than because they could receive high-quality medical services and treatment at a modest cost and in their native language and culture.

In the end, the most important lesson I learned in this case was that being a Mexican immigrant and a Spanish-speaker was itself evidence of guilt.

∴ 3 ∴

Domestic Violence

Xavier, the Painter

Querido Alfredo,

I want to thank you for your patience, as I have been extremely busy and have not had the time to write. I have been running around quite a bit, teaching and continuing my work with Milagro. Enclosed you will find a picture from a recent immigrant rally in Phoenix, and yes, the one on the left is me, albeit unrecognizable with such a dark tan!

Thank you for your letter and for incorporating the new edits on your previous chapter. I must confess I was very intrigued by the child abuse case. It had all of the elements of an exciting case that would be presented in a law and murder television show. You are right, being a zealous advocate is a basic truism in law. In your case, it was easy to be a zealous advocate for the couple because you believed in their innocence. Even the field notes of your assistant, Alma, reflect the same sentiment toward the young couple. You also related that it would be difficult to be a zealous advocate for someone accused of committing a heinous crime, such as the one the young couple was accused of—yet advocating for María came naturally to you. How do you think you would have represented María if you were not as confident in her innocence? What does a rascuache lawyer do when the presumed innocence of a client is not evident? I ask this because, as a young lawyer, I find myself constantly having to deal with my biases. In other words, how does a rascuache lawyer continue being a zealous advocate? Do you believe there are times when it is better to drop a case?

Your reflections on this case were very insightful. It is still quite startling to see the type of "evidence" that the detectives introduced against the couple, and if you had not been such a zealous advocate, I can envision the case with a completely different outcome. What a great case, truly showing the trials and tribulations of a rascuache lawyer. Sorry, but I have to go now. I must return to the Milagro clinic!

Hasta la próxima,
Fermina

∴ ∴ ∴ ∴ ∴

Hola Fermina,

I want to thank you for your letter, your edits, and your comments on my last chapter. Your comments were very helpful and I will incorporate them into my revisions. I am glad that all is well at your work and with the adjunct teaching and at the immigration clinic. Thanks for the picture. I have posted it on my bulletin board. I wish that I could have joined you at the protest in Phoenix, but I was teaching a three-week summer-school class and just couldn't get away. The work at Milagro must be keeping you busy with all of the anti-immigrant bashing and xenophobia that is going on in the country. Before getting into the next case, I wanted to briefly respond to your question. I think that our job as lawyers is to be zealous advocates for our clients, not to judge their guilt or innocence. I really never want to know about my client's culpability. It is the responsibility of the courts to determine guilt or innocence, and it is our responsibility to give people the best representation possible and to be a zealous advocate for them, irrespective of the charges.

The next case I'd like to tell you about revolves around an immigrant mexicano who was accused of domestic violence. But before getting into the case, I want to go back to a comment that you made about Oscar Zeta Acosta, the Brown Buffalo, in your letter a couple of weeks ago. You were critical of me for lauding Acosta and not acknowledging his sexism and misogyny. Let me clarify: My intent was not to glorify Acosta or to defend his sexism and homophobia, but to recognize his contributions to rascuache lawyering. Lawyers simply do not talk about Acosta because they tend to see him more as a Chicano movement figure and as a creative writer than as a lawyer. As you know, he is credited with creating the gonzo journalism style that was popularized by Hunter S. Thompson and his Dr. Gonzo in *Fear and Loathing in Las Vegas*, a character modeled after Acosta.[1]

I realize that Acosta is openly sexist and homophobic in his writing, and most women are understandably turned off by his sexist and essentializing portrayals of Mexican identity, masculinity, and machismo. But some critics, like Michael Hames-García, have a different spin on Acosta. Hames-García offers an intriguing new vision and interpretation of Acosta, which he describes as a "postpositivist realist" interpretation of his work. Without going into the details of it or trying to explain postpositivist realism, I can say that Hames-García sees Acosta's work as grotesque satire that is critical of certain elements of Chicano cultural nationalism, specifically the sexual chauvinism and excessive masculine displays that characterized Chicano cultural nationalism.[2] "The pomposity and self-centeredness of Acosta's protagonists are components of the satire directed at the idea of the Chicano-warrior hero. Acosta inflates the egos of Oscar [the protagonist] and Brown [the lawyer] at least as much as he exaggerates their bodily characteristics."[3] What is clear in this conception of identity is that Chicano heterosexual masculinity has no meaning in itself, the Chicano-warrior hero coming into existence only in relation to other identities, and that "these relations are frequently relations of domination over Chicanas and Chicano gay men."[4]

The next case I'd like to tell you about is not about machismo and heterosexual masculinity as such, but it does deal with the related issue of domestic violence. My client, Xavier González, was a forty-five-year-old man who was born in Los Altos de Jalisco, a region of Mexico that is famous for a number of things, including *charros* (cowboys) and the production and consumption of tequila. Los Altos is also a strongly Catholic region where traditional gender roles are said to predominate. Xavier was born and raised on a ranch and grew up in a traditional Mexican family where men were expected to be the primary breadwinners and women, wives, caretakers, and mothers.

The state of Jalisco has also long been recognized as a place where machismo and male dominance prevail. According to Trinidad Terrazas, "Jalisco has been the cradle of machismo, and in particular the man of Jalisco has been the prototype of the Mexican macho in Mexican films and this image has been seen around the World."[5]

After migrating to the United States, Xavier settled in Orange County and began working in construction. He had a knack for painting, and he eventually landed a regular *jale* (job) as a commercial painter, painting newly constructed homes. Xavier had been married to "Juanita Doe" for two years, a forty-five-year-old woman with several adult children. They lived in an apartment complex next door to Juanita's eldest daughter,

Ema, and Ema's husband and two children. Xavier was a good provider and had few vices, except for the fact that he drank an "occasional" beer after work. It was also not uncommon for him to go drinking with his coworkers after work, especially on Friday afternoons after picking up his weekly paycheck. In fact, it was not uncommon for Xavier to have one or two too many beers and to drive home when he had too much to drink and really should not have been driving. Xavier's drinking irritated his wife and was a source of conflict and tension between them.

I met Xavier through the ex-wife of a former client, Juan Diego. Juan Diego's ex-wife called me and asked whether I could represent Xavier, after Xavier was arrested and charged with domestic violence following a domestic dispute. Juan Diego's ex-wife is the sister-in-law of Juanita Doe, Xavier's wife.

Domestic Violence

According to the police report, Officer John Tyler and Sergeant Joe Medina of the Santa Ana Police Department were dispatched to 2400 Avondale Ave. in response to a domestic disturbance. Dispatch advised that the victim, Juanita Doe, had fled her apartment (number 9) and was now waiting in apartment 7. Doe claimed she was the victim of domestic violence. Dispatch further advised that the named suspect, Xavier González, was still inside apartment 9. González was said to be a forty-five-year-old man and was last seen wearing a black tank top and Levi's jeans.

Upon arrival, Officer Tyler drove to the rear carport of the apartment building at 2400 Avondale. As he rounded the corner, he saw a male approximately forty-five years old, wearing a black tank top and black jeans. Tyler and Sergeant Medina approached the male and asked what his name was, to which he replied, "Xavier González." González was detained without incident pending the investigation.

Sergeant Medina served as a Spanish-language interpreter for both González and Doe. According to the report, González, who appeared to be under the influence of alcohol, stated he had been arguing with his wife (Doe), but denied striking her. González claimed he had to push Doe away from him. González did not provide any further details.

Medina and Tyler then made contact with Doe in apartment 7. Doe was in the company of her adult daughter (not the biological daughter of

González), who lives in apartment 7. Doe was visibly upset and crying. Doe, in substance, described her version of what happened:

On the date in question, at approximately 1500 hours (3 p.m.), González returned home. González already appeared to be intoxicated. González became very argumentative with Doe over various issues. Doe simply ignored and avoided González for most of the afternoon. At approximately 1900 hours (7 p.m.), González became more agitated, grabbed Doe by both of her arms, and squeezed tightly. González shook her several times and pushed her against a wall in the living room. González then struck Doe across the face, using his open right hand. Doe was able to get away from González and ran to the front door. Doe stated she was going to leave. González followed her and held the front door shut using his body weight, preventing her from exiting the residence. González told Doe she was not going anywhere. González then pushed Doe again to get her away from the door. González prevented Doe from leaving the residence for approximately twenty minutes. González eventually strayed away from the door and Doe was able to open it and run out. As she did so, González attempted to stop her but was only able to grab the end of her blouse. Doe was able to break free and run to apartment 7, where the police were notified of the incident.

Doe stated that she and González had been married and cohabitating for the past two years. They did not have any children in common and were the only two residents in their apartment. Doe said González constantly drank and verbally abused her. González had never struck Doe in the past, she said, but he had pushed her several times. Doe stated she was fearful of González. Doe complained of pain in both her arms where he grabbed her. Officer Tyler stated, "I saw they were red and slightly swollen from her forearms down to her hands. There was a small scratch on top of her left hand." Officer Tyler took digital photographs of Doe and her injuries and later booked the photographs into property as evidence.

Tyler placed González under arrest for domestic violence and false imprisonment. Officer Jones transported González to the station for booking. At the station, Officer Jones read González his Miranda rights, as per the department-issued form. González declined to speak with Officer Jones about the incident. Officer Tyler contacted Judicial Officer Sawyer and advised him of the circumstances. Mr. Sawyer granted an emergency protective order (EPO) against González. I gave Doe a copy of the EPO and a domestic violence pamphlet. González was served a copy of the order while in custody at the county jail.

A supplemental report was filed on February 13 by Detective Pat Furnell, assigned to investigate domestic violence incidents and assaults and battery. On February 12, Furnell spoke to Ema Méndez via telephone. She identified herself as Doe's daughter but stated that she was not related to the suspect, González. Furnell reported that Méndez stated that on the date of the incident, she was standing outside of her apartment speaking to a neighbor. She then saw Doe run out of her apartment, and she saw González chasing Doe. Méndez saw that Doe was crying, so she let her inside her own apartment and immediately called the police.

Doe told Méndez that González had hit her. She then showed Méndez her wrist, and Méndez saw that she had redness on both wrists near the area where she was wearing bracelets. Méndez further explained that Doe was wearing bracelets on both wrists. Méndez stated she knows of no past domestic violence incidents between Doe and González.

Xavier's Story

I made arrangements to meet Xavier on the east side of Riverside, since he said he was familiar with this area. We met at a Mexican restaurant, Los Tres Cochinitos, on University Avenue. Xavier was about five-foot-seven-inches tall and weighed about 190 pounds. He had a stocky build and was dressed like a Mexican charro, with boots, Levi's jeans, a checkered Levi's-type shirt, and a Mexican sombrero. He also wore a thick charro belt made from *pita*, which is string made from the maguey plant.

The meeting was a bit awkward initially. It was awkward, I think, first because Xavier struck me as a fairly traditional and macho man and he was, therefore, embarrassed by the whole situation. For me, it was also awkward because he brought his wife to the meeting. I knew that his wife, Juanita Doe, was likely to be called as a witness in the case, and I wanted to speak privately with my client. But how do you tell a traditional Mexican male who you just met that you want to speak with him alone without his wife being present?

My first task was to explain the situation to Xavier, so that he understood why I preferred to talk to him privately. Xavier said he understood and asked his wife if she minded waiting in the car for a few minutes while we talked. I began the conversation by trying to explain my role to

Xavier, telling him that my job was not to pry or to judge but to represent him to the best of my abilities. He admitted sheepishly that he and his wife had been arguing but said that he would never hit her. Xavier said that his wife was upset because he had gone drinking with his friends earlier in the day. She was also upset because he had drunk too much and they had spent most of the day Saturday arguing. Xavier said that they had argued and that his wife was angry and crying, so he grabbed her by the wrists in order to try to keep her from hitting him or scratching him.

Xavier explained that they had been together for two years and that they were married both by the church and civil court. He said he had been with his friends in Chino and had been drinking and had lain down. Xavier and his wife had been arguing for about a week and were not talking during that time. He said that she wanted to go to her daughter's next door and he grabbed her. Though he had said he grabbed her by her arms to prevent her from hurting him, he also said he had a scratch on his chest. He said he held her for two minutes, not twenty minutes, like his wife was saying. He added that she did not have any marks or *moretes* (black and blue marks) until later.

Xavier did not know who had called the police, but he assumed it was the neighbors. He said he tried to leave so that the neighbors would not see anything. The police had him in handcuffs down below and asked him to put his leg out. He had drunk four beers. They talked to Doe in her daughter's apartment. There was no bail, and he had to spend four days in jail until he went to court for his arraignment and they released him. Xavier also indicated that the police took pictures.

When I spoke to his wife separately, she told me that an investigator had gone out to see where they lived. She said that Xavier pushed her against the door and would not let her leave and that she got angry when he locked the door. She also said that she hit him on the chest. She added that a neighbor heard the argument and may have seen him push her. She said the police took pictures and that it was the first time this had happened and that the incident had lasted about ten minutes. Juanita said she was sore the next day and went to her doctor but there was no report to the police.

Near the end of my interview with Xavier, he went on to explain that his wife was sorry that they had called the police and that she did not want him to be prosecuted. I explained to Xavier that it was not uncommon for victims of domestic violence to recant their stories after reporting the abusive behavior to the police, and that most jurisdictions would proceed to charge the person, even when the victim had recanted. They simply went ahead and used the statements that the victim made at the time of the incident as evidence against the accused.

I was careful to explain the law to my client and the various elements of the offenses that he was charged with. I explained that he was charged with violation of California Penal Code § 273.5(a), corporal injury on a spouse, in that he did "willfully and unlawfully inflict a corporal injury resulting in a traumatic condition upon JANE DOE, who was the spouse of said defendant." He was also charged with violation of Penal Code § 236, false imprisonment by violence, in that he "did willfully and unlawfully violate the personal liberty of JANE DOE, said violation being affected by violence, menace, fraud and deceit."

I explained to Xavier that even though the charges would not be dropped, it would be difficult for the prosecution to obtain a conviction without his wife's testimony. I also explained that the state would have to subpoena and personally serve any possible witnesses, including his wife and her daughter. I stressed that by law, they could not be compelled to testify unless they were personally served with a subpoena.

As I reflect on my preliminary conversations with Xavier and his wife, it becomes clear that initially it was very difficult for Xavier to talk about the allegations of domestic violence with a stranger. Even though I was in my role as his attorney and tried very hard to be nonjudgmental, I know that we were talking about intimate and private details of their marital relationship. I also know that Xavier was embarrassed by the entire situation. As I mentioned, it was especially awkward when I asked to speak to his wife without him being present. In my conversations with his wife, I also stressed to her that she would be compelled to testify if she was personally served with a subpoena and notice to appear.

The Trial

We made several appearances and had preliminary discussions with the assistant district attorney about a possible settlement of the case. Xavier would have pled guilty to a lesser offense such as disturbing the peace, but he would not plead guilty to the domestic violence or false imprisonment charges, since he had proclaimed his innocence—although he might have pled if his punishment was credit for time served. The district attorney made several offers, but they entailed additional jail time, so we decided to move forward with the trial. Up until the end, I felt that the district attorney believed that we were bluffing and would not go to trial. He was wrong, because we felt like we had nothing to lose by going to trial.

As we prepared for the trial, the district attorney provided the following witness list to the defense:

1. Juanita Doe (alleged victim)
2. Ema Méndez (Doe's daughter)
3. Santa Anna Police Department Officer J. Tyler
4. Santa Anna Police Department Sergeant J. Medina

In the opening statement, the assistant district attorney told the jury that the evidence would show that the defendant had inflicted corporal injury on the victim and held her against her will. I reserved my opening, and the people began with their case in chief. The first prosecution witness, Sergeant Medina, said that he had extensive domestic violence training, with forty to fifty hours beyond the training given at the police academy, and that he had undertaken about a thousand investigations of domestic violence cases, resulting in approximately a hundred arrests. He testified that he and his partner had responded to a call regarding a family dispute at 7:30 p.m. on the date of the incident and had arrived within five minutes.

When they arrived, he said they spoke with the suspect first and then went to apartment 7 to speak with the victim. They encountered the suspect in the courtyard of the apartment complex. The sergeant testified that González told them he and his wife had been arguing and that he had to push her away but that there was no physical contact. Medina added that the suspect spoke in Spanish.

Sergeant Medina also noted that the victim had given them a statement. He said she was crying, upset, and shaking and her voice was "cracking." He described her demeanor as "normal to quiet," noting she was cooperative but was upset and fearful of her husband. He further testified that the victim had told them that her husband had slapped her, and that she ran to the door, that he pushed her away from the door, and that there was no other physical contact. She allegedly waited for about twenty minutes until he wandered away from the door and she escaped.

The victim had said that her husband had arrived home around 3 p.m. and was argumentative. She tried to ignore him for most of the afternoon, but around 7 p.m. he grabbed her wrist and slapped her. He appeared to have been drinking. She said that she broke away from him and ran to her daughter's house.

The second witness was Ema Méndez. When asked to describe what happened, she said that her mother had arrived crying and that she had called the police. She did not remember the time, but said it was in the evening. Ema acknowledged she did not see any of the incident, and on cross-examination, she admitted that she had never seen Xavier hitting her mother. She said that her mother had told her that González had grabbed her by the wrists, that she was wearing bracelets on both arms, and that her arms were red. She could not describe why the couple had been fighting. She said that she asked her mother, but she did not respond. Méndez added that her mother was crying in anger and was nervous, but that she calmed down when the police arrived. Ema said that it was more like she was emotionally upset than angry and added that she had not seen her stepfather, Xavier, that night.

The last prosecution witness was Pat Furnell, a detective who had worked with the Santa Anna Police Department investigating domestic violence cases for some eight years. She was also a crisis-hostage negotiator and trained to investigate domestic violence cases; she had investigated approximately three hundred domestic violence cases.

Furnell testified that she spoke with the victim's daughter, Ema Méndez, by telephone on February 12, approximately two weeks after the incident. According to Furnell, Méndez said she was outside her apartment talking to a neighbor when her mother came running from her own apartment. She said her mother was wearing bracelets on each of her wrists and that there was redness on both wrists in the area where she was wearing the bracelets. I should mention that Juanita Doe did not testify at the trial. She had apparently gone out of town to visit one of her other daughters and was not available when they tried to serve her. I believe that ultimately her unavailability helped us in the end.

After the prosecution ended its case in chief, the defense rested and the trial concluded with closing arguments. I opted not have Xavier testify because I did not believe that his testimony would help us that much and I felt that the prosecution might try to discredit Xavier during the cross-examination, so it would have been risky to have him testify. We did not have anything to hide, and much to potentially lose if he testified, so it was not worth the risk. More importantly, I also did not feel that the prosecution had met its burden of proving beyond a reasonable doubt that Xavier had inflicted corporal injury on his wife. If I had felt that the prosecution had met their burden, we might have had no choice other than to put him on the stand.

The Closing

I believe that this is a case where the closing argument mattered a great deal because the case could have gone either way based on the witnesses' testimony and evidence. From the testimony offered to the jury, it was clear that Xavier and his wife had argued and that a domestic dispute had occurred. It was also clear that Juanita Doe had attempted to leave the apartment and that Xavier had grabbed her wrists and prevented her from leaving and that she had redness around her arms. But no evidence was offered that showed that Xavier had inflicted corporal injury or falsely imprisoned his wife.

In the closing, it was important to remind the jury members of their instructions. I was careful to tell them that they were to presume the defendant's innocence and to remember that the prosecution had the ultimate burden of proving each and every element of the crime beyond a reasonable doubt. I was also able to take the elements for each crime and put them on a large poster board, so that the jury could follow along as I discussed the elements and the evidence and argued in each instance that the people had failed to meet their burden of proving each element beyond a reasonable doubt.

As per § 273.5(a) of the California Penal Code:

> Every person who willfully inflicts upon a person who is his or her spouse, former spouse, or cohabitant a corporal injury resulting in a traumatic condition is guilty of a violation of § 273.5 subdivision (a) of the Penal Code, a crime. "Corporal injury" means bodily injury. [As used in this instruction, "inflicts" means that the corporal injury results from a direct application of force by the perpetrator upon the victim.] A "traumatic condition" is a condition of the body such as a wound or internal injury, whether of a minor or serious nature, caused by a physical force.

The thrust of my argument in the closing was that the prosecution had failed to prove beyond a reasonable doubt that my client had willfully inflicted "a corporal injury resulting in a traumatic condition" on his spouse. In fact, even though there was hearsay evidence that Xavier had slapped Juanita Doe across the face with an open hand, the only alleged injuries that she suffered was what was described as a "small scratch" on her left hand and redness to her arms and wrists.

There were at least three major weaknesses in the prosecution's case, which I sought to exploit with the jury in the closing. First, as noted, the prosecution had failed to show that the defendant had inflicted corporal injuries on the victim. Second, even though photos were taken of the victim, the prosecution had failed to produce the photos. Finally, and most importantly, the prosecution had not produced the victim at the trial.

Besides the themes that Xavier was presumed innocent until proven guilty and that the burden was on the prosecution to prove each and every element beyond a reasonable doubt, a third and most important theme was captured by the phrase, "What is the prosecution trying to hide?"—a theme that I was able to exploit successfully. For example, the prosecution called Sergeant Medina to the stand. While Medina was present during the investigation, he was not the officer who wrote the police report. This effectively prevented me from pointing to inconsistencies between what was written in the police report and the testimony provided under oath. I was able to exploit this by asking the jury during the closing, "Where is Officer Tyler, the one who wrote the report?" and directly asking, "What are they trying to hide?" I was similarly able to exploit the fact that the prosecution was not able to produce the victim and asked once again, "What are they trying to hide? Where is the victim? Why isn't she here?"

It was also important for me to discredit or explain the only real corporal injury that was offered as evidence, and that was the alleged "redness" on the victim's arms. What I was able to do successfully in the closing was to remind the jury that there had been testimony that Doe was wearing bracelets on both of her arms and by pointing out that the "redness" on her wrists was likely caused not by my client hitting or striking Doe but by his grabbing her wrists in a defensive posture as she tried to hit and scratch him and that he had attempted to stop her. As I gave the closing, I felt that this was the most important point that I had made because it showed that it was the victim who was the aggressor.

The false-imprisonment charge was a secondary charge tagged on by the prosecution in order to build a stronger case against my client, but

I still had to address it. In the charging documents, the defendant was charged with violation of § 236 of the Penal Code, false imprisonment by violence or menace. "Every person who by violence or menace violates the liberty of another person by intentionally and unlawfully restraining, confining or detaining such other person and compelling such person to stay or to go somewhere without her consent, is guilty of the crime of false imprisonment by violence or menace in violation of Penal Code § 236." Here, "violence" means the exercise of physical force used to restrain someone over and above the force reasonably necessary to affect restraint. "Menace" means a threat of harm express or implied by word or act. In order to prove such a crime, each of the following elements must be shown: (1) a person intentionally and unlawfully violated the liberty of another person by restraining, confining, or detaining that person, compelling her to stay or to go somewhere without her consent; (2) such an act was done by violence or menace.

Once again, I was able to argue that the prosecution had failed to prove beyond a reasonable doubt that my client had violated the liberty of the victim or that he had done so by violence or the threat of violence.

After the closing, the jury was sequestered and we were ordered by the judge to wait for the verdict. It is never easy to await a verdict. Xavier and I decided to wait for the verdict in the hallway of the court. We tried not to talk about the case, but we would inevitably come back to doing just that—reconstructing some part of the trial, especially the closing. We had spent quite a bit of time together during the course of the trial and had developed a close rapport, so we were also able to kid around about certain aspects of the trial. Xavier had confided in me that he felt very proud in seeing how well I, a fellow mexicano, could speak English. He was very complimentary and said that he had taken a lot of pride in listening to me giving my closing argument. We waited for about an hour and a half and started to get more nervous as the time elapsed, but the bailiff soon thereafter came out into the hallway and said the jury had a verdict.

We returned to the courtroom. After the jury was seated, the judge asked my client to stand. He then had the bailiff go to the jury foreperson to pick up the verdict. The judge then read the verdict: "As to count 1, we the jury find the defendant not guilty. As to count 2, we the jury find the defendant not guilty." Xavier extended his hand to thank me and gave out a big sigh of relief. After the verdict, we stayed to see if any of the jury members had anything to say to us. A couple of middle-aged female jurors stayed and talked to us. They complimented me for my work and told me that Xavier should be careful so that this does not happen again.

Reflections

Xavier and I had never settled on a fee for my services, but we had discussed the possibility of having him paint one of my houses. After the trial ended, he asked about payment for my services and I asked him whether he could paint the exterior of a house that I owned and used as a rental. He agreed. I purchased the paint and he provided the labor. Xavier turned out to be an excellent worker and a very good painter. I got to know him even better than I had during the trial. He and his wife would come out on the weekends. She would serve as his "helper" and would keep him company while Xavier did his thing and painted the house. After he finished the first house, we negotiated and he agreed to paint the outside of my home residence for a discounted fee. I provided the paint and paid him a minimal sum, and he provided the labor. In the end, the compensation arrangement turned out to be mutually satisfactory. It was much easier for Xavier to spend a few days on the weekend painting my house than it would have been to pay me in cash for my services. It also worked out well for me because it would have cost me several thousand dollars to contract with someone to paint my two houses. A side benefit is that we were able to spend more time together and to develop more of a friendship. As we spent more time together, Xavier and I began to develop a strong mutual respect for each other.

As I reflected on the trial, I had very positive feelings about the experience. Even though Xavier had not testified during the trial, I believe that his appearance and demeanor had made a positive impression on the jury. I haven't yet said anything about Xavier's appearance, but he was a good-looking, distinguished-looking man, with graying salt-and-pepper hair and a gray mustache. He looked kind of sophisticated and could have easily passed for a college professor or lawyer. He didn't dress up for the trial but wore jeans and a clean plaid shirt. I felt proud to have him as a client because he looked like such a decent man.

I think, now, that the most lasting memory that I have of the case is the relationship that I developed with my client. Because I spoke Spanish and was born in México, I had the cultural capital to relate to Xavier. We were, after all, both middle-aged Mexican men. And we both had roots in rural Jalisco, since my mother was from the small village of Sayula, which is about thirty miles south of Guadalajara. In the end, perhaps what was most satisfying about the case is that I was able to effectively articulate the needs and aspirations of my client. As I noted, Xavier told me that he felt very proud when he heard me using such "beautiful" words in English as I represented him. Because of my education and fluency in English and training as a lawyer, I was able to defend him in a way in which he could not have defended himself, and in a way that made him feel proud that I was representing him—and this in and of itself was satisfying.

Another source of my satisfaction in the case was that I won the trial simply by effectively cross-examining the prosecution witnesses and without calling any witnesses. Another unintended consequence of the trial was that we were able to refute some misconceptions about Latino men and masculinity. In embracing my client's background and treating him with care and dignity throughout the course of the proceedings, I believe that I was able to refute myths such as that Mexican males are violent and relish beating up on women. In fact, Xavier told me that he was brought up to believe that a man should never hit a woman. I could relate to this because I had a similar upbringing; I was raised with the same ideology and learned early in life that one of the worst or lowest things that a man can do is to hit a woman.

Reflecting further on the case, I think I derived the most satisfaction of all from the fact that I was able to effectively and competently represent my client. It's hard to describe exactly how I felt about my client, but the truth is that we had developed a genuine friendship during the trial. Xavier was a man of few words and one who lived his life and carried himself with dignity and pride. The nature of the case and the fact that it was a domestic violence case had put me in a position where I was privy to Xavier's personal life and intimate marital relationship. But the fact that I was able to be privy to this information and to treat it in a confidential, professional, and discreet way further increased my rapport with Xavier, in the sense that he felt like I was someone he could trust and confide in.

In the end, I felt that I had made a lifelong and loyal friend in Xavier. He even called me periodically after the trial to see how I was doing. In the ensuing years, he would also recommend a number of family members and friends as clients.

Denial of Due Process

⁖ 4 ⁖

Concealed Weapon

Carlito's Güey (Way)

Amiga,

I want to tell you about Carlito Cruz, my youngest and most precocious client. Carlito, a bright nine-year-old fourth-grader, faced possible expulsion from school after being suspended and charged with carrying a concealed weapon to school. The tale is pretty incredible, and it is best captured in Carlito's own words in the statement he prepared at the time of the incident.

> It started with a blue pencil sharpener. One day, I found a blue pencil sharpener. I got it and I got a scissors and I opened it. Then I screwed out the screw, and I got the blade. The first time I got it, I cut papers that needed to be cut and shaved pencils that had to be shaved. Then one day, Robert, a boy in my class, got cut because he tried to cut himself to see if it was sharp. He told the teacher that he got cut by the blade; then all she said was, "Give me the blade." I did not hear her, so I took the blade and put it in my desk, and she did not even stand up. It was like she didn't care. A few days later Robert brought a big blade; then I said, "Where did you find it?" and then he said, "I didn't find it. I brought it from home." Just to show off, he cut everything he saw. He cut a test that we were taking. He cut his lunch and even papers that were not used. Then one time the teacher saw him using it; then, when she was going to call the office, he said, "Teacher, Carlito has one, too." Then we both got in trouble. He got to say his side of the story and I had to say mine and we both had to write what happened.

Carlito's mother, Magdalena Cruz, was a graduate student at a nearby university. Magdalena was shocked when the school called her to inform her that her son had been suspended. He was facing possible expulsion for, of all things, bringing a little pencil sharpener to school. She thought it was ridiculous that he was being charged with a violation of California Education Code § 48900(b) and that it was alleged that he "possessed, used, sold, or otherwise furnished any firearm, knife, explosive or other dangerous object."

The incident occurred on January 28, and the mother and father received a letter from the principal of the school, Tory Matrix, dated January 29, "inviting" them to attend a principal's conference on Tuesday, February 2, at 10 a.m. at the principal's office. According to the letter, the "purpose of the conference was to determine possible expulsion from Riverdale Unified School District." The letter concluded by noting, "It is very important that you and your son attend this meeting."

On January 31, Magdalena wrote the following response to the principal, which I helped her draft:

> Dear Ms. Matrix:
> I was shocked to receive the notice of suspension and your letter "inviting" me to attend a principal's conference on Tuesday, February 2, to determine possible expulsion of my son, Carlito Cruz, from the school district. I was shocked and dismayed that you have opted to unilaterally suspend my son, Carlito, and to consider expulsion from the district, without first informing me of the allegations against him, without advising me of my rights under the California Education Code, and without affording me a conference prior to imposing the suspension. This is a violation of my son's due process rights under the due process clause of the U.S. Constitution and the due process clause of the California Constitution. The notice of suspension indicates that Carlito was suspended under Education Code § 48900 because he allegedly "possessed, sold, or otherwise furnished any firearm, knife, explosive, or other dangerous object." My son Carlito did not furnish, sell, or possess any firearm, knife, explosive, or other dangerous object, as defined in the Education Code.
>
> The notice of suspension also erroneously states that "review of the above data prior to this suspension was held with all individuals involved in this incident on January 27 at 11:00 a.m." I was not informed of the suspension until after it was effected, when I was called on January 28 and asked to pick up my son because he had been suspended from school. . . . These are very serious allegations with grave consequences for my son. I am prepared to

pursue all available remedies, up to and including initiating charges for malicious prosecution and civil action for violation of my son's civil rights.

I hereby request a formal hearing or conference with the superintendent on the suspension as provided under Education Code § 48914. I also request that the conference to determine possible expulsion, which is set for February 2, be cancelled, since it has not been concluded that there was any basis for the suspension. Finally, please provide me with a copy of my rights under the Education Code and the rules and procedures governing suspension and expulsion proceedings in the district.

Best wishes,
Magdalena Cruz
Mother of Carlito Cruz

The Case against Carlito Cruz

The expulsion hearing against Carlito Cruz proceeded as scheduled. The case against Carlito was initiated by an "indictment" by the principal of the school, Tory Matrix, who sent a memorandum dated February 2 to Robert Kincaid, the coordinating principal in charge of the expulsion hearing. The charging document listed the name of the accused, Carlito Cruz; his identification number; and the name, address, and telephone number of his parents. It described the violation as follows: "*Specific Violation.* On Jan. 28, Ms. Morton [Carlito's teacher] called the office to report that two boys had razor blades. Carlito admitted to having a razor blade for about a week. He used the razor blade to cut up papers. He showed several students the razor blade. This is in violation of the Ed. Code § 48900(b)." A copy of the notice of suspension, dated January 28, followed the charging document. The document stated that the date and time the accused left school was on January 28 at 2:38 p.m., that he was released to his mother, and that he was suspended for five days. He was scheduled to return to school on February 4. The document further indicated that the reason for suspension under Education Code § 48900 was that Carlito "possessed, sold, or otherwise furnished any firearm, knife, explosive, or other dangerous object," and that law enforcement was notified and filed a report, PN99028124. The school principal signed the document and described the reason for the suspension in the narrative as follows: "At approximately 10:50 a.m. on January 28, Ms. Thornton called the office to report that two boys had razor blades. Carlito admitted to having a razor blade for about a week. He used the blade to cut up papers. He showed several students the razor blade."

The charging document and notice of suspension were accompanied by some supplementary materials, including a Xerox copy depicting the razor blade in question next to a ruler, presumably placed next to the blade so that the reader could get a sense of how long the blade was. The blade appeared to be approximately one and one-quarter inches long. Also included were several statements from witnesses and the following "narrative of due process":

Narrative of Due Process
1. Carlito Cruz has been a student at Glendale Elementary School for two and one-half years. He has attended school assemblies during his time at Glendale. During the past academic school year, Carlito and his parents received a copy of the school rules. He also has met with the principal to review the rules. The principal met with Carlito on January 25 to discuss discipline and a possible track change. The principal called Carlito's mother, Ms. Magdalena Cruz, and she agreed to the track change to help Carlito academically and behaviorally.
2. Carlito was brought to the office at approximately 11 a.m. on January 28.
3. He was interviewed by the principal and allowed to tell what happened regarding the blade. He then voluntarily wrote a statement regarding the incident. Carlito admitted to having a blade at school.
4. After meeting with Carlito and reviewing statements from other students, the principal suspended Carlito from school for five (5) days pending possible expulsion. Carlito's mother was called at approximately 1:50 p.m. to inform her of the suspension and pending expulsion. Ms. Cruz then came to the school at approximately 2:20 p.m. to meet with the principal to discuss what had happened, the role of the principal's conference, and possible outcomes.
5. The principal's conference was set at a time that Ms. Cruz noted would be convenient for her.

6. The parent received a written notification of the principal's conference (please see attached). This was delivered by employee Susana Jimenez.

※ ※ ※ ※ ※

Robert, a student, wrote the following statement:

> I found a razor blade by the slide in the sand. When I had it in the bathroom, I showed it to Michael in the bathroom. When we got to class, I showed it to Carlito. As soon as Carlito seen it, he said, "Dang, can I see that?" I said, "Yes, you can." He said, "Where did you get that?" "Out on the playground," I said. As soon as I got back from the office, I took it out of my desk and cut a piece of paper; then Ms. Morton seen it and took it away. I should have given it to one of the duty guards. I shouldn't have touched the razor at all.

Another boy, Walter, provided the following declaration:

> Robert was in the bathroom this morning with a razor in his pocket. He had pulled it out when I came in the bathroom to show me. I had forgot to tell the principal because I was not thinking about it. Carlito had a little razor that had come off my sharpener. Carlito and Robert would cut themselves and say to Ms. Morton, "I just got cut and I need first aid," right to Ms. Morton. Ms. Morton would say, "Why do you have a razor anyways?" Ms. Morton told Carlito to give her the razor, but Carlito would make Ms. Morton forget about it. Robert had the razor getting tape off his desk. Carlito was getting the black stuff off of his desk, too. Robert got his from home or he found it.

※ ※ ※ ※ ※

On February 2, we attended the expulsion hearing at the school. I was dressed like a lawyer for the hearing and wore a black pinstripe suit and a red tie. I met the mother, Magdalena, and her husband, Gabriel, as well as a friend of the family, Karla, and Carlito in the parking lot. Everyone was fairly dressed up, especially Carlito, who wore a bright red tie, a white shirt, and black pants. He looked very dapper. Magdalena commented in her notes:

February 3
Yesterday was dedicated to Carlito's case. At 10 a.m. we went to the meeting Ms. Matrix called to discuss Carlito's suspension pending expulsion. Carlito was all dressed up. Gabriel, Karla, and I were also relatively well dressed. We waited for Mirandé for about ten minutes, and after he came, we walked to Ms. Matrix's office. A while before, the district representative had passed by us when we were still waiting for Mirandé. The principal as well as other school people were fairly surprised (and even a bit scared) regarding the number of people there to defend Carlito. Of course they weren't expecting that! As soon as we got home, Gabriel, Karla, Carlito, and I tape-recorded our accounts of the meeting. We found out during the meeting that Ms. Matrix, in response to my letter asking for clarification (in fact the letter written by Mirandé), had recommended Carlito's expulsion.

The expulsion hearing, euphemistically termed "principal's conference," was chaired by Robert Kincaid, the principal at a local high school and an ex–football coach; it was attended by the principal (Ms. Matrix), the vice principal, and the child-welfare and attendance manager for the district.

Mr. Kincaid was a large man with a crew cut who adopted a take-charge stance at the meeting. Early on, he said that this was "his" hearing. I corrected Mr. Kincaid and told him it was Carlito Cruz's hearing, since he was the party who was facing possible expulsion, and that his due process rights were at issue. Mr. Kincaid proceeded to present the case against Carlito. The hearing was tape-recorded, but there were no witnesses or formal testimony. In fact, all the evidence against Carlito was hearsay evidence and consisted of the charging document and all the supplementary materials, including the various declarations by Carlito, Robert, and the other so-called witnesses, which were introduced as exhibits. I objected to the introduction of the exhibits because it was all hearsay and we would not have the opportunity to question or to cross-examine the witnesses. Also included in the record was a copy of Carlito's academic record and his most recent report cards or progress reports.

Our case in chief consisted largely of going over the charges against Carlito and stressing that he was not guilty of violation of Education Code § 48900(b), which alleged that he "possessed, used, sold, or otherwise furnished any firearm, knife, explosive or other dangerous object." We acknowledged that he had the blade from a pencil sharpener but argued that the blade was only one and one-quarter inches in length and was not a knife or inherently dangerous object. We further argued that he did not furnish anyone with firearm, knife, explosive, or other dangerous object; that he had not posed a threat to himself or others; and that there was no justification for his suspension or possible expulsion from the school district.

Finally, we argued essentially that Carlito's suspension and the expulsion hearing were in violation of the California Education Code, that the February 2 meeting was illegally constituted, and that Carlito's due process rights under the California and U.S. constitutions had been violated.

Carlito Cruz's Suspension Was Illegal and in Violation of Education Code § 48911

The Education Code states that the principal of the school, the principal's designee, or the superintendent may suspend a student for any of the reasons specified in § 48900 for five or fewer consecutive workdays. However, the Education Code clearly specifies that a suspension shall be preceded by an informal conference held by the principal or the principal's designee, or the superintendent. The code dictates: "At the conference, the pupil shall be informed of the reason for the disciplinary action and the evidence against him or her and shall be given the opportunity to present his or her version and evidence in his or her defense." Carlito's notice of suspension was, therefore, not in compliance with Education Code § 48911.

Section 48911 provides that the principal, the principal's designee, or the superintendent of schools "may suspend a pupil without affording a pupil an opportunity for a conference but only if the principal, the principal's designee, or the superintendent of schools determines that an emergency situation exits." An "emergency situation" is defined as a situation in which the principal, principal's designee, or superintendent determines that the student "constitutes a clear and present danger to the life, safety, or health of pupils or school." In this case, Carlito was suspended without having had an opportunity for a conference, but there was no determination that he constituted a clear and present danger to the life, safety, or health of other pupils or the school.

At the hearing, we argued that Carlito was not a clear and present danger to anyone. We further argued that he was an intelligent and curious boy who needed to be in school, and we demanded his immediate reinstatement. We also demanded the production of evidence, including statements of witnesses, recordings, and police reports.

The Principal's February 2 Conference Was an Illegally Constituted Meeting

You will recall that Carlito's parents received a notice of suspension "inviting" them to attend a principal's conference and that the purpose of the conference was to "determine possible expulsion" from the school district. The meeting was illegal and in violation of the California Education Code. There is no provision for a "conference" on expulsion under the Education Code. Education Code § 48918 provides for a "hearing" on expulsion and states that written notice of the hearing shall be mailed to the pupil at least ten days prior to the hearing, along with a statement of the specific facts on which the suspension is based and a copy of the disciplinary rules of the district. Education Code § 48918 says:

> (b) Written notice of the hearing shall be forwarded to the pupil at least ten calendar days prior to the date of the hearing. The notice shall include all of the following:
>
> (1) The date and place of the hearing.
>
> (2) A statement of the specific facts and charges upon which the proposed expulsion is based.
>
> (3) A copy of the disciplinary rules of the district that relate to the alleged violation.
>
> (4) A notice of the parent, guardian, or pupil's obligation pursuant to subdivision (b) of § 48915.1.
>
> (5) Notice of the opportunity for the pupil or the pupil's parent or guardian to appear in person or to be represented by legal counsel or by a non-attorney adviser, to inspect and obtain copies of all documents to be used at the hearing, to confront and question all witnesses who testify at the hearing, to question all other evidence presented, and to present oral and documentary evidence on the pupil's behalf, including witnesses.

At the conclusion of the "conference," we argued that Carlito's suspension and the expulsion conference were an infringement of his rights under the Education Code and a violation of the due process clause of the California and U.S. constitutions.

During the conference, Mr. Kincaid kept saying that the meeting was about suspension, but Carlito has already been suspended prior to the meeting. We also complained that we did not receive the packet of materials we should have received, including a copy of the district rules and procedures and the exhibits, or have an opportunity to review the materials prior to the meeting. When we asked for a copy of the rules and procedures, Mr. Kincaid said he had them and he would give us a copy "later." Of course, it would not do us any good later.

There Were No Grounds for Recommending Expulsion

Under Education Code § 48915, a principal or the superintendent of schools shall recommend expulsion for any of the following acts, unless the principal or superintendent feels that expulsion is inappropriate under the circumstances:

(1) causing serious injury to another person, except in self-defense;
(2) possession of a knife, explosive, or other dangerous object of no reasonable use to the pupil;
(3) unlawful possession of any controlled substance listed in chapter 2 (commencing with § 11053) of division 10 of the Health and Safety Code, except for the first offense for the possession of not more than one avoirdupois ounce of marijuana, other than concentrated cannabis;
(4) robbery or extortion;
(5) assault or battery, as defined in sections 240 and 242 of the Penal Code, upon any school employee.

Section 48915 further stipulates that the principal or superintendent of schools shall immediately suspend, and shall recommend expulsion of, any student that he or she determines has committed any of the following acts at school or at a school-sponsored activity off the school grounds:

(1) possessing, selling, or otherwise furnishing a firearm;
(2) brandishing a knife at another person;

(3) unlawfully selling a controlled substance listed in chapter 2 (commencing with § 11053) of division 10 of the Health and Safety Code;

(4) committing or attempting to commit a sexual battery sexual assault as defined in subdivision (n) of Section 48900 or committing a sexual battery as defined in subdivision (n) of Section 48900;

(5) possession of an explosive.

Another important point is that under § 48915, *knife* "means any dirk, dagger, or other weapon with a fixed, sharpened blade fitted primarily for stabbing, a weapon with a blade longer than three and one-half inches, a folding knife with a blade that locks into place, or a razor with an unguarded blade."

In sum, the small blade on a tiny pencil sharpener does not qualify either as a knife or as a "dangerous object," and there was insufficient grounds for either a suspension or expulsion of a nine-year-old boy who essentially used such a blade to cut up paper.

Reflections

As I reflect on the case, I have a clear image of my client, Carlito, on the date of the principal's conference, dressed up like any other client in his black pants, white shirt, and bright red tie. Although I spent a lot more time speaking with Carlito's mother than with Carlito, there was no doubt that he was my client. As we walked into the hearing room, I could sense that Carlito knew that this would be his day in court and that he was represented by a zealous advocate. I could also sense a certain amount of pride in his demeanor, pride perhaps in the fact that so many people were advocating on his behalf.

On the surface, the case may appear trivial. We are talking, after all, not about a serious or a violent crime but about a nine-year-old playing and cutting papers with the blade of a small paper cutter. The case was not trivial, however, as it entailed violation of due process, one of the most fundamental rights that we are granted by the U.S. Constitution.

The due process clause of the Fourteenth Amendment provides that no person may be deprived of life, liberty, or property without due process of law. Similarly, the California Constitution, article 1, Declaration of Rights, section 7, provides that "a person may not be deprived of life, liberty, or property without due process of law or denied equal protection of the laws...."

In *Goss v. Lopez* (1975),[1] the Supreme Court considered the issue of whether the imposition of suspensions without preliminary hearings violate students' due process rights guaranteed by the Fourteenth Amendment. Nine students at two high schools in Columbus, Ohio, had been given ten-day suspensions from school by their principals without being provided with a hearing and where state law did not require the school district to provide a hearing prior to suspension. In a 5–4 decision, the Court held that because Ohio had chosen to extend to its citizens the right to an education, it could not withdraw that right "on grounds of misconduct absent fundamentally fair procedures to determine whether the misconduct ha[d] occurred." The court held that Ohio was constrained to recognize students' entitlements to education as property interests protected by the due process clause that could not be taken away without minimum procedures required by the clause, and that students facing suspension should at a minimum be given notice and afforded some kind of hearing.

Here, the school's action was a clear violation of Carlito's property interest protected by the due process clause that could not be taken away without minimum procedures such as notice and a hearing. Carlito did not have proper notice of either the suspension or the recommended expulsion. The suspension was imposed without prior notice or a hearing. As noted, California Code § 48911(b) states,

> Suspension by the principal, the principal's designee, or the superintendent of schools shall be preceded by an informal conference conducted by the principal or the principal's designee or the superintendent of schools between the pupil and, whenever practicable, the teacher, supervisor, or school employee who referred the pupil. ... At the conference, the pupil shall be informed of the reason for the disciplinary action and the evidence against him or her and shall be given the opportunity to present his or her version and evidence in his or her defense.

As I have made clear, this conference may be waived only where an emergency situation exists and there is "a clear and present danger" to the life, safety, or health of pupils or school personnel. Obviously, no clear and present danger existed in this case and the suspension without notice or a hearing was a violation of Carlito's right to due process.

Similarly, the factual allegations against Carlito did not constitute grounds for expulsion under Education Code § 48915. Even though the principal had recommended expulsion and had invited the parents to attend the conference, noting, "The purpose of the conference is to determine possible expulsion from Riverdale Unified School District," Carlito was not afforded the right to a hearing as is mandated under Education Code § 48918; nor was he provided with ten days' notice of the hearing.

Carlito was suspended without a hearing, and even though the February 2 meeting was termed a principal's conference rather than an expulsion hearing by the hearing officer, it was in fact an expulsion hearing—held without proper notice or procedural safeguards.

In recent years, public concern with school violence and the prevalence of weapons and drugs on school campuses has led to increased pressure to make schools safer and more accountable for school violence and for drugs on campus. The result has been a movement toward zero tolerance for drugs or weapons on campus and a call for increased policing, vigilance, and control. Unfortunately, in their quest to make schools safer and drug free, school administrators have failed to protect students' fundamental constitutional rights.

As I think about the case, I can't help but wonder, as you did, whether it was worth getting involved in representing Carlito Cruz in a relatively minor incident in school. Carlito, after all, was not charged with criminal misconduct and he was only suspended for five days. While the case may appear trivial, it was not—because it involved the violation of one of my client's most basic constitutional rights: the right to due process of the law. Although the case was not a criminal case, it illustrates the biases and injustices inherent in the educational system. Carlito was not charged with a crime, but the charging document read very much like an accusatory pleading, and a police report was even issued (although not produced). In addition, Carlito faced possible expulsion, which entails not only a denial of his property interest in a public education but deprivation of his freedom. He was treated unfairly by the educational system in the sense that as a nine-year-old, he was held to an adult standard of conduct, so that opening a pencil sharpener and using the blade to cut papers was likened to bringing a concealed weapon to school, allowing him to be charged with "possessing, selling, or otherwise furnishing any firearm, knife, explosive, or other dangerous object." The case is important, moreover, because it shows how Latino children are stereotyped and subject to differential and unequal treatment by the educational system.

The biases of the educational system and the high dropout or "push-out" rate of Latinos has been widely documented,[2] as has the relationship between school failure and juvenile delinquency and involvement in gangs, because many Latino children who experience rejection and failure in school have inevitably turned to their peer group for identity and support. James Diego Vigil, a renowned expert on gangs, notes that gang members usually have difficulty adjusting to school and that most drop out of the educational system by the age of sixteen because of "language problems, cultural and ethnic identity conflict, a general malaise, and discrimination."[3] According to Vigil, "What is important to note is that school problems generally precede and contribute to involvement in the gang."[4]

I thought about Marcos and Mario, the boys I described to you in previous letters—and many other Latino youth who get into trouble in school and grow increasingly alienated from and disaffected by the educational system. Carlito was lucky in that he was not expelled, and his mother, Magdalena, was cognizant of her son's educational rights and ready to defend them. Carlito was also lucky to find a lawyer who was willing to take on the case and become his zealous advocate.

⁖ 5 ⁖

Trespassing

Benny, the Homeless Man

Querida Fermina,

I hope this letter finds you in good health. I am really excited because I am teaching law and subordination. Before describing my current case, I want to tell you a little bit about the class. I feel privileged to have the opportunity to work with these young people. Actually, they are not all that young. We have an interesting mix of people. It's the kind of class that would normally be taught at a fancy law school, and here I am teaching it to undergraduates through ethnic studies. The class is supposed to be joint-listed with sociology, but because of an oversight, it did not appear on the schedule under the sociology listings.

What is law and subordination? The class is modeled after some of the classes we took in the lawyering for social change (LSC) curriculum at Stanford—like classes in teaching self-help and lay lawyering. The program became defunct once Gerald López left for UCLA. With classes like these, the goal is simply to have people reading about advocacy on behalf of subordinated groups and then applying the things that they learned in a placement setting, working with those subordinated groups. It is interesting because Gerald ("Jerry") was a lawyer who believed that people who are working with the poor and people of Color have to know something about the cultures and experiences of these groups. He was, in fact, a lawyer who believed that you have to know something about sociology and anthropology and the cultures of subordinated groups in order to be an effective advocate. In other words, he was a lawyer who wanted to integrate sociology and anthropology into law, and I'm a sociologist who became a lawyer and wants to integrate law into sociology and ethnic studies. Being a sociologist and a rebellious lawyer is a lot like being bilingual and bicultural, because you are knowledgeable and live in two distinct worlds that may touch but seldom intersect. And this may sound pretentious, but you end up feeling like you know more than people in either of these two worlds. Don't misunderstand! I can talk to lawyers and to sociologists and anthropologists, but they can't usually talk to each other.

One of the goals of my class is to train students to serve as lay advocates for subordinate groups who do not normally have access to law, lawyers, or advocates. The class is unique in that it normally involves a placement working with a subordinated group and doing simulation exercises, where students can practice, in front of the class, the presentations that they will be making in the field, with the goal of having the presentations critiqued by the class. I limit the enrollment to ten to twelve students.

The students in the class work in one of several placements, including the Day Laborers Group (DLG), At Risk Youth or the Youth Advocacy Project (YAP), and the Homeless Advocacy Group (HAG). The third component of the class, in addition to the placement and simulation exercises, is doing theoretical readings about law and subordination and advocacy on behalf of subordinated groups.

The class is an ambitious enterprise because I am teaching, in fact, a critique of traditional law doctrine and the hierarchical view of lawyering and law practice—but one can't critique something unless one first understands that something; in other words, my class and I have to know a little bit about law in order to better critique it. The class is not a law class. It is an advocacy class, or a cross between lay lawyering and community organizing. Yet my students are going to have to learn about law. For example, you can't talk about developing a know-your-rights workshop on the Fourth Amendment or immigration unless you know something about these doctrines. At the same time, a philosophical principle underlying the class is that law should be something that is readily accessible to everyone, not only to lawyers or law scholars. It is based on a bottom-up view of law and law practice.

I have asked the students to write weekly field reports. The goal is to report on and critically evaluate their field experiences, the readings, and class discussions. However, since we will not be discussing the readings until next week, I have asked the students to write something about who they are, how they got to be in this class, and what they expect to get out of the class.

I should note that when I first created the class several years ago, I asked Benny, a homeless man, to serve as the supervisor for the homeless group, and he agreed. He would regularly attend class, participate in class discussions, and provide input and direction to the class on various topics, including homelessness. However, the most important function that he served was that of an informal supervisor and mentor for the homeless field placement. He took the students out into the field and proved to be an invaluable resource not only for students in the homeless placement but for the class as a whole. Whenever he attended class, I felt like we had a second teacher because he knew so much—not only about homelessness, but also about race and subordination.

Fermina, I visited the At Risk Youth group on Monday in the field the other day, and the group blew me away. It gave me a nice feeling of satisfaction to see all these smart young people eagerly working with at-risk youth. It was so great that I felt like a proud parent. I hope I didn't surprise the group and make them nervous. My intent was to express an interest and to satisfy my own curiosity about them.

Benny came to the class last Tuesday. It felt like the old days. He is always full of ideas and is extremely knowledgeable of the issues. It was interesting that he disagreed with some of the ideas that were being expressed relative to pedagogy in the at-risk group. I think Benny is an organic nonregnant advocate. He wants to take a bottom-up rather than a top-down approach. This is what I wanted to get at in my discussion with you of the Brown Buffalo,[1] but we didn't get very far. We didn't get far beyond saying that the Buffalo was *firme* (cool) because he tells things how they are. I was looking for more depth in the discussion . . .

Benny Mattumbo, Recycler and Lay Advocate

Benny Mattumbo was a fixture on the University of California, Riverside, campus (UCR campus). Almost everyone knew Benny at least by sight, not only because he could be seen walking around, tirelessly pushing his grocery cart filled with empty cans and other recyclable materials, but because he was very active in a number of campus clubs and organizations and because his shopping cart was adorned with progressive political signs and posters. Benny had a slender build but was in incredibly good shape. He was around five-foot-seven and weighed approximately 160 pounds. Another of his distinctive features was that he wore his hair in braids and dreadlocks and had black horn-rimmed glasses, which were cracked and held together with Scotch tape.

It would be an understatement to say that Benny was a politically active person—he seemed involved in virtually every progressive cause on the campus. It was not uncommon for him to attend MEChA (Movimiento Estudiantil Chicano de Aztlán) or Native American Student meetings at the respective offices of Chicano Student Programs or Native American Student Programs; he also wrote articles and editorials in different campus newspapers such as *The Highlander* and *Nuestra Cosa*, the Chicano student newspaper; his topics included the Iraq war, police abuse, and civil-liberties and human-rights violations. Benny was such a fixture on the campus that he became almost synonymous with progressive campus causes. One longtime lecturer at UCR commented that Benny had some clear ideas and progressive theories regarding how to organize subordinated communities, adding, "but I am not sure I fully understood them."

I do not know much about Benny's background or how or why he became homeless, except that he was clearly a very educated man who was respected by students, faculty, and staff at the university. Despite his visibility, Benny remained a mysterious figure. He was reportedly born in Uganda and was said to have received a master's degree in economics from Oxford University, the London School of Economics, or some other fancy school. A reliable source who had known Benny since he first arrived on the campus in the late 1980s mentioned that Benny had reportedly lived in Europe for some time and had "taught rich people how to play tennis"—but the source was not sure if this was true.

Although Benny's story was something of a mystery, he remained a fixture on the UCR campus for many years. Benny would park himself outside of the university commons, or student center, with a couple of shopping carts that contained all his worldly belongings and antiwar messages and signs. He would plug his portable radio into an outdoor outlet at the student commons and listen to 90.7 KPFK FM, the so-called "people's station," spending the day chatting with students or anyone who would stop to say hello or discuss current political issues. If there was an issue or progressive cause mentioned, it seemed Benny would be in the middle of it and would readily discuss it. Although the phrase is overused, Benny was what I would call an "organic intellectual." His early mornings and afternoons were devoted to recycling; he would alternate between using the recycling center at the Canyon Crest Shopping Center and the recycling center in the Kmart parking lot, which were close to the university.

However, as the student population expanded and student enrollment almost tripled in the 1990s and 2000s—going from approximately seven thousand to more than twenty thousand students—the university became increasingly less tolerant of Benny and persons like him and began to pressure him directly and indirectly to stay off the campus. When I asked why he stopped coming to the university, Benny mentioned that there was a woman at the student commons who was giving him a hard time and that he no longer felt welcome on campus. He said people there used to let him hang out around the student center, but they had become increasingly less tolerant.

Benny was especially visible at campus protests against the Iraq war or the University of California administration. On April 14, for example, a campus coalition of students united to voice its dissent regarding the war going on in Iraq. According to staff writer Pamela Shen in an article in the student newspaper, "In an effort that they said was to garner support for the troops in Iraq and to end the ongoing war, the UCR Student Coalition for Peace and Human Rights held a noontime speak-out against the war on Friday." The event was held on Speakers' Hill, near the commons. Many students stopped at the rally on their way to and from class to listen to the speakers, as well as what Shen's article described as "the Deep Stirring" of KPFK FM. The article quoted a number of speakers who protested the war and the senseless killing of thousands of people, including innocent women and children. Benny Mattumbo, acting as a community member, commented on the absence of President Bush on the war front: "Why is Bush not on the front line, followed by his daughters?"

On May 14, Benny attended a meeting of the University of California Regents in San Francisco to protest proposed increases in student fees. According to a news release, in addressing the regents, Mattumbo—who was identified this time as a UCR student—"stated that the Regents should not meet out of public view and should ask the public to participate in solving the budget problem. He also believed that Regents should be elected rather than appointed."

In the spring of the same year, Benny was arrested for trespassing at the recycling center of the Canyon Crest Shopping Center near the campus, and I agreed to represent him. Although this was a relatively simple case, which I was able to resolve fairly quickly, it proved to be an important one because it did much to inform my view of advocacy, rebellious lawyering, and homelessness. While I had known Benny for almost a decade, I came to view him differently once he became my client. The case was also important because it occurred while I was teaching my class on law and subordination, which focused largely on homelessness, so it served to illustrate many of the concepts and issues that we had been addressing in the class.

People of the State of California v. Benjamin Mattumbo

After class one day, Benny took me aside and confided that he was being harassed by security at the Canyon Crest Shopping Center. He mentioned that one security guard there in particular had been giving him a hard time and told him that he would be arrested if he continued recycling at the center. Benny felt that the people in charge of the shopping center did not want him there because of the political and antiwar protest signs on his shopping carts. He believed there was a double standard, pointing out that security never harassed other people who recycled there, including the homeless veterans who had pro-war propaganda on their shopping carts. After the harassment had continued for several days, Benny asked me if I could do anything as a lawyer so that security would stop harassing him—one security guard in particular. Though there were a few security guards at the shopping center, he was having problems primarily with a heavyset African American security guard—the one who had threatened to have him arrested if he returned to the shopping center. If this were to happen, what the security guards would do is make a citizen's arrest, detain him, and then call the Riverside Police Department and press charges against him.

After attempting to contact the manager of the shopping center repeatedly by telephone and getting no response, I finally decided to send the manager a demand letter, explaining how Benny was being singled out and harassed by security because of his political views and beliefs and that this was clearly a violation of his First Amendment constitutional rights to free speech and assembly. I also added that Benny was not trespassing and that he was simply going to the center to recycle, which was presumably the intended purpose of the recycling center.

I never received a response to that letter, but Benny was subsequently arrested and charged with misdemeanor trespassing. What is ironic is that we had been discussing homelessness in my class and several of the readings had focused on the theme of an article titled "Annihilation of Space by Law."[2] We discussed how more and more cities were moving to criminalize many of the activities that are normal for any human being, like sitting, sleeping, defecating, or urinating, just because these activities are taking place in a public space—as when a homeless person sleeps on a park bench or sits on a sidewalk.

After conferring with Benny, I agreed to represent him. My first strategy was to file what is referred to as a "demurrer" to the complaint against him.

The Demurrer

A demurrer is essentially the first line of defense for a criminal defense lawyer. Rather than addressing the substantive charges, a demurrer is an attack on the pleadings or filing document; it says that the complaint itself is faulty and that the charges should be dismissed because no crime was committed—because no legitimate cause of action has been stated. Below I share what I communicated in the demurrer I filed for Benny.

> The defendant, Benjamin Mattumbo, hereby defers to the complaint on the grounds of uncertainty, and on the grounds that no offense is stated in the complaint. Even if the facts alleged in the complaint were true, they would not constitute a violation of Penal Code § 602(1), a misdemeanor, which entails entering and occupying real property without the consent of the owner or his or her agent without permission.
>
> I. GROUNDS FOR THE DEMURRER
>   1. Uncertainty (Penal Code § 1004[2])
>   A defendant may demur on the ground that a complaint or information does not substantially conform to the requirements of Penal Code § 950 and § 952 relating to statement of offense. See, for example, *People v. Horiuchi* (1931).[3] Literal compliance with Penal Code § 952 is insufficient in the face of a demurrer if the accusation fails to give constitutionally adequate

notice of what the accused must defend against. See *People v. Jordan* (1971).⁴

Here, the defendant is charged with trespassing at a recycling center at the Canyon Crest Shopping Center. The defendant is a recycler and was using the center for its intended public use, which is recycling.

2. No Offense Stated (Penal Code § 1004[4])

It is a ground for demurrer that the facts stated in the complaint do not constitute a public offense. This ground, like lack of jurisdiction, may be used to raise questions of constitutionality, inoperative legislation, and limitations. See, for example, *People v. Superior Court* (Caswell) (1988)⁵ and *People v. Heitzman* (1994).⁶

The complaint charges that defendant committed a violation of Penal Code § 602(1), a misdemeanor, in that on or about May 9, in the county of Riverside, California, he did willfully and unlawfully commit a trespass by entering and occupying real property and a structure located at 5225 Canyon Crest Dr., Riverside, California, without the consent of the owner, his agent, and the person in lawful possession thereof.

The police report alleges that the security guard at the Canyon Crest Shopping Center had told the defendant not to be in the area on several occasions, and that the defendant entered the area of 5225 Canyon Crest Dr. The court should take judicial notice that 5225 Canyon Crest Dr. is the Canyon Crest Shopping Center, which is privately owned but open to the public, and that it has a recycling center, which is open to the public.

In order to prove this crime, each of the following elements must be proven:

(1) A person willfully entered upon the land [or buildings of any kind] of another person;

(2) the person did so without the consent of the owner;

(3) the person occupied some portion, or all thereof, continuously or until ousted therefrom; and

(4) the person entered and occupied the property with the specific intent to dispossess those lawfully entitled to possession from that portion of the property actually occupied.

The defendant entered the Canyon Crest Shopping Center with the express purpose of recycling. He was on the property and intended to use the property to recycle, which is the intended purpose of the recycling center, and which is on private property but open to the public. There is no allegation that the defendant "occupied" some portion of the property until ousted. In fact, the police report alleges that defendant was "detained" by the security person, who signed a private person's arrest form. Further, the complaint fails to allege that the defendant occupied some portion or all of the property "continuously or until ousted." On the contrary, the defendant was detained against his will. Finally, there is no allegation that he entered the property with "the specific intent to dispossess those lawfully entitled to possession of that portion of the property actually occupied." There was substantial evidence upholding the defendant's conviction of violation of Penal Code § 602(j), where the defendant entered land with the intention of interfering with the lawful business carried on by the owner, where the defendant set up a table in a passenger tram at the Disneyland parking lot for the purpose of gathering signatures and soliciting donations and where there was testimony that his activities interfered with the loading and unloading of the tram.[7]

Here, however, the accused was not alleged to have interfered with the intended use of the property. He was using the property for the intended use of recycling. The defendant was subjected to false arrest and malicious prosecution simply because the security guard did not want him on the property.

The demurrer should be granted because no public offense is alleged in the complaint. Even if all of the allegations in the complaint were true, it would not constitute a violation of § 602(1) in that there is no allegation that the property was occupied continuously with the purpose of interfering or the specific intent to dispossess those lawfully entitled to possession from that portion of the property actually occupied.

Alfredo Mirandé
Attorney for defendant, Benjamin Mattumbo

My Client

Once I decided to represent Benny, I had to make the transition from viewing him as a campus icon, organic intellectual, and supervisor of the homeless placement to viewing him as my client. This might seem like an easy task, but it was not. Although I had known Benny for a number of years, he remained an enigma to me. Up until I represented him, I had known him as a master recycler who worked tirelessly recycling on and near the university campus and as a person who knew a great deal about recycling and homelessness. I had also known Benny as a community activist and organizer who was involved in virtually every campus issue or progressive political agenda, ranging from the war to protests against raising student fees. Finally, I had known Benny as a homeless advocate who took time to share his knowledge and wisdom with my students and other progressive people.

One of the first things I learned after making our first court appearance was that Benny, like many homeless persons, had a number of other unresolved misdemeanor and failure-to-appear charges on his record. After I decided to represent him, I focused on clearing all the other charges pending against him. The major problem was that on paper at least, Benny appeared to have a serious criminal record, but the reality was that he had a number of cases for which he had failed to appear and that warrants had been issued for his arrest for failure to appear. After a while, the failure-to-appear warrants had piled up. In fact, he was almost placed under arrest when he made his first court appearance because I was coming from another court and I was delayed in making my own appearance. The bailiff wanted to arrest Benny because he had a number of outstanding warrants.

The unfortunate reality is that the police routinely charge homeless people with miscellaneous crimes and infractions in order to get them into the criminal justice system and keep them under control. Perhaps the most difficult thing about representing a homeless client is precisely the fact that they are homeless and are without food or shelter. Benny did not have a telephone or home address. I would, therefore, rely on seeing him after class or calling him at the Chicano Student Programs office, and there were times when I had to actually go out looking for him on the streets near the university, trying to catch him as he made his daily trips to recycle. Benny spent a lot of time hanging out at the Chicano

Student Programs and Native Student Programs offices, so people would leave messages for him there. I generally left messages at Chicano Student Programs to have Benny contact me.

On court days, I would offer to meet Benny at a certain designated place so that I could give him a ride and we could drive to the court together, or he would simply agree to meet me downtown outside the courthouse. Like other people entering the courthouse, we had to go through the security checkpoints. Benny had a large kerchief that he used to hold some of his more important worldly possessions. He would take the kerchief and carefully hide it in the bushes outside the courtroom. After court, he would retrieve his worldly belongings and would be on his way.

The next problem with representing Benny is more difficult to talk about because it entails stereotypes surrounding the homeless. One of the things that I had to learn to do was to normalize my relationship with Benny, who was a homeless person. I do not know exactly how to say this, but I could not help but notice how people responded to him outside the secure confines of the university. As we entered the courtroom, for example, the security tended to treat Benny the way they would normally treat other homeless persons, and that is with derision and disrespect—even initially attempting to deny him access to the court.

The Shopping Center Cases and the Annihilation of Space by Law

As I mentioned previously, there are issues we had been discussing in my class that relate directly to Benny's case. One of the issues comes up in what are known as "the shopping-center cases." In my journal to you, Fermina, on April 24, I began by complaining that the students were not doing the reading. Then, I wrote:

> Reflections: April 24
>
> Walter started off the discussion by raising the issue of stare decisis from the shopping-center cases. You remember those cases; in fact, they were the first cases we read during the one-week orientation at Stanford. I do not think that we have adequately discussed either the shopping-center cases or the concept of stare decisis. Historically, law has sought to distinguish itself from politics. Hence, we talk about

things like the rule of law and legal reasoning. Duncan Kennedy[8] thinks this is all nonsense and part of the training for hierarchy that goes on in law school, and he debunks the idea that there is a separate entity called legal reasoning that is somehow separate from other kinds of moral, logical, or ethical reasoning. Kairys is similarly critical of the doctrine of stare decisis, which is the idea that legal decisions are based on legal precedent, so that in any particular case there is a "correct" legal decision that flows automatically from the precedent. Kairys shows effectively how precedent is a sort of shell game or sleight of hand, whereby courts are able to make political judgments and legitimate them by employing the doctrine of stare decisis and creating the illusion or fiction of continuity.

The shopping-center cases are interesting because they show how courts must sometimes balance competing rights or interests. Since shopping centers are private or semipublic property, the court must balance an individual's right to exclude people from his or her private property, which is fundamental, with the First Amendment right to free speech, which is no less fundamental. Since *Marsh v. Alabama* (1946),[9] a case that upheld the right of a Jehovah's Witness, Mrs. Staples, to distribute religious literature in the downtown of a company town, the Supreme Court has been wrestling with this issue. In *Amalgamated Food Employees Union Local 590 v. Logan Valley Plaza* (1968),[10] the court upheld the right of union members to picket a grocery store at a private shopping center, ruling that free speech outweighed the private property interests of shopping-center owners. However, only four years later, in *Lloyd v. Tanner* (1972),[11] the court distinguished the facts in *Lloyd* from *Logan Valley*, holding that antiwar demonstrators did not have a constitutional right to distribute antiwar leaflets at a shopping center. But in *Hudgens v. NLRB* (1976)[12] contrary to the explicit language in *Lloyd*, which distinguished it from *Logan Valley*, the court said that *Lloyd* had actually "overturned" *Logan Valley* and concluded that it was bound by *Lloyd*, and that union members picketing a store do not have a constitutional right to picket at a private shopping center.

The common gut-level response, and the one articulated by Walter during the class discussion, is something to the effect that the concept of stare decisis is nothing but a smoke screen that masks blatant political moves by courts, but I think the issue is more complex. One of the things that you have to remember is that law and courts are more concerned with appearing to be right than with actually being right. Hence, since courts are ostensibly bound to follow precedent, the concept of stare decisis can serve as a powerful catalyst for social change. In *Brown v. the Board of Education* (1954),[13] for example, the Supreme Court was able to overturn *Plessy v. Ferguson* (1896)[14] and to hold that separate facilities are inherently unequal and unconstitutional; this decision set a precedent for subsequent decisions. The problem is that no two fact patterns are ever the same, so you can always distinguish cases from each other.

What is clear from the shopping-center cases is that shopping centers are not simply private property. They may be privately owned, but they are sanctioned and often indirectly supported by the state.

Benny's case can be distinguished from the shopping-center cases in that the First Amendment issue was never directly at issue in the court pleadings. The First Amendment issue would have come into play only because the security guard was said to have arbitrarily denied Benny access to the recycling centers because of his "speech," as reflected in his political signs and placards, while permitting recycling by other homeless people who did not show themselves to be antiwar or progressive. Consequently, one could argue that this was a content-based regulation of speech by the state.

In defending Benny, I never raised the First Amendment issue in my pleadings, instead focusing on the narrower issue of whether he was guilty of trespassing. I would have raised the First Amendment issue as needed, especially in an appeal, but the truth is that this was an easy case in the sense that my client was simply not trespassing.

The second issue that we had been addressing in class that is relevant to Benny's case is the so-called "annihilation of space by law." As described in the book *Sidewalk*, sociologist Mitchell Duneier[15] spent five years living with and talking to street people who made their living on the streets of Greenwich Village selling secondhand goods, selling printed materials, or panhandling.

In the chapter in the book called "Space Wars," Duneier discusses how business owners, politicians, and the police worked to control the activities of the street vendors. Duneier notes that there was a movement in the 1990s for formal social control for small infractions. Leading the way in the movement for formal social control for small infractions were the business-improvement districts (BIDs). These are geographic areas within the city in which property owners agree to pay for enhanced services and capital improvements to benefit an area. Many of the BIDs in Manhattan "employ uniformed safety officers who patrol their areas from 7:00 a.m. to 11:00 p.m., with the objective of providing a deterrent to crime and a radio link to the local New York Police Department precinct."[16]

According to Duneier, the BIDs emerged as a significant political force in the 1980s: "By employing their own security forces and sanitation workers, the BIDs have brought about the degree of civic order called for by the "broken windows theory." Duneier added that "some BIDs are politically powerful and work closely with the mayor and City Council."[17]

In the 1980s, the New York City Council passed Local Law 33, which banned unlicensed street vending. However, because of objections from the American Civil Liberties Union and mindful of First Amendment protections of free speech, the City Council had already passed a written-matter exception intended to protect pamphleteers. The attorney for the midtown BIDs who had introduced the exception commented, "Unfortunately, that well-intentioned minor exception grew into a loophole big enough to spawn a table-based sidewalk industry which has clogged the sidewalks to the point where pedestrians cannot pass."[18]

The City Council subsequently passed Local Law 45, which included "prohibitions on the mandatory number of feet between a vendor's table and a street corner, the entrance to a building, or a subway entrance." The new law had immediate implications for the street vendors within the jurisdiction of the Grand Central Partnership and the Thirty-fourth Street Partnership. According to Duneier,

> In Greenwich Village, the amount of sidewalk space was cut in half. For quite a while, instead of bringing about greater order on the streets, Local Law 45 led to further deterioration of sidewalk life on Sixth Avenue. Those vendors who did remain would routinely fight with the police and with another for the remaining legal sidewalk space.[19]

Don Mitchell has similarly analyzed the nature and implications of anti-homeless laws in major cities in the United States like Seattle,

San Francisco, New York, Atlanta, Phoenix, and Santa Cruz, concluding that these ordinances have led to the annihilation of space by law.[20] More specifically, the anti-homeless laws have led to the criminalization of activities that all of us engage in in order to survive, like sleeping, sitting, urinating, and defecating. The intent of these laws is to control the behavior of homeless people in a public space so that homeless cannot do what they must do in order to survive without breaking laws and having the behavior criminalized.[21]

Anti-homeless legislation,

> by seeking to annihilate the spaces in which homeless people must live—by seeking, that is, to regulate the public space of the city such that there literally is no room for homeless people, recreates the public sphere as intentionally exclusive, as a sphere in which the legitimate public only includes those who ... have a place governed by private property rules to call their own. Landed property thus again becomes a prerequisite of effective citizenship.[22]

"Invisible Man"

I am an invisible man. No, I am not a spook like those who haunted Edgar Allan Poe, nor am I one of your Hollywood-movie ectoplasms. I am a man of substance, of flesh and bone, fiber and liquids—and I might even be said to possess a mind. I am invisible, understand, simply because people refuse to see me. Like the bodiless heads you see sometimes in circus sideshows, it is as though I have been surrounded by mirrors of hard distorting glass. When they approach me they see only my surroundings, themselves, or figments of their imagination—indeed everything and anything, except me.[23]

In the above quote, Ralph Ellison is referring to the "invisibility" of Black people in a racist society, but there is a sense in which the metaphor of invisibility is also applicable to homeless people like Benny. Although Benny was extremely noticeable on the university campus, his visibility may have been more transparent than real. Let me be clear on what I mean. While Benny was extremely visible on campus, he was not visible as a complete person with blood and bones but rather as an icon, an advocate for progressive causes or a defender of homeless people.

Others did not necessarily see him as a human being with special needs, problems, and concerns.

There is a very real sense in which homeless persons are invisible to society. What society and the public see is not a real person but a faceless label. They see a category, such as a homeless person, a panhandler, a derelict, or a mentally ill street person, rather than an individual. In fact, it is the label itself that enables the observer to dismiss a person simply as "homeless."

While concern with pauperism and poor people dates back not only to the colonial United States but to medieval Europe, homelessness was not recognized as a serious social problem in the United States until the 1980s.[24] Amir Marvasti begins the story of the treatment of the poor and the mentally ill in the United States in the 1640s and traces it to the mid-1840s with the emergence of some of the early "poor laws," which attempted to control paupers and the mentally ill by institutionalizing them.[25] In the classic book *The Mentally Ill*, published in 1845, Albert Deutsch notes that "the individual in need of assistance was apt to receive public attention only when his condition was looked upon as a social danger or public nuisance—and was then 'disposed of' rather than helped."[26] Deutsch adds that economic class was a major factor in determining who came to the attention of public officials and that the problem of mental illness was closely linked to poverty. While rich people were able to be protected, as Marvasti paraphrases Deutsch, "poor people, if in any way deviant, were more visible and consequently more likely to be subjected to official scrutiny and formal processing."[27] Between the 1840s and the 1950s, the movement to institutionalize the mentally ill corresponded with an explosive growth in asylums to house them.[28]

One of the first sociological studies that contained the word "homelessness" in the title was Alice Solenberger's *One Thousand Homeless Men*, first published in 1911. Nels Anderson's book *The Hobo*, a study of homeless men in Chicago, was published in 1923 and is recognized as "one of the first in-depth qualitative studies of life on the streets."[29]

Despite increased interest in the problem of homelessness and a growing concern with homelessness as a societal problem, there has been little consensus on the definition of homelessness. Marvasti notes that "defining homelessness has proved to be a sticky business," and that while some approach the problem with methodological rigor, others "rush to romanticized literary descriptions that single large numbers."[30]

Drawing on Harold Garfinkel's focus on the importance of institutional practices for producing official data, Marvasti opts for what he refers to as the "constructive demography" of a problem, or "the social construction of problem populations through institutionally grounded demographic data."[31] Perhaps what is most ironic about the elusiveness of the concept of homelessness is that, in the end, one cannot define homelessness without first defining "home" or the antithesis of homelessness. Homelessness is obviously more than having adequate shelter or a roof over one's head—it entails a sense of belonging. After all, there are people without roofs over their heads who do not see themselves as homeless, just as there are some people with adequate shelter who feel displaced or homeless.

In an interesting article called "The Unaccommodated Woman," Julia Wardhaugh notes that home and homelessness are binary opposites, so that you cannot define one without defining the other.[32] The concept of *home*, as opposed to *house*, cannot exist without the concept of homelessness, just as Durkheim noted that "normalcy" cannot exist without "deviance."[33] That is, just as "good" people define other people as bad or deviant in order to define themselves as good or "normal," so do people who are not homeless ultimately define homelessness. Drawing on the *Concise Oxford Dictionary* (1991) definition of "home," Wardhaugh defines it as "the place where one lives; a dwelling-house; the members of a family collectively; the native land of a person or a person's ancestors; an institution for persons needing care, rest or refuge; the place where a thing originates or is most common."[34] She adds that "home" can mean a private residence or public institution, "a place of refuge or a prison,"[35] noting that for many homeless-at-home women—those who experience violence, abuse, and the suppression of self within the confines of the home—the home is a prison.[36] The so-called "unaccommodated woman" is "a particular aberration and a contradiction in terms: the gender renegade who has rejected, or been rejected by, traditional family and domestic structures."[37]

As I reflect on Benny, I have come to the strange realization that for a number of years, his home—the place where he belonged—was the university. When I first met him, he was a recycler who had a pickup truck and would collect items to recycle around the baseball diamond and sports complex, which were on the outskirts of the university. My recollection is that he would park, and presumably sleep in, his vehicle in the vicinity of the sports complex. Eventually, however, Benny was without the pickup truck. Thus, while those of us who were employees or students at the university—those who would spend time at the university attending classes, attending meetings, going to the library, or engaging in other miscellaneous activities away from home—for Benny, the university *was* home. Ironically, I believe it was the massive growth in student enrollments and the attendant changes in the campus itself that eventually led to Benny's displacement and cemented his status as a homeless person.

Another thing that has struck me as I think about Benny is the extent to which people really do tend to stigmatize the homeless, treating them essentially as non-persons. As I have mentioned, a lawyer is supposed to be a zealous advocate for his or her client, and when I went to court for Benny, I could not help but notice that he was being treated in a demeaning and condescending manner by everyone he came into contact with. People would treat him basically as though he did not belong or was invisible—a non-person. Although they feigned otherwise, all the people in the courtroom, including the bailiff, court clerk, and other defendants, stared openly at Benny and did little to hide their disapproval of him.

The tactic that I used with Benny was to treat him with the same care and compassion that I would show toward any cherished and respected client. I did this in both direct and indirect ways. I did it directly by always referring to him as "sir" or "Mr. Mattumbo" when addressing him or the court. I did it by carefully explaining to him the courtroom procedures and the law. I did it by making sure he understood what was going on at all points in the proceedings. But mostly, I did it by treating him the same as I would any other client.

Though I did not put extra effort into my appearance when I first started going to court with Benny, I could not help but notice the contrast between us when we did go. Of course, whether I was with Benny or not, when I went to court I made sure that I was dressed properly in my suit and tie. But after a while, I put more effort than usual into looking nice when Benny and I appeared in court together. I noticed that people stared when Benny's case was called—especially, I think, because he was a homeless man who was being represented by a lawyer. And as I made my appearance before the court, I would proudly announce, "Good morning, Your Honor, Alfredo Mirandé, representing Mr. Benny Mattumbo, who is present and not in custody." No one said anything, but I am sure that people were wondering how a homeless person could afford to hire a lawyer—not a public defender, whose job it was to represent indigent people, but a not-so-fancy private attorney.

I was proud to have had Benny as a client and got a lot of satisfaction from working for him and from successfully working out a plea that allowed him to plead guilty to trespassing without having to pay a fine or do jail time, and that compelled the court to dismiss his previous cases. However, as I look back, I am left with the realization that my efforts, while genuine and well-intended, probably did little to help homeless people as a group or to counter the biases and injustices that are perpetrated by the society and the legal and judicial system against the homeless. Lawyering on behalf of the homeless and the poor is different from lawyering on behalf of ordinary people because the problems of the poor and the homeless are endemic and part and parcel of their daily existence in a hostile world. Stephen Wexler notes that practicing law for poor people is unique because lawyering on their behalf requires that we abandon the traditional law-school model of law practice, in which the practitioner helps a client solve a specific legal problem and then simply return to his or her harmonious life. According to Wexler, "Poor people are not just like rich people without money. Poor people do not have legal problems like those of the private plaintiffs and defendants in law school casebooks. People who are not poor are like casebook people. In so far as the law is concerned, they live harmonious and settled private lives. . . . [The lives of the casebook people] usually do not demand the skills of a lawyer."[38] Poor people, on the other hand, especially poor homeless people, do not live settled and harmonious lives and their experiences are inconsistent with the law-school model of personal legal problems. This is because "poverty creates an abrasive interface with society; poor people are always bumping into sharp legal things."[39]

Rather than being unusual or aberrant experiences, for poor people and the homeless, legal problems are endemic to daily existence. No-trespassing, no-loitering, no-blocking-the-sidewalk, and other ordinances are part and parcel of the way society seeks to control the lives of homeless people. They are part of the larger movement by society to annihilate space by law. That is, anti-homeless legislation seeks to annihilate the spaces in which homeless people must live; as Mitchell has noted, "landed property thus again becomes a prerequisite of effective citizenship."[40]

Effective solutions to the problem of homelessness, therefore, require political solutions that address broader societal issues such as poverty, housing, and the need for drug and mental-health treatment for indigent persons. Effectively dealing with the legal problems of the homeless and the poor requires that we replace the law-school model of legal advocacy with collective strategies that address the endemic and recurrent nature of legal problems poor people face every day. Wexler notes that even if all the lawyers in the country were to work full-time, they would not be able to address the legal problems faced by the poor.[41] Moreover, "traditional practice hurts poor people by isolating them from each other, and fails to meet their need for a lawyer by completely misunderstanding that need,"[42] in the sense that poor people's legal problems are not anomalies that can be solved and moved on from, but the result of poverty and/or homelessness.

Effective legal representation for the poor and the homeless will require collectively performed and ongoing solutions to the problems they face. The nonprofit organization LA CAN[43] is an example of a collective solution to the problems faced by the homeless. Located in a downtown Los Angeles Skid Row community, it was established in 1999 and is made up of homeless and extremely low-income people living in the community, as well as volunteers who work with the homeless. The group's membership roster includes seven hundred individuals (both homeless and non-homeless), with approximately three hundred of those being volunteers, and seventy-five "core members" (presumably the group's leadership). Significantly, the majority of the seven hundred members generally live in Skid Row. In addition to a housing committee, LA CAN has a Community Watch Program in which members go into the field to document police interaction with community residents, as well as a weekly legal clinic that addresses the citations homeless people receive for minor infractions and the impact of these infractions on their lives.

When we discuss rebellious or nontraditional lawyering, the focus is generally on the client, not the attorney. In other words, we usually focus on how the client feels about the representation and not on how the lawyer feels. As I reflect on my representation of Benny, I can say that I derived a certain amount of satisfaction in representing him. And the satisfaction that I got was not because his was a major case or because I did a stellar job representing him. It was a simple case, after all, in which

I was able to get the trespassing charges against Benny dismissed and to settle his other cases that were on the books without his getting any fines or jail time. I think the reason that I got a certain amount of satisfaction in representing Benny is simply that I felt like I was doing something to recognize him not as a nameless homeless person but as, in Ellison's words, "a man of substance, of flesh and bone, fiber and liquids." In fact, I was proud to represent Benjamin Mattumbo and to do whatever was within my power to have him treated with the dignity and respect he so richly deserved.

∴ 6 ∴

Speedy Trial

Rodrigo Torres

Querida amiga,

Like the story of the twins I told you about (Marcos and Mario), this is a case about two brothers, Rodrigo and Rodolfo Torres. But before getting into the case and talking about the brothers, I want to talk a bit about my practice. As I reflect on the practice, one of the things that intrigues me most is the intricate relationships and links that have existed among many of my cases and clients. Since I was a part-time attorney who charged little or nothing for his services and devoted a lot of time and attention to each case, perhaps it is not surprising that a demand for my services would develop and that my client base would be based on personal referrals.

Although I had an unlisted telephone number and have never advertised or sought out clients, I did not have to advertise because the word got around quickly and I was able to build a reputation for being a competent, honest, reliable, and most certainly affordable lawyer. An additional factor is that I was readily accessible, approachable, and capable of communicating well with my clients, especially my Spanish-speaking, immigrant clients. I soon learned that if you help someone in distress and they are satisfied with your services, the next time that a friend, relative, or acquaintance has a legal problem and needs a lawyer, he or she is likely to recommend you. For example, Xavier, the painter I told you about in a recent letter, was the person who first referred Rodrigo Torres to me, and Rodrigo himself also referred several other clients, including his nephew, whom I represented in a DUI case.

When I first got a message from Xavier about a year after his case had closed, I feared he had gotten into some kind of legal trouble again, but after a brief exchange of greetings, Xavier assured me that he was fine and he was not in any trouble. As it turned out, he was calling *por un favor* (for a favor) and asked whether I would be willing to represent a fellow painter, Rodrigo Torres—a *compañero* who had failed to show for a recent court appearance and had an outstanding warrant for his arrest. The story is somewhat complicated because Rodrigo was in Mexico at the time, and Xavier had asked whether it would be okay for him to give my name and contact information to Rodrigo's brother, Rodolfo ("Rudy") Torres. I agreed and spoke with Rudy, who gave me more background information on the case and the whereabouts of his brother.

Rudy confided that in recent months he had been very worried about his younger brother Rodrigo because the brother had been heavily involved with alcohol and drugs. He explained that Rodrigo had received a notice to appear in court but that he could not appear because he was interned in a drug/alcohol rehabilitation program across the border in Baja California. Rudy said that his brother had been in really bad shape prior to being interned but would not seek help. Rudy had grown increasingly frustrated and desperate and eventually decided that it would be necessary to use deception in order to get help for his brother. He explained that he had devised a plan in which the two brothers would go to Tijuana, ostensibly to buy a car but in reality to allow Rudy to get Rodrigo into a Mexican rehabilitation center—without his prior knowledge. The ruse worked well; when Rodrigo crossed the border, he was met by staff from the rehabilitation center and forcefully detained and interned.

I ultimately agreed to appear for Rodrigo without first meeting him or knowing exactly what the charge against him was. Rudy assured me that the charge was minor and involved trespassing in a department store at a local mall. Even though the charge did turn out to be a minor violation, the case was complicated by the fact that Rodrigo had failed to appear and that the court had issued a warrant for his arrest, and his failure to appear itself was a separate and more serious offense. Rudy said he needed a lawyer to appear and explain the situation to the court and to tell the judge that Rodrigo could not attend because he was interned in a drug rehabilitation program. It was odd that I agreed to represent Rodrigo because I was about to represent someone whom I had never spoken with or met. I had to keep in mind that although Rudy retained me, the mystery man, Rodrigo, was in fact my client.

Factual Background

On September 19, Rodrigo Torres had been charged with violation of Penal Code § 555, entry/remaining on posted property without permission, committed on August 20. On October 16, a "failure to appear" warrant was issued for § 853, a violation of a written promise to appear, on September 27.

On November 13, I appeared #977(a)[1] in Department C51 before Judge M. J. O'Brien. At the hearing, I informed the court that the family had retained me and that Rodrigo Torres was interned in a treatment center in Baja California, Mexico, and could not appear. A ten-thousand-dollar warrant was issued and held by the court, and arraignment and a second hearing were set for February 7, on the Penal Code § 555 charge. On February 7, I appeared #977(a) once again and was able to delay further court action until November 3.

Rodrigo Torres finally returned from Mexico, and on November 3 he appeared in court with me, his attorney, as promised, and entered a guilty plea on his trespassing charge. He was ordered to pay a modest fine.

Appearances Can Be Deceiving

At the conclusion of Rodrigo's arraignment and guilty plea, to all appearances the case was closed and had resulted in a satisfactory outcome for my client. Unfortunately, I soon learned that appearances could be wrong. Once Rodrigo entered his plea, he was ordered to pay a victim restitution fee and the penalty assessment, in addition to his modest fine. The penalty assessment is a special fee that is added to a fine and is approximately two and one-half times as much as the initial fine. When I accompanied Rodrigo to the clerk's office to pay the fine after the hearing, we discovered that he had several outstanding traffic infractions and thus other fines to pay. These were minor infractions, like having a broken taillight, and Rodrigo had to go to work soon after learning of them, so we agreed that he would return to the court another day to take care of his various fines. A few days later, I received a call from a distraught Rodrigo telling me that when he returned to the clerk's office, he was told that he had an outstanding warrant on a domestic violence case that he had no knowledge of.

When we appeared in court to answer for the domestic violence charges, we were shocked to discover that, unbeknownst to us, shortly after Rodrigo was interned in Mexico and about a month before my first appearance on his trespassing case, a separate complaint had been issued in the same judicial district. It charged Rodrigo with Count 1, Penal Code § 273.5, inflicting corporal injury on a spouse; Count 2,

Penal Code § 273a(b), inflicting physical pain or mental suffering on a child; Count 3, Penal Code § 136.1(b)(1), attempting to dissuade a witness; Count 4, Penal Code § 243(e)(1), battery against a spouse; and Count 5, Penal Code § 594(a), vandalism in an amount less than four hundred dollars. The charges allegedly arose from incidents that were said to have occurred on or about May 21 and June of the same year in which I had first appeared regarding the trespassing case. The court had apparently issued an arrest warrant on October 15 and bail was set at fifteen thousand dollars for failure to appear.

Significantly, Rodrigo was never served with the domestic violence complaint or the summons and had no knowledge that domestic violence charges were pending and had been filed on October 9, or that a warrant on those charges had been issued on October 15, just one day prior to the issuance of the warrant on the trespassing charge. Having no knowledge of the domestic violence charges, I had previously told the defendant via his brother Rudy that he was only facing a charge on a minor violation of Penal Code § 555.

The Right to a Speedy Trial

Under both the Sixth Amendment of the U.S. Constitution and article 1, section 15, of the California Constitution, a defendant has a right to a speedy trial, and unless the defendant knowingly waives this right, the state has an obligation to bring the defendant to trial in a timely manner. While there are no hard and fast rules as to when this right has been violated, it is generally recognized that the right is triggered either by the date on which charges are filed or when a person is arrested, whichever occurs first.

As I reflected on Rodrigo's situation, I was really struck by the fact that there had been an inordinate delay in bringing charges against him. At the same time, I also realized that Rodrigo had been out of the country and had failed to appear, so on the surface it did not appear that I would have much luck in bringing a "denial of right to a speedy trial" due process violation, or what is called a "*Serna* motion" in California. However, when I discussed the matter with my good friend and mentor, Juan Guerra, he calmly pointed out that although Rodrigo had been out of the country, I could argue to the court that he had "appeared" when I appeared for him #977(a). I decided that prior to addressing the substantive charges, I would prepare a "denial of speedy trial" due process violation motion. It was interesting because I had previously prepared other speedy-trial motions with some success. What follows is a slightly revised and condensed version of the motion.

The Speedy-Trial (*Serna*) Motion

I. *In Order to Establish a Violation of Sixth Amendment Right, Defendant Must Show a Presumption of Prejudice*

Under both the California Constitution and the U.S. Constitution, the speedy-trial right of a defendant attaches in a misdemeanor case when either formal charges are filed or the defendant is subjected to the restraint of arrest, whichever comes sooner.[2]

While a federal speedy-trial evaluation is to be done on a case-by-case basis, the speedy-trial clause of the Sixth Amendment requires that an accused allege that the interval between the date the right was triggered and the ultimate trial date crossed the threshold dividing ordinary delay from presumptively prejudicial delay.[3] However, a defendant cannot establish a federal speedy-trial claim if his or her case has been prosecuted with "customary promptness."[4]

"Prejudice is presumed when it is reasonable to assume sufficient time elapsed to affect adversely one or more of the interests protected by the speedy trial clause."[5] The dividing line for "presumptive prejudice," depending on the charges, is generally one year.[6] The California Supreme Court found that a one-year delay was presumptively prejudicial in a misdemeanor case because that was the length of the statute of limitations for misdemeanors.[7] Thus, in California, the statute of limitations provides the standard when a delay is deemed to be presumptively prejudicial.

In this case, a delay of more than two years is presumptively prejudicial in California, because enough time has elapsed to adversely affect one or more of the interests protected by the speedy-trial clause of the Sixth Amendment. The prejudice toward the defendant is substantial in this unjustified delay because within two years it can be expected that memories of the alleged victim, of witnesses, and even of the defendant have faded.

The initial incident in question occurred some two and one-half years ago. The police officers, the witnesses, and the defendant have fading memories of the incident and the facts, which are in dispute.

II. There Was a Speedy Trial Violation under the Barker v. Wingo Four-Factor Balancing Test

Once the federal right to a speedy trial has been triggered and the threshold of presumptive prejudice has been reached, then the court must determine whether there has been a violation of the speedy-trial right using the four-factor test laid out in the case Barker v. Wingo (1972). The four factors of the Sixth Amendment balancing test are "[t]he length of the delay, the reason for the delay, the defendant's assertion of his right, and prejudice to the defendant."[8] The defendant need not establish actual prejudice as a prerequisite to obtaining a hearing at which evidence relevant to this four-factor balancing test is heard.[9]

1. *The Length of the Delay.* The length of the delay is the first of the four factors that is used by the court in determining whether a federal speedy-trial violation has occurred.[10] Once the threshold dividing line of "presumptive prejudice" has been crossed, as it has in this case, the presumption that pretrial delay has prejudiced the rights of the accused increases over time. In this case, a delay of more than two years in an uncomplicated misdemeanor case warrants granting the defendant's motion to dismiss the case, especially since the delay was not justified or necessitated by pretrial investigation, and it was not otherwise unavoidable.

2. *The Reason for the Delay.* The Supreme Court of the United States has said that the courts should generally deny a speedy-trial claim when the government has pursued a defendant with "reasonable diligence." The court attaches "great weight" to certain "inevitable and wholly justified" pretrial delays, such as when there is a need to collect witnesses, gather necessary evidence, or pursue an evasive defendant.

However, the court has stated that a defendant will surely prevail where the delay is intentionally undertaken by the prosecution to gain some advantage.[11] In such instances, dismissal is "virtually automatic."[12] Official negligence in bringing an accused to trial occupies the middle ground between diligent prosecution and bad-faith delay. Official negligence is not tolerated even in cases where the accused cannot demonstrate actual prejudice. "Although negligence is obviously to be weighed more lightly than a deliberate intent to harm the accused's defense, it still falls on the wrong side of the divide between acceptable reasons for delaying a criminal prosecution once it has begun.... [T]he weight we assign to official negligence compounds over time as the presumption of evidentiary prejudice grows."[13]

In *Doggett v. United States* (1992), the court found the government did not exercise reasonable diligence in trying to find the defendant, who had been living openly under his own name in the United States for six years. A simple credit check located his current address. The government's six-year delay caused by official negligence, coupled with the greater presumption of prejudice—though unspecified—due to such a long delay led the court to conclude that a speedy-trial violation had occurred.

A factor that weighs heavily in favor of the prosecution is whether the authorities acted with customary promptness.[14] Adequate justification for the delay occurs, for example, when a defendant's case is part of a continuing undercover operation by law enforcement that would be jeopardized by an early arrest and prosecution.

Here, however, there is no apparent justification for the delay, since the delay was at worst intentional and at best the result of official negligence. Moreover, official negligence is not tolerated even in cases where the accused cannot demonstrate actual prejudice. The accusatory pleadings were filed on October 9 (see appendix B)[15] and the warrant was signed on October 10 and issued on October 15, but there was no effort to find, serve, or give notice of the charges to the defendant. Because the delay is sufficient to be presumptively prejudicial and because there is no apparent justification for the delay beyond official negligence, the motion to dismiss the charges should be granted.

3. *The Defendant's Assertion of Speedy-Trial Rights.* The third factor in a federal speedy-trial analysis is whether the defendant promptly asserted his or her rights. A defendant who does not promptly assert his speedy-trial rights will not generally prevail. In other words, if a defendant knew or reasonably should have known of the pending case, the failure to seek a speedy trial can be dispositive against the defendant.[16] In this case, the defendant could not assert his right to a speedy trial because he did not know of the domestic charges pending against him.

When, as in this case, the defendant's own conduct did not contribute to the delay, the defendant can rightfully claim a Sixth

Amendment speedy-trial violation. The Sixth Amendment to the U.S. Constitution says, "In all criminal prosecutions, the accused shall enjoy the right to speedy and public trial. . . . The right to a speedy trial is fundamental and is imposed by the Due Process Clause of the Fourteenth Amendment on the States."[17] A defendant has no duty to bring himself to trial; the state has that duty, as well as the duty of ensuring that the trial is consistent with due process.[18] However, where the delay was caused directly by the defendant's wrongful act and justification is demonstrated by the prosecution, the harm to the defendant may be outweighed by the justification. "It is an established maxim of jurisprudence that 'no man can take advantage of his own wrong.'"[19]

4. *Actual Prejudice to Defendant.* The final factor in the *Barker v. Wingo* four-factor balancing test is actual prejudice. Actual prejudice to the Sixth Amendment right to a speedy trial can relate to several other factors, such as oppressive pretrial incarceration, anxiety and concern of the accused, and the possibility of dimming memories and loss of exculpatory evidence.[20] However, "[a]ffirmative proof of particularized prejudice is not essential to every speedy trial claim."[21] And in the absence of such proof, the court simply looks at the length of the delay and the presumption that prejudice increases with the length of the delay.

In order to demonstrate actual prejudice, a defendant must present proof that the defendant's ability to defend against the charges has been impaired by the delay. Bare conclusionary statements are not sufficient to establish actual prejudice.[22] In other words, "the showing of actual prejudice which the law requires must be supported by particular facts and not . . . by bare conclusionary statements."[23]

Here, the defendant is able to establish not only presumed prejudice caused by the length of the delay but actual prejudice in that the memories of the accuser, of witnesses, and even the defendant have faded. The initial incident occurred about two and one-half years ago. The police officers involved, the witnesses, and the defendant have fading memories of the incident and the facts, which are in dispute. The defendant and the accuser were separated at the time of the incident. They have now reconciled, and much has happened since the incident. The defendant went into a treatment center in Mexico a few months after the incident. He was not working at the time, and he now has fading memories of the time period in question and the incident.

Even more significant than the faded memories is the fact that exculpatory evidence has been lost because of the delay. In sum, because of the length of the delay, the absence of "reasonable diligence" or justification for the delay, the fact that the defendant asserted his speedy-trial rights in a timely manner and took no evasive action, the fact that he has shown the occurrence of actual prejudice by having endured unnecessary anxiety and concern, and because his defense was impaired by dimming memories and loss of exculpatory evidence, under the four-factor *Barker v. Wingo* balancing test, the defendant has shown that his Sixth Amendment speedy-trial right was severely impaired. The court must, therefore, grant the motion to dismiss.

III. *The Defendant's State Constitutional Right to a Speedy Trial and Due Process Was Also Violated by the Delay*

Article 1, section 15, of the California Constitution states that the "defendant" (and not "accused") in a criminal case has the right to a speedy trial. The Sixth Amendment right to a speedy trial attaches in misdemeanor prosecutions, as it does in felonies, with the filing of the accusatory pleading, here a misdemeanor complaint, or arrest, whichever is first.[24]

But the test under the state constitutional speedy-trial provision is different from the federal speedy-trial standard.[25] Although no actual prejudice need be shown under the U.S. Constitution, under the California Constitution there is no presumption of actual prejudice, so the defendant must show it.[26]

Once the right to speedy trial attaches, as it did in Rodrigo's case on October 9, two and one-half years ago, the court must determine whether the defendant has been deprived of his constitutional due process right by balancing the resulting prejudice against the justification for the delay. In *Jones v. Superior Court of Los Angeles County* (1970),[27] the Supreme Court explained the process by which a defendant's speedy-trial right is determined under the California Constitution.

In the case in question, the petitioner's right to a speedy trial came into play later than the filing of the charge against him, and since no legislative implementation of that right has been violated, this court must balance the competing interests involved to determine whether the petitioner has been denied his right to a speedy trial, and in doing so, the court must weigh the prejudicial effect of the delay on the petitioner against any justification for the delay.

In *People v. Pellegrino* (1978),[28] the Court of Appeal explained the analysis by which deprivation of due process is established based on the prosecution's failure to file formal charges.

A three-step analysis is employed to determine if a defendant's due process right to a fair trial has been violated because of the delay in filing an information or seeking an indictment: (1) the defendant must show that he has been prejudiced by the delay, whereupon (2) the burden shifts to the People to justify the delay, and (3) the court balances the harm against the justification.

In this case, the prejudice to the defendant is substantial, as has been noted, and there is no justification for the delay. The length of the delay is well beyond the one-year statute of limitations and it is presumptively prejudicial. In addition, the defendant asserted his right in a timely manner and took no steps to avoid prosecution, and there has been actual prejudice to the defendant not only because of fading memories but because exculpatory evidence has been lost because of the delay. In balancing the prejudice to the defendant against the justification, which is official negligence or intentional delay, the court must rule in favor of the defendant and grant the motion to dismiss.

IV. *Fading Memories of Witnesses May Be Sufficient to Establish Prejudice*

In *People v. Hill* (1984),[29] the California Supreme Court held that fading memories of prosecution witnesses that prevent adequate cross-examination on a material issue may constitute sufficient prejudice to warrant a finding of denial of due process.

The Court of Appeal in *Ibarra v. Municipal Court* (1984)[30] also stated that the fading memory of the defendant must be considered by the court in determining prejudice. Even in instances in which the defendant deliberately flees, the court must balance factors to ensure that the justification for the delay outweighs the prejudicial effect. "Even when the defendant has made a concerted effort to avoid prosecution, a court must give effect to the holding of *Barker v. Wingo* by weighing the conduct of both sides."[31]

Far from deliberately fleeing to avoid prosecution, Rodrigo Torres went out of his way to make himself available, making every effort to comply with the order to appear. The defendant's attorney appeared #977(a) on November 13 and February 7 of the subsequent year. He presented himself before the court again on November 4, pled guilty to the Penal Code § 555 charge, and paid a fine plus the penalty assessment.[32] In short, the defendant made no effort to evade law enforcement or to avoid detention and arrest, instead making three separate appearances before the court over a period of approximately one year. The government, on the other hand, made no effort to contact him or to apprise him of the domestic violence charges pending against him. In addition, the mere fact that the memories of the parties and of witnesses has faded is sufficient to establish prejudice and warrant dismissal.

V. *Even Minimal Prejudice Must Be Balanced against the Justification for the Delay*

Even if the prejudice to the defendant appears to be minimal, which it is not in this case, the court must conduct a hearing, using the four factors identified in *Barker v. Wingo* to balance the prejudice against the justification for the delay in order to determine whether a defendant has been deprived of his right to a speedy trial.[33]

Because a one-year delay is unreasonable and presumptively prejudicial to the defendant,[34] a delay of more than two years is clearly excessive and prejudicial to the defendant, especially given the nature of this case and the subjective aspect of the allegations. Potential witnesses have moved, are unavailable, and have fading memories of the facts. In addition, the memory of prosecution witnesses will have faded. The elapsed time and fading memories of witnesses prevents effective cross-examination and violates the defendant's due process right to a fair trial.

Closely related to the length of delay is the reason the government assigns to justify the delay, and different weights are assigned to different reasons. In this case, the reason for the delay appears to be negligence on the part of the government, and the delay is in no way attributable to the conduct of the defendant. Whether and how a defendant asserts his right is closely related to the other factors mentioned above. Here, the defendant could not possibly assert his right because he had no knowledge that accusatory pleadings had been filed and reasonably assumed that no charges were pending against him.

Prejudice is presumed when it is reasonable to assume, as it is in this case, that sufficient time elapsed to adversely affect one or more of the interests protected by the speedy-trial clause. Further, when the defendant had nothing to do with the delay, law enforcement conduct becomes a paramount concern in assessing prejudice and other key factors. In this case, the defendant's failure to assert his speedy-trial rights is meaningless when he is unaware of the pending charges, and his ability to prepare a defense will be impaired.

VI. *Charges Should Be Dismissed Because a Delay of More than One Year Is Presumptively Prejudicial and Was Not Caused by the Defendant*

The Sixth Amendment right to a speedy trial attaches in misdemeanor prosecutions, as it does in felonies, with the filing of the accusatory pleading, here a misdemeanor complaint, or arrest, whichever is first, and "a delay between the filing of a misdemeanor complaint and the arrest and prosecution of a defendant which exceeds one year is unreasonable and presumptively prejudicial."[35]

Under the California constitution, the defendant must show actual prejudice.[36] Under the federal standard, there is no need to show actual prejudice and a fourfold standard is used to balance prejudice against the justification: the length of the delay; the reasons for the delay; the defendant's assertion of the right; and any prejudice toward the defendant.[37] However, under the California Constitution, only two factors need to be balanced: actual prejudice and justification.

For the foregoing reasons, the motion to dismiss should be granted.

Alfredo Mirandé
Attorney for defendant, Rodrigo Torres

Reflections

On the day of the hearing for the speedy-trial motion, I learned that the judge in the department was absent and that I would be appearing before a temporary judge, or "judge pro tem." Prior to the case being called, I had an opportunity to speak with a public defender in the attorney conference room. The public defender told me she had just done a *Serna* motion before the judge pro tem and that he had denied it. She therefore strongly recommended that I ask for a continuance so that I could have the hearing with the regular judge, who would be more sympathetic to the motion.

When the case was called, I started to ask for a continuance and the judge pro tem stopped me in mid-sentence. He said, "I have had an opportunity to read your motion. I can tell you that I have read a lot of *Serna* motions over the years, but I have never read one that is as thorough or complete as this one. I am ready to rule on the motion, but you may request a continuance if you like. It's your call." I felt torn and was forced to make a decision on the spot, without much reflection. On the one hand, the public defender had told me that her motion had been denied and she recommended that I continue the matter. The judge, on the other hand, was extremely complimentary of my motion and seemed positively disposed to rule in my favor. After some reflection, I decided to roll the dice and told the judge that I wanted him to hear the motion. The judge proceeded to tell me that I had done an excellent job in preparing the motion and with little or no comment, he granted the motion to dismiss based on denial of the constitutional right to a speedy trial.

Rodrigo was surprised and extremely happy and grateful. He asked me how much he owed me. He did not have any money but wondered whether he could pay me on time. I knew that Rodrigo was a painter and so I asked him whether he could paint some rooms at my house in exchange for my services, and he jumped at the opportunity. Since Rodrigo had a regular job, he had to do the painting at my house on the weekends. I therefore got to know Rodrigo very well, as he spent four or five weekends painting several rooms of my house. I also got to know his seven-year-old boy, Edgar, who accompanied his father on the weekends. I provided the paint and paid him some money for his services, since the painting turned out to be more than we had expected initially. He ended up painting nearly all of my house, the family room, three bedrooms, and a bathroom.

It might appear that Rodrigo's story ended on a happy note, but it did not. About two years after the successful *Serna* motion, Rodrigo called me once again. He had picked up a couple of misdemeanor charges for carrying drug paraphernalia, like a pipe, in his car, as well as for a minor hit-and-run accident. I wasn't taking any new clients at the time, so I recommended another attorney. After the attorney failed to show up for one of the court appearances, Rodrigo called me again and asked if I would represent him, so I agreed to appear on his behalf. I soon learned that he also had three or four misdemeanor drug-possession cases, which had been continued. Rodrigo pled guilty to the hit-and-run in exchange for a fine and I continued the drug-possession and drug-paraphernalia misdemeanor cases. Unfortunately, while he was out on bail and waiting for the next court appearance, Rodrigo picked up a felony charge for possession of a controlled substance with the intent to sell. This more serious drug charge was assigned to a public defender and was continued in order to give the public defender time to prepare for trial. The lesser charges were also continued until there was a disposition on the felony. Although he was eligible for a public defender, Rodrigo wanted me to also take over the more serious drug charge; unfortunately, I simply did not have the time to prepare for the trial because I was teaching, serving as chair of the Ethnic Studies Department, and writing this manuscript. I represented Rodrigo on the misdemeanor charges but not the felony. The DA offered a three-year package deal in exchange for all the charges, but Rodrigo insisted on going to trial because he felt that the police did not have any evidence against him for the felony charge. He said the police had planted the drugs and blamed him for it. After about six months of continuances, the public defender struck a deal and Rodrigo pled guilty in exchange for credit for time served. The misdemeanor charges were dropped.

 Fermina, as I thought about Rodrigo, I realized that although I had done a good job in filing and prevailing on the speedy-trial motion and getting the minor drug charges dismissed, I had not done much to counter the injustices and biases inherent in the legal and judicial system against people like Rodrigo. In fact, I may have failed Rodrigo in the sense that I didn't address the real, much deeper problem that he was facing: drug addiction. Rodrigo's problems—the petty possession of drugs, the drug paraphernalia charges, the minor hit-and-run incident, and even the domestic violence charges—all stemmed from the fact that Rodrigo had a serious addiction to methamphetamines. His brother Rudy was very much aware of the problem, and this is why he opted to put Rodrigo in the drug rehabilitation program against his will. But after his stay at the rehabilitation center in Mexico, Rodrigo had obviously relapsed. In fact, Rodrigo was for a time eligible for a diversion program that would help him with his addiction, and I was about to strike a plea bargain with the DA to take advantage of this opportunity. But before I could do that, he picked up the felony drug-sale charge, which made him ineligible for the diversion program.

The Substance Abuse and Crime Prevention Act, also known as Proposition 36, was passed by 61 percent of California voters on November 7, 2000. This vote permanently changed state law to grant first- and second-time nonviolent, simple drug-possession offenders the opportunity to receive substance-abuse treatment instead of incarceration. Proposition 36 went into effect on July 1, 2001, with $120 million for treatment services allocated annually for five years. More than thirty-six thousand Californians enter treatment each year thanks to Proposition 36, codified under 1210 of the Penal Code.[38]

Rodrigo Torres was someone who needed medical treatment rather than criminal punishment, and he was an ideal candidate for the diversion program. Ironically, his relatively long period of incarceration while he was awaiting trial enabled him to undergo withdrawal from drugs and alcohol and to clean up his life. Rodrigo called me shortly after he was released and offered to do some painting jobs for me as payment for his representation. Almost a year has elapsed since then and I haven't heard from Rodrigo, but I am hoping that he has stayed clean and has not gotten into any trouble. For a defense attorney and his clients, no news is generally good news.

Morals Charges

∴ 7 ∴

Indecent Exposure

The Story of Bud Black

Querido Alfredo,

I hope this letter finds you smiling and enjoying the wonderful Southern California fall weather. The busy season at El Sombrero has just ended, so I have been able to devote more time to teaching and working at Milagro. Also, I am looking forward to starting my new poetry project, *Silent Earthquake*, a series of vignettes written in honor of the women of my family. I am glad to hear that this school year is going well for you, and your law and subordination class intrigues me. I might have to adopt a similar curriculum for my adjunct teaching. It is very rascuache of you to have Benny supervise the homeless group, and that truly is a bottom-up approach to teaching advocacy to young students. I also commend you on your meticulous approach in representing Benny and your other clients. I can just imagine the facial expressions of the people in the courtroom when they saw a lawyer in a nice suit representing a homeless person.

    I enjoyed your discussion of your practice in the last chapter, but it raised some questions for me. There are many aspects of your practice that are notable. First, your services are entirely unadvertised, yet they are very accessible to both low-income and Spanish-speaking clients. Furthermore, the personal attention and time that you spend on each case speaks volumes on your commitment to people, and as a result, the intricate and meaningful bonds you are able to build with your clients. At times, I feel that calling them "clients" is not appropriate in rascuache lawyering. Is it not regnant to call them clients? What are your thoughts on that? Also, I wanted to mention the fact that your practice is part-time (since you also have your work at the university, which provides you with a standard of living). This brings up a question: Can one be a rascuache lawyer full time? Can rascuache, rebellious lawyering also provide a living wage for an aspiring rascuache lawyer? Or is this something that you see working only on a part-time basis? Please share your thoughts on this.

Enjoy yourself, and don't forget to tell me how the aloe vera cream that I got you is working for the rash on your arms!

Con cariño,
Fermina

❖ ❖ ❖ ❖ ❖

Querida Fermina,

I am glad to hear that you are doing well. First, the aloe vera cream has done wonders for the rash on my arms. Thanks. I really appreciate it. Thanks also for your kind words about my practice. You raised some intriguing questions in your last letter, and I am not sure that I have adequate answers but I will attempt to respond. The first question was whether it is regnant to call the people that I represent clients, since the word "client" implies a more distanced relationship than I have with most of the people I serve and suggests an economic relationship or bond. Even though I do develop long-term relationships with many people, they are still ultimately my "clients" in the sense that I provide legal services for them and have an ethical duty to represent them to the best of my ability and to put their interests above everyone else's, including my own. I also have a duty to respect the attorney-client privilege and to make them feel like anything that they share with me is confidential. I don't frankly think it's regnant because I am actually being deferential in calling them my clients, so it does not reflect a hierarchical approach to law practice.[1]

The second question is more difficult: Is the rascuache approach to lawyering available to everyone, or is it something that can only be practiced by people who have a secure day job, like I do? I firmly believe that you can make money as a rascuache lawyer, but you would have to make the money from fees collected on a sliding scale. You could also make money from defendants in civil litigation, including employment-discrimination and civil-rights litigation, since rascuache lawyers would represent plaintiffs suing defendants with deep pockets.

I remember speaking to Gerald P. López, whom I know as "Jerry" and who was my teacher and mentor in law school as well as the creator of the rebellious approach to law practice. Jerry said that when he left law school and set up a community law practice in San Diego with some of his Harvard Law School buddies, they had to take on ordinary cases like criminal defense, immigration, divorces, and personal injury in order to pay the bills. They were then able to take on civil rights litigation, in which the odds were stacked heavily against victory and lawyers did not get paid unless clients won. Surprisingly, López and co-counsel Roy Cazares won a sizable settlement from the city of Riverside in a case for "police use of excessive force" involving fifty-six young Chicanos, who were beat up by the police while attending a bachelor party in the Casa Blanca Riverside barrio.[2] In fact, the defendants obtained damages and fees in excess of $275,000. López said that he also started teaching at a nearby law school so that he could support the community law practice.

I want to begin this letter by telling you about a case that I had a couple of years ago. Maybe it is not a case that sounds all that important to you, but it certainly was important to me and to my client. I guess this case was a personal referral because the client, Bud Black, is one of my son's close friends and I first met him through my son's band. As you know, Alejandro ("Mano") is in a local reggae/ska band called the Debonaires. The boys were all in their twenties at the time of the case, but they had been playing together since they were around fifteen years old. It was about as close to a garage band as you can get, without literally being one. They started out by practicing in the family room of our house, which was a converted garage and a rather large room that still barely accommodated all of the boys and their instruments. Bud was not in the band, but he was one of the crowd of young people that supported the band, and I would often see him at their practices and shows. On occasion, Bud would even help out by selling band merchandise and CDs. It would be a stretch to call him a "groupie," although he was a strong supporter of the band and a friend of several of its members, including my son.

Bud was rooming at the time with two brothers, Joseph ("Joey") and James ("Jim") Cooper, also close friends of my son (and Joey is also a member of Alejandro's band). The brothers worked in the same restaurant as Bud, Mario's Restaurant—an upscale Mexican place at a local shopping mall. My son told me that Bud had been charged with a crime that he did not commit. He suggested that I speak with Joey, because he could fill me in on the details of the case. But before I tell you about the specifics of the case, I want to tell you a little bit more about my client.

Bud Black

Bud Black was born and raised in Riverside, California. He has a scraggly beard and shoulder-length, curly, sandy hair; he is about thirty but looks and acts much younger. He is one of those tough, lean, and wiry young men. According to the police report, Bud is five-foot-ten and weighs 150 pounds, but he somehow seems taller and thinner. Bud is not skinny, but he is lean—and, I think he would say, "mean." He works out and was apparently in pretty good shape at the time I met him. I got to know Bud better after taking the case. I remember joking with him once when he told me that one of his fantasies was to become a professional body builder. His father was a local mechanic and had been the owner of Jack's Garage on the north side of Riverside for many years. Bud was not exactly a master mechanic, but he could do basic work on cars, and when I met him, he was working at the Alamo Muffler and Brake Shop on Riverside's East Side. He told me he liked to lift weights at home and would do push-ups and chin-ups during his breaks at Alamo to help him stay in shape and retain what he called his "cat-like reflexes." Bud's parents are older now. His father retired a few years ago, and both parents moved to the high desert near Victorville; since then, Bud has been pretty much on his own.[3] Bud is White, but he grew up around Chicanos and most of his friends are not White. At the time of the incident, Bud was working at Mario's Restaurant part-time, and the restaurant would prove to play a key role in the case, since several of the employees were potential witnesses.

Aside from his slim body build, curly hair, and beard, there is not much that is distinctive about Bud's appearance, except for the fact that one of his front teeth is missing. Bud's appearance was a relevant factor in this case because he had to be identified by the alleged victim of his crime.

The Original Police Report

The charging document ordered Bud Black to appear in Department 11 of the Riverside Superior Court on July 8, stating that "the above named defendant, BUD WILBUR BLACK, committed a violation of Penal Code § 314, subdivision (1), a misdemeanor, in that on or about February 11, in the County of Riverside, State of California, he did willfully, unlawfully, and lewdly expose his person and the private parts thereof in a public place and in a place where there were present other persons to be offended and annoyed thereby." The document added, "Pursuant to Penal Code section 1054.5, subdivision (b), the People are hereby informally requesting that defense counsel provide discovery to the People as required by Penal Code section 1054." Bud was advised of his constitutional rights and entered a not-guilty plea.

According to the police report, on February 23 at approximately 18:00 hours, the victim (named Martínez) came to the police storefront at the Westridge Shopping Mall at 500 Riverside Dr. and reported seeing a suspect in the parking lot of the mall who had previously exposed himself to her. The victim said she had called the Riverside Police Department at the time of the incident but that a police report was not filed then.

Martínez felt uncomfortable about what had happened and had trouble expressing exactly how the crime of indecent exposure took place. She did not tell the Riverside Police dispatcher that she saw the suspect's penis during her initial report of the incident.

Martínez said she went for a walk in the neighborhood of her apartment complex, which is near the University of California, Riverside, and was walking northbound on Lawton Avenue approaching Spruce Street. As she began to step off the curb to cross Spruce, she said, a burgundy suspect vehicle traveling northbound on Lawton made a right turn onto Spruce in front of her and came to a stop, blocking Martínez's way. The vehicle came so close to the curb, Martínez said, that she had to step back onto the curb to avoid being hit. The driver of the suspect vehicle then allegedly said something that Martínez could not understand, to which she said, "Excuse me?" as she stepped forward and leaned into the passenger-side window. The suspect then allegedly said, "Hey baby, show me your titties." Martínez said she was in shock and thought she misunderstood the suspect; she continued to look at the suspect's face for a moment, after which point she looked down and saw the suspect masturbating. The suspect allegedly had his penis sticking out of the top of his shorts, with one hand wrapped around his penis and being moved up and down.

Martínez said she then stepped back from the vehicle and said, "You are so rude," turning around and beginning to walk southbound on Lawton. The victim said she was overcome with fear and started running home. Martínez said that as she ran, she looked back and saw the suspect vehicle driving away northbound on Lawton.

Then on February 23, Martínez said, she was walking around at the Westridge Shopping Center when she heard a male voice "catcalling" a female in the parking lot. Martínez recognized the male voice to be that of the suspect in the indecent-exposure incident. She turned around and saw the same suspect in the same suspect vehicle making comments to a female walking in the lot. Martínez wrote down the suspect vehicle's license plate. A DMV check on the license plate said it belonged to a 1987 Toyota, which was owned by a Judith Mercer from San Leandro.

The following is a paraphrased extract from the police report. (Note that the subject's hair is described as black, while Bud's hair is in fact sandy-colored.)

> Martínez thought she saw the suspect park in the parking lot of Mario's Restaurant. I went to Mario's and asked the manager, García, if he had seen a White male with black curly hair inside Mario's. García said that Bud Black had purchased food from Mario's and he fit the description. García recognized the suspect as Bud because Bud used to be an employee at Mario's. To García's knowledge, Bud still lived at 187 University Ave., in apartment 16. Martínez was positive that she could identify the suspect if she saw him again and wanted him prosecuted.
>
> On March 3, I was patrolling in the area of 187 University Ave. I saw a male subject on an apartment patio who matched Bud's description and asked him if I could speak to him. He said, "Yeah, sure" and walked through the apartment and out the front door. The subject identified himself as Bud Black.
>
> Prior to me mentioning anything about indecent exposure, Bud denied exposing himself to a female. He said he'd heard from people at Mario's Restaurant that I was looking for him. Bud said he was at work all day on the day of the incident. When I went to Mario's, I had made no mention of indecent exposure, and I had made no mention of when the incident occurred to Bud at that time—he produced these facts on his own. I did a records check and discovered that Bud had two warrants for his arrest. I cited and released Bud on the two warrants.
>
> During our time together, Bud volunteered his photograph for file. Officer Flynn #0319 took several photographs of Black. Nothing further.

Supplemental Report

The following is a close paraphrase of part of the supplemental police report:

> On May 13, Detective Ron Garret of the Riverside Police Department contacted Martínez at her place of employment to view a photo line-up with Black among the photos. The victim read and signed the photographic line-up admonition. Detective Garret then showed her six pictures of six White males, with one of the photos being S/BLACK.[4] She immediately pointed at Black's picture and said that he was the person she saw exposing his genitals in the original report. The victim said that she would testify in court.

Bud's "Rap Sheet"

This was not the first encounter that Bud had had with the law. His "rap sheet" included several charges of vandalism and one charge involving a confrontation with a police officer. Earlier in his life, Bud was involved in graffiti and was arrested several times for vandalism and defacing private property. He was also allegedly in a confrontation with some skinheads at a fast-food restaurant and had been charged with interfering with or obstructing a police officer in his duties. Unfortunately, at the time of the arrest, he had two outstanding warrants because he had overdue court fines.

Bud first got in trouble with the law at age twenty, when he was arrested for vandalism after he and another young man were suspected of spray-painting a building in the downtown area. They were booked, but neither was charged or convicted.

Two years later, Bud was arrested and charged with resisting/obstructing a police officer. Two officers responded to a report of a man with a knife at a Jack-in-the-Box restaurant near a Riverside shopping mall. Upon their arrival, the two officers spotted four White men, any one of whom could have fit the description of the man with the knife inside the fast-food restaurant. Three of the men stopped, but one of them allegedly ran. The arresting officer reported, "I chased Black and apprehended him approximately one hundred yards west of the restaurant. Black continued to struggle and attempted to reach into his rear right pocket. I then took Black to the ground, and handcuffed him.

A check of the area revealed that Black's knife fell out of the sheath during the foot pursuit." According to the police report, Bud was inside the restaurant, and according to witnesses who would not identify themselves, he threatened and got into a verbal confrontation with an unknown customer. According to the police report, the witnesses said that Bud told the man "he had a knife and was not afraid to use it." Bud pled guilty to and was convicted of violation of Penal Code § 148, a misdemeanor. He served five days in jail, was assessed a fine, and was placed on twenty-four-month probation.

Three years later, he was taken into custody, cited, and released after being charged with vandalism again. He had reportedly been observed by a police officer writing on the windows of a business in downtown Riverside at the corner of Fifth and Market with a white wax marker. Bud was questioned by police and brought to the back of a police car, where he was reportedly "identified" by the victim, the owner of an antique shop. One officer reported that he found "GRIP" and "5D" beneath the window at three different locations in the vicinity of University and Fifth. There were also scratches at the windows at two other locations in the area. According to the police report, Bud was taken to the police station, where he was read his Miranda rights. He waved his Miranda rights and told the officer that he did write "GRIP" and "5D" on the windows. He said that "GRIP" stands for his loneliness. He further told me that "5D" simply stands for "fifth dimension." Bud pled guilty once again, paid a fine and restitution to the victims, and was placed on probation for twenty-four months.

The following year, Bud and another person, identified as Harrington, were charged with vandalism and conspiracy to commit vandalism at a business in downtown Perris, California. According to the police report, Bud and Harrington were found hiding under an air-conditioning unit on the roof of a business establishment at approximately 00:22 hours, after the officers were called to investigate a possible commercial burglary. Bud was said to have waived his Miranda rights. He said that he and Harrington were at a party earlier in the evening and talked about doing a mural on the above-mentioned building. Said the police report: "Black told us he and S/Harrington climbed up on the above mentioned roof for the purpose of spray painting a 'mural' on the roof of the business. He told me it was a good spot because the 'mural' could be seen from the 91 Freeway." Prior to Bud's sentencing, a probation search was conducted of his apartment, and the police confiscated markers and papers, three cans of spray paint, posters with graffiti, and miscellaneous items. Bud was charged with violation of his probation because the terms of his probation stipulated that he was to "violate no law or ordinance and not to possess items commonly used for tagging including: spray paint/paint or ink markers/metal scribers/aerosol nozzles/related or functional items." Bud pled guilty to violation of Penal Code § 594 once again and was sentenced to four and one-half days in jail, as well as being assessed a restitution fine and placed on probation for thirty-six months. On the violation-of-probation charge, he was sentenced to an additional ten days in jail and was assessed another restitution fine and given twenty-four months of probation.

Bud Black's Account

By the time I took over the case in October, Bud had already been arraigned on one count of indecent exposure and was being represented by the public defender's office. The office had started its investigation of the case, but when I spoke with Bud, he told me that his attorney had a heavy caseload and he asked me whether I would take the case. Bud explained that he could not understand why he was being charged with the crime in the first place. He did not even own a car and rode his bicycle to and from work. He also told me that he was working all day on the date of the incident and his manager and coworkers could verify that he had been working.

Although the incident took place on February 11, a holiday (President's Day), the district attorney was delayed in filing charges and the complaint was not filed until June 12. Bud was arraigned and pled not guilty on July 8. The case had already been continued several times when I "substituted in" in October.

The Alamo Muffler and Brake shop is a dilapidated garage on a busy stretch of North Main sprinkled with auto repair shops, radiator shops, auto-part stores, and small taco stands. When I visited Alamo, I found that I generally had to park on the street because the driveway of the shop was filled with cars in various states of repair (or disrepair), and it honestly looked more like a junkyard than an auto repair garage. The shop is operated by two thirty-something Chicano brothers, Armando and Rolando Cruz. The "office" for the shop is a small adjoining room, separated from the shop by a rack of used tires. The office is littered with papers, miscellaneous car repair orders, bills, and a greasy fax machine.

Armando Cruz, the manager at Alamo, confirmed that the shop had been open on President's Day and that Bud had worked his full shift on that day. He assured me that the records at the shop would confirm that Bud had been working. He also told me that he had already been interviewed by an investigator and answered all of his questions. I got a sense from Armando that he was sympathetic to Bud but was less than eager to get involved in the case.

In an interview on August 19, Armando had told an investigator from the public defender's office that he has been the manager of Alamo for the past eleven years and that it was a small, family-owned and -operated business. He added that Bud had been working at Alamo for the past five years and that his performance had been exemplary. The Cruz brothers knew Bud's father, Elmer ("Jack") Black, a longtime mechanic in the city, and they had known Bud since he was a kid, for approximately twelve years. Bud had been very reliable and had only been absent from his job at the shop about five times in the past five years. Armando added that Bud is very punctual and works well with peers.

The regular work hours for all employees at the shop were from 7:30 a.m. until 5 p.m., Monday through Friday; they normally break for lunch around 1 to 2 p.m., and their food is always ordered and delivered to the shop. Armando said that because the shop is so small and the number of employees so few, they are like a family and almost always eat lunch together. All of the employees are required to wear the same type of uniform—blue pants with light blue shirts, which have the business name ("ALAMO") written on the top left side and the employee's name ("Bud," in this case) is on the upper-right side.

Armando stated that Bud was definitely at work on February 11 and that he arrived on time and did not leave until 5 p.m. He added that this could all be verified not only by a personal calendar that he uses on a daily basis but also by payroll records. Armando indicated that his "accountant" would ensure that the records were brought to the investigative bureau of the public defenders' office on the following day, August 20.

Armando added that Bud had not owned a car since he began working at Alamo, saying that he always rode his bicycle to and from work and everywhere else he went on a regular basis. Finally, Armando stated that since he had known Bud, Bud had always had long brown hair and maintained a neatly trimmed full beard with a mustache. He further stated that Bud had always been missing his top right front tooth.

The manager at Mario's Restaurant, Victor Lara, also told the defense investigator that Bud was formerly employed at the restaurant as a cook but had been terminated for being involved in a fight with another cook. At the same time, the manager characterized Bud as "personable" and "reliable." Lara added that Bud was a very religious person and a conscientious employee who never took off from work without first receiving permission. Finally, he said Bud had never owned a car and always rode his bicycle everywhere, including to and from work.

Bud reiterated to me that he was at work at Alamo all day on February 11. He always wore his uniform when working, and he said there was "no freaking way" that he could have gone out at eleven in the morning to commit the crime he had been charged with, adding that he "wasn't a pervert and wouldn't go around exposing himself to some woman." He said that his boss at the shop or any of his coworkers would vouch for the fact that he was at work on the date and at the time of the incident.

As I reflected on the case, I concluded that Bud had a foolproof alibi and that the best strategy for getting the charges dropped would be to get a signed declaration or affidavit from Manager Armando Cruz and a record from the accountant substantiating that Bud was at work on February 11. I asked the manager to sign an affidavit declaring under penalty of perjury that Bud Black worked at Alamo and that Armando was his immediate supervisor, that he had known Bud for approximately twelve years, and that they were open for business on February 11, when Bud had been at work all day.

Unfortunately, I soon discovered that Armando would prove to be uncooperative and evasive. I had to go back to Alamo several times, because the manager was often either busy or out of the office when I came. And when I did find him, he said he had to get the affidavit approved by the owner and receive authorization before he could sign it. It took me awhile to discover that the so-called "owner" turned out to be Armando's brother, who was in the small office next door. Armando also made it very clear that this was a small business and that they did not have time to testify or to get involved in a trial. I assured him that my hope was that if we could get the statement, we could avoid going to trial. After numerous attempts and revisions, Armando refused to sign the original document, but he subsequently agreed to sign a shorter declaration affirming that Alamo was open for business on February 11 and that Bud was at work all day on February 11. However, he would not sign the document under oath. The fact that Armando refused to sign the document under "penalty of perjury" was unfortunate because this is critical to obtaining proper verification of any legal document.

Before continuing with my description of the case, I should say something about the common perception of the Riverside courts among lawyers in Southern California. First, there is a view that Riverside has a very weak defense bar. A friend and mentor of mine, an experienced defense attorney, had warned me that Riverside's very weak defense bar has given too much power to the local district attorney's office. My experience in this and other cases in Riverside was that the Riverside assistant DAs did not do much in the way of plea bargaining, so that defendants generally had to either plead guilty or go to trial. This obviously clogged up not only the courts but also the jails.[5] I felt that the case against Bud was weak, but I feared that a jury could conceivably be persuaded by the testimony of the witness, who seemed very credible and had unequivocally identified him as the perpetrator. I did not want to risk a trial, because if Bud was convicted he would surely serve additional time for violating the conditions of his probation. I continued the case a number of times, hoping it could be resolved without going to trial. The district attorney refused to consider a dismissal, particularly since they had a very credible witness, a clean-cut twenty-eight-year-old Latina social worker, who had identified Bud and was willing to testify at the trial.

I believe that another factor precluding early settlement of this case was Bud's rap sheet. One of the things that I pointed out to the various deputy district attorneys with whom I negotiated during the four months that the case was continued was that Bud had a criminal record, but his previous convictions were largely for vandalism, not for morals charges. In the past, Bud had clearly been involved in tagging and petty vandalism of business establishments, but he had never been involved in anything even remotely related to indecent exposure. I also pointed out that the victim had described the suspect as being seventeen to twenty-five years old and clean-shaven, and she had not noted a missing front tooth. Bud, of course, was thirty, had a full beard, and was missing a front tooth.

Mario's Restaurant

In assessing the case and looking over the statements that had been made by potential witnesses, it was clear that Mario's Restaurant and the employees of the restaurant would play a critical role in the case. The manager of the restaurant, Victor Lara, and a hostess named Bonnie Smith would be especially important witnesses for the prosecution, although they had no personal knowledge of the case. The manager was particularly important, since he had said that Bud fit the description of the perpetrator and gave the police Bud's name and address.

Victor Lara told the defense investigator on August 8 that he had been the manager of Mario's Restaurant for eight years and that on February 23 a female, later identified as Martínez, entered the restaurant visibly emotionally upset and crying. One of the hostesses, Bonnie Smith, and another employee, "Jason," approached Martínez and asked her what the problem was. Lara said that Martínez told Bonnie that she heard and recognized a man who was outside, near the bar patio, and that she had reason to be afraid of him.

Lara stated that Martínez told Smith that she had met the man approximately two weeks earlier. She stated that she had been walking in the nearby area when the man who was now outside had approached her in a red vehicle. The man supposedly stopped his car, got out, and began yelling at Martínez. The man then allegedly began to "feel on" Martínez all over her body. The man returned to his vehicle a short time later and drove away.

Lara stated that at the conclusion of her story, another employee, named Jason, had escorted her to a nearby storefront police station and that police officers had come to the restaurant to inquire about Smith and Bud Black. The manager said the officers made additional inquiries about Bud because Lara had told them that Bud had been terminated for being involved in a fight with another cook while at work. Lara added that the other employee had provoked the fight. He went on to say that on one occasion he had to counsel Bud regarding a complaint initiated by Smith, who had indicated that Bud was overly "friendly" and that this was beginning to annoy her. Bud apologized to her and they worked fine together, without any further incidents. Lara added that Bud was "predictable" and "even-tempered" and indicated that he worked well with his peers.

Victor Lara's statement struck me as inconsistent and contradictory. On the one hand, he pointed to problems with Bud allegedly being "overly friendly" with Smith and mentioned his being fired for fighting with a fellow employee. Then, in the next breath, he said Bud was "predictable" and "even-tempered" and worked well with his peers. I did not understand how one could say that he had to be counseled for being overly friendly with a female employee and he was fired for getting in a fight with a coworker—and then say that he got along well with his peers. The manager's story just did not add up.

His account of the incident was also not consistent with the victim's account and involved a bizarre allegation that the perpetrator had "groped" the victim, rather than that he had exposed himself to her, as was indicated in the police report. It was also clear that Smith had negative feelings toward Bud and would likely be biased against him. I therefore felt that although Smith's story was consistent with the victim's account, she lacked credibility. Another inconsistency is that in the initial report to the police, the victim did not tell the police that the person had exposed his penis to her. In any event, I was confident that during cross-examination, the manager, Victor Lara, and hostess, Bonnie Smith, could be effectively impeached and neutralized. Lara had no personal knowledge of the incident and was wrong even about the allegations. His testimony was hearsay at best, since he had no personal knowledge of the events. Smith had a grudge against Bud and was not credible.

Bonnie Smith was contacted on August 8. She said that shortly after she began her duties as a hostess, a female later identified as the victim entered the business crying hysterically. Martínez informed Bonnie that there was a man outside whom she had encountered approximately two weeks ago. After she explained the nature of the encounter, Martínez described the man and asked if someone could escort her to her vehicle.

Another employee, Jason, informed Martínez that there was a storefront police station within the shopping mall and escorted her there. When Martínez returned, she entered Mario's and re-contacted Smith. She advised Smith that she had just seen the perpetrator sitting in the eating area outside of Mario's. Martínez and Smith positioned themselves inside the restaurant in a place that would give them a clear view of the outside eating area. Martínez pointed to a White male adult and asked Smith if she knew him. Smith identified the man as Bud Black and informed her that he was a former employee.

On August 12, Joey Cooper—an employee at Mario's, one of Bud's roommates, and a member of my son's band—also provided a statement to the investigator at the restaurant. He stated that a few days after the incident involving Smith, Jason, a female customer, and the owner of Mario's had informed him that on the night of the incident, Martínez left Mario's and was on her way toward her vehicle in the parking lot. Shortly thereafter, she returned and asked for an escort, saying that she had seen a man sitting outside eating along with a few other men. She informed the manager and Smith that this man had exposed his genitals to her a few weeks prior at another location.

Joey said the victim also told management staff that the suspect had been driving a red vehicle at the time of the incident and that she had obtained the license plate number. After being pointed out by the female, the man in question was identified by Smith as a former employee, Bud Black.

Joey went on to say that his first impression was that the entire incident had to be a joke. He stated that he and his brother James had been roommates with Bud for more than a year. Joey also stated that Bud had a strange sense of humor, but that this sort of behavior would be totally contradictory to his character and personality.

Joey indicated that Bud was a normal guy, and that he had several female friends but was not going steady with anyone in particular at the moment. He added that Bud did not own a vehicle, and nor did Joey or his brother or any of their friends own a vehicle that matched the description provided. Joey confirmed that Bud's only source of transportation was a bicycle, which he rode everywhere, including to and from work every day. He admitted that when he initially learned about the allegations, he telephoned Bud at home and made him aware of them. Joey also had no direct knowledge of the incident but could serve as a character witness for Bud.

"Remember the Alamo": Preparing for Trial

When I substituted in for the public defender on October 10, I was concerned because I discovered that the case was set for trial, and I certainly was not ready for trial. Before I came onto the case, Bud had been arraigned July 8 and entered a not-guilty plea. On August 28, counsel stipulated to a continuance, and a trial date was set for September 24. On that date, the matter was continued by stipulation of counsel to October 2. The matter was continued on October 2 to October 7, and on October 7, at the request of the defense counsel, Bud's trial was set for October 10.

Once I substituted in for the public defender, the judge granted me a reasonable amount of time to prepare. The October 10 trial date was immediately vacated, and the case was re-assigned from Department 31 to Department 11 for all purposes. In addition, a trial-readiness conference was set for November 6, and the defendant agreed to a time waiver, plus forty-five days.[6]

I appeared #977(a) at the trial-readiness conference on November 6, and the case was continued several times by stipulation of counsel on November 20, January 6, January 21, and January 27.

I had subpoenaed the custodian of records at Alamo, Armando Cruz, to appear on January 27. The parties were ordered to return on February 2, at 8:30 p.m. in Department 31, and the last day for trial was February 7, within the time allotted in a ten-day waiver. Cruz was ordered to return and to provide copies of the requested documents to counsel. The matter was trailed and/or continued several times during the month of February, drawing the process out significantly.

In retrospect, it is difficult to understand how or why a case would be endlessly continued. First, I should note that there is an old adage among defense lawyers that says, "No case is ripe before its time." What this essentially means is that delays generally favor the defense. They favor the defense for a number of reasons—first, because it is more difficult to locate prosecution witnesses than it is when there's a timely trial. Second, even if witnesses are located and produced, their memories are likely to fade or blur over time. Finally, the drive to prosecute vigorously is likely to wane with the passage of time. A substitution of attorney is certainly good cause for continuing a case and for a defendant to waive his constitutional right to a speedy trial, since the new attorney obviously needs additional time to talk to the client, investigate the case, and prepare for trial.

Another factor that contributed to the delay was that once I substituted in and the case returned to Department 11, it was no longer a priority for the court. Being transferred back to Department 11 was like starting over, because the department is not a trial court but a general-purpose court that handles preliminary and routine matters, such as pleas, misdemeanor sentencing, and infractions. It's hard to explain how being in Department 11 felt, but I might go so far as to say it was like an *Alice In Wonderland* out-of-body experience.

I went into the case—naively, perhaps—thinking it could be quickly resolved. All I needed was an opportunity to speak with the deputy district attorney assigned to the case, or a conference with the prosecutor and the judge in chambers, so I could explain that my client had witnesses who could verify that he was at work at the time of the incident and the charges would be dismissed. Unfortunately, each time I went to court, I was faced with a different district attorney. Also, the DA was generally someone who was just filling in for someone for the day and was not familiar with the case or authorized to settle it. Each time I appeared, my experience was like going through a revolving door or like re-inventing the wheel, especially because there were many cases on the docket and the DAs were busy. I guess the best way to put it is that there was no continuity between one court appearance and the next, so the simplest thing was to continue the case and to gain additional time.

Another complication was the fact that one of my star witnesses, the Alamo manager, turned out to be elusive and inaccessible. Initially, he had assured me that Bud was at work on February 11, from 7:30 a.m. until closing at 5 p.m. and that he could not possibly have committed the crime. However, even after I kept trying to get him to sign a declaration of this statement under penalty of perjury, he would not. Finally, he signed a declaration indicating specifically that he was the manager at Alamo Muffler and Brake at 2143 Main Street, that Bud Black was an employee at the shop, and that Bud was at work the entire day on February 11.

This would have been a good declaration, except for the fact that it was not signed under penalty of perjury, and this severely limited the utility of the document. In fact, it was practically useless. It is obviously preferable to have "in-person" testimony from a witness so that the witness can be subjected to cross-examination by the opposition. However, signed affidavits or declarations are admissible in court as business records and can be offered in place of in-person testimony if they are properly verified and authenticated. A critical element of verification is that the person must have personal knowledge of the matters that are averred in the statement *and* the declaration must be made under oath and under penalty of perjury under the laws of the state of California.

It took me awhile to figure out why Armando Cruz and his brother were so reluctant to get involved in the case. At first, I thought that they did not want to get involved because they were busy and hoped that if they ignored a problem it would go away. I soon learned, however, that there was more to the story than met the eye. I believe that Armando did not want to get involved because Alamo was running a questionable operation. He and his brother did not wish to get involved because they were engaged in some shady employment and business practices and wanted to avoid any sort of contact with the law.

The Alamo shop was part of the underground economy. At ten dollars per hour, Bud earned more than minimum wage. He was paid by check but he did not receive any benefits, like health insurance, social security, or unemployment or disability insurance. In short, I believe that the primary reason for the lack of cooperation by Alamo was that the Cruz brothers did not want to subject the records of the shop to close scrutiny.

Unfortunately, it was necessary for both attorneys to involve Alamo in the trial. I needed Bud's employment record for February 11 because it would exonerate Bud, and the prosecution needed invoices of the cars that were worked on in the period in question to see if the suspect vehicle had been at the shop for repair work. On the eve of trial, I served a subpoena on Armando Cruz at Alamo, ordering him to appear in Department 31 of the Riverside Superior Court at 8:30 a.m. on January 27, and to produce the following business records: (1) employment records and/or check stubs for Bud Black for February 11 of the previous year; and (2) invoices of vehicles worked on at the shop between February 11 and February 23. The DA served the custodian of records at Alamo with a separate subpoena, requesting copies of invoices and work orders performed at Alamo during the entire month of February. I obtained copies of the invoices, and there was no record of the suspect vehicle having been serviced at the shop.

I made five appearances in the case between October 10 and January 21, and it was difficult because I had to deal with five different deputy district attorneys. It was not until January 21 that I began to get some semblance of continuity in the case, when Michael Bloom, the deputy DA who would take the case to its conclusion, first appeared on the case. Then, I was finally able to establish a continuous dialogue with the DA. Bloom was originally from New York and had graduated from an elite law school in the East. He was young and aggressive but smart. Although he proved to be a difficult adversary, I was relieved when he appeared because I finally had someone I could contact and talk to about the case.

One of the first things that I had pressed for (unsuccessfully) since I had come onto the case was to get the district attorney to check out the owner of the red Toyota. Bud did not have a car, as I have established, and was not driving at the time of the incident. In addition, the victim had taken down the license plate of the suspect vehicle and the registered owner was a Judith Mercer from San Leandro. Bud had no obvious connection to the vehicle or its owner. During my many conversations with Bloom, I repeatedly requested that he check on the owner of the vehicle to determine whether the vehicle was in the area during the date of the incident. Another possibility was the owner of the vehicle having a son or daughter attending the university, since it is not uncommon for college students to drive vehicles that are registered to their parents.

When Bloom first came onto the case on January 21, he promised to "check out the suspect vehicle." I had a number of subsequent discussions with Bloom, but he was slow to contact the owner. In a chambers conference on February 3, after I told the judge that my client had no known connection to the suspect vehicle, we agreed to continue the matter in order to give the prosecution an opportunity to speak with the registered owner of the vehicle.

We were on the eve of trial, and one of the things that had always concerned me was that if Bud was convicted he would not only have to register as a sex offender for life but he would also be facing added time for probation violation, as I've mentioned. I should also note that on January 10, the deputy DA filed a new, separate charge against Bud Black, and he was ordered to appear in the Riverside Superior Court on January 21 to answer the charge of violation of probation on the existing conviction for violation of 594(a)—for allegedly violating the term of his probation that he should violate no law. I therefore decided to pay Bud's outstanding fines prior to the trial, on February 6. Bud owed an $85 fine on one case, $36 on a second case, and $410 on another case, and all three fines had been due on October 1, nine days before I substituted in on the sex-offense case. He owed an additional $332 on another case, which had been due on November 1, three weeks after I substituted in. The total amount on the outstanding fines was $863.

As noted, I had previously asked Bloom not only to check on the suspect vehicle but also to check with the university police to see if the registered owner was a student at the university. On February 20, I received a fax from Bloom showing that on February 16, two years prior to the incident, and on October 9, two and a half years prior to the incident, a four-door red Toyota with the suspect license plate number had been cited for parking in an expired meter in parking lot 14 at the university. The fines and the late fees had been paid and there was no balance due on either citation, but this was an important development. It was the first lead that we had in the case, and it supported the theory that the suspect vehicle was still in Riverside and in the vicinity of the university campus. But there was no evidence that the vehicle was registered to a student at the university.

An alternative theory proposed by Bloom was that the vehicle might have been serviced at Alamo and that Bud or another employee would have had an opportunity to take the car out for a test drive and, in the process, to commit the crime. This seemed pretty far-fetched to me, and when I asked Armando about it, he quickly dismissed it, saying that Bud did not have a driver's license and that he never took cars out for a test drive. He also checked his records and said they had not serviced a car with that license-plate number.

On February 20, Bloom told me that an officer had attempted to make contact with the owner of the suspect vehicle but that she was not home. The prosecution requested that the matter be trailed to February 26, so that they could have an officer go out to talk to the owner of the suspect vehicle.

Bloom was not only young and aggressive, but also extremely confident and a bit cocky. He was certain that the prosecution would prevail in the trial, and he repeatedly advised me to convince my client to plead guilty. He felt the judge would be more lenient in sentencing if Bud pled guilty. The prosecution, after all, had a very credible young witness who would identify Bud as the perpetrator, the person who had exposed himself to her and traumatized her. They also had several witnesses at the restaurant that would testify that the victim had "immediately" identified Bud Black as the perpetrator of the crime some two weeks after the incident.

On Wednesday, February 26, Bloom came into court acting strangely. He wasn't the same aggressive and cocky young district attorney, and for the first time, he appeared nervous and unconfident. He told me there had been an important development in the case and requested a conference with the judge in chambers. In chambers, he told the judge and me that the police in San Leandro had finally been able to speak to the owner of the red Toyota, Judith Mercer. The owner said that her son was not a student but that he lived in Riverside and worked at an Indian restaurant at the Westridge Mall, a restaurant two doors down from Mario's. He said that this was incredible, but it turned out that there was an uncanny resemblance between the suspect and my client. They looked like twins and both had long curly hair. The victim had identified the new suspect, and Bloom was sorry that Bud had been falsely charged. He needed to clear up a few loose ends, but he expected that the charges against my client would be dropped and that he would be charging the new suspect with the crime. Bloom requested that the matter trail until Friday, which it did. We proceeded to open court, and the indecent exposure charge against Bud Black was dismissed.

Reflections

Fermina, although I was successful in having the charges against Bud dismissed, his case illustrates some of the limitations and pitfalls faced in a rascuache law practice. I also feel that my efforts did little to counter the biases and injustices that are inherent in the criminal justice system, particularly against Latinos and other people of Color or a young man like Bud with limited resources who is on probation and has a rap sheet for petty offenses. Most juries would take the word of an educated professional woman like the victim in this case over the word of a working-class man like Bud Black. The truth is that regardless of the evidence, Bud was presumed guilty not only by the district attorney and the court but also by his ex-coworkers at Mario's Restaurant, though they had no personal knowledge of the case. If the public defender had continued to represent Bud, he would have pressured him to plead guilty, even though he was not guilty and had an alibi and witnesses who could verify that he was at work at the time of the incident.

In retrospect, it is clear that my defense of Bud Black was severely hampered by my lack of money and resources. I didn't have the resources of the state or of a regular attorney to hire an investigator to question possible witnesses and key people in the case. A private investigator could have spoken to Armando Cruz and Bud's coworkers at Alamo and could have testified that they told him that Bud was at work from 7:30 a.m.

to 5 p.m. during the day in question. More importantly, an investigator could have spoken to the owner of the suspect vehicle, who would have told him that her son drove the vehicle and worked in a business that was two doors from Mario's Restaurant. This is a case of mistaken identity, but it is also one in which my lack of resources required that I spend a lot more time on the case than should have been necessary in order to exonerate my client. Finally, it is a case in which, in addition to the time and energy that I put in defending my client, I also had to contribute my own money for his outstanding fines and court fees. I have no regrets, however, and I am confident that Bud will ultimately reimburse me for my efforts.

Bud was elated and relieved by the news of the charge against him being dropped. He thanked me, saying he did not know how he could ever repay me for my work, and he promised to stay out of trouble and to pay me back my money. I went with Bud to a local credit union and helped him open a savings account. I suggested that he set up the account and try to save a small amount, like twenty-five or thirty dollars per week, so he could eventually pay me back. I still see Bud occasionally at some of my son's band's shows, and he confessed once when he saw me at the Riverside Orange Festival that he feels bad every time he sees me because he has not paid me back my money, but that he intends to pay. I told him not to feel bad and to pay me back a little bit at a time, whenever he could. I am still waiting, but I am glad that the case against Bud was finally dismissed and he was able to clear his name and reputation and return to his normal life and routine.

∻ 8 ∻

DUI

A Bag Full of Tricks

Querida amiga,

I want to apologize for the long delay since my last letter. I have been teaching an undergraduate sociology class called "Law, Race, Class, Gender, and Culture." It is a large class with about a hundred students, and I do not have a teaching assistant. I decided not to do weekly letters or field reports for you in this class, not because I did not want to but because I was not sure that the letters would mesh with the large and somewhat impersonal nature of the class. The class is almost over, but it has been a very difficult—yet interesting and challenging—quarter. I want to share with you what happened these past few months, not so much with the class but with issues that arose.

First, I was sick with the flu and got off on the wrong foot in the class. It was not so much because of the sickness itself but because I had a negative reaction to the antibiotics that were prescribed. It took me several days to figure out that what was making me so sick was not the flu, but the medicine.

The first day of class was on a Thursday, April 4. I did not feel well, so I simply asked one of my colleagues to pass out the syllabus and reading assignments for the class. The following Tuesday, I remained sick and did not know until the last minute whether I would be able to teach. Unfortunately, I mistakenly thought the class was at 2 p.m. and was surprised when I talked to my staff assistant at about 12:30 p.m. and he informed me that the class was about to start. I immediately left the house and got to class about fifteen minutes late. The students waited and were very nice, kind, and enthusiastic, so even though I was feeling terrible I was actually energized by the class. It was strange because I felt a lot better after teaching the class than I did before. I do not recall much of what happened, but I apparently had quite a bit to say and the students were gracious and seemingly attentive. I am not sure where I picked up my work ethic, but it is very strong, and so it is hard for me to cancel or to not show up for a class, or to feel like I am not doing all that I could or should be doing. On the other hand, I wanted to wait until the last minute to decide whether I would show up, hoping that I might feel better. It is strange, but when I miss class I feel like I am somehow shortchanging my students, not giving them their money's worth or letting them down, even though most of them are happy when class is cancelled.

Unfortunately, the next day (Wednesday), I had an important oral argument with the California Court of Appeal on an employment-discrimination case. It has been a very time-consuming case that has been going on for about four years. I knew that it was too late to cancel or reschedule the oral argument and that it was very important. I only had fifteen minutes to convince the court to reverse its tentative decision, denying our appeal of the trial court's summary judgment motion against us, which effectively dismissed the suit. Believe me, it was much harder than teaching the class, not only because it was a tougher, more demanding, and less sympathetic audience, but also because I was even sicker this time. In addition to feeling the pressure of having to make an effective and persuasive argument, I feared that I might pass out in front of the three-person appellate panel, or get sick and vomit on the large, fancy wooden counsel table and podium.

In retrospect, thinking about the difficult and challenging quarter, I am looking forward to the end of the class. Do not misunderstand—I really love the class. It is a very good group. The class is extremely diverse with more than half of the students being Chicano and about one-third Asian. This is not surprising, because almost half of the campus student body is Asian. There are also at least a half-dozen African Americans, a handful of Anglo students, and several Middle Eastern students in the class.

I do not know if I mentioned this to you, but my daughter is getting married at the end of next month (June 30) and is moving to Oaxaca, Mexico. Her fiancé is from Oaxaca, and she had previously lived there for almost a year. One of the things that I had to do in the middle of this quarter was to go up to San Francisco, where she had been living, and help her move down to Southern California. I went up with a good friend and we did one of those old-fashioned moves where you rent, load, drive, and unload the truck yourself. I have to admit that it was a lot of fun, but I would have liked to have had more than a weekend to complete the job.

But what really added to the stress this quarter, over and above the class and my illness and the move, was that I also did a driving-under-the-influence (DUI) trial. It went down as a "refusal," in which there was no alcohol/drug test when the defendant was arrested, so I figured that the case would take three or four days and it would not disrupt my class schedule because I could schedule the midterm during the trial. Unfortunately, because the judge continued to hear his regular calendar in the mornings, and sometimes during parts of the afternoons, the trial took much longer than expected and it really cut into my class. The trial started on Tuesday, May 8, and we got the verdict the following Thursday, May 17. I had the midterm on May 8, there was a quiz on May 10, and I showed a film on May 15, but it was stressful because I had to continue to plan and arrange for someone to cover my class and carry out my normal responsibilities at the university in addition to doing the trial. Another unique complication is that the person who was supposed to help me with the class as a "reader," or assistant, also happened to be my client. Fermina, the DUI case turned out to be a very interesting one, so I want to share the story with you. I will start by telling you a little bit about my client.

Aberlardo "Lalo" López

When I first met Lalo López a few years ago, he impressed me as a kind of imposing man who is about six-foot-two and weighs approximately two hundred and fifty pounds. In short, Lalo is "big for a Mexican." He is in his early forties, but has a much younger demeanor and generally dresses Chicano-style in neatly pressed, clean Dickies pants and short-sleeved checkered shirts. Lalo is also definitely one of those "what you see is not what you get" types of people, because his size and imposing physical presence are deceiving, very quickly offset by his laid-back, unassuming, nonthreatening demeanor. Do not misunderstand! Lalo is not shy or meek. He is simply very personable and charismatic, with a pleasant personality and gentle manner. He is one of those people who in a church retreat, or among any group of strangers—like, even on a jury—would easily emerge as a leader or foreperson, as someone that people not only would listen to and respect but would follow. One could summarize his physical presence as at once imposing and extremely personable.

Lalo is a student in the doctorate program in anthropology at the university. He is not a typical student in any sense of the word, not only because he is older than most students but also because he arrived at the university through a nonconventional route. Lalo was born and raised in East Los Angeles. He says he was too individualistic to be in a gang, but he grew up surrounded by gangs and is very familiar with gang culture. In fact, he has a strong professional interest in gangs and has done research on gangs.

His father was a carpenter and handyman, and Lalo learned the trade at an early age, spending a good part of his young adult life working in the small family construction business with his dad. I will not dwell on his past, except to say that he somehow got on the wrong path and spent about ten years on drugs and was arrested about forty times. He was on heroin, but was arrested mostly for petty theft, possession of drug paraphernalia, and other misdemeanor drug-related charges. This was prior to the passage of Proposition 36 in California, which as you know allows minor drug offenders to opt for treatment instead of jail. I am not sure how he got off drugs, but at some point he got clean and started getting serious about school. He ended up getting a tuition scholarship to the University of Southern California, excelled as a student, and graduated with honors and a BA in anthropology.

Lalo contacted me last December. He was distressed, telling me he needed a lawyer and confiding that he had a legal problem. I feared that he had gotten busted for some sort of drug violation, and I was actually relieved to learn when we met for coffee that he had been stopped for a DUI. I told him that I was reluctant to take the case because I was trying to wind down my cases, so that I could focus on my research and teaching. I explained that I did not want to take on additional cases, ironically because I needed the time to write a book about my cases. Lalo had recently had all of his convictions expunged, and he told me that he could not afford to get a DUI on his record or to have his license suspended because it would be impossible for him to get a teaching job after he graduated, so I agreed to represent him in the initial court appearance, but I told Lalo he should get another attorney for the criminal trial. Lalo had put a lot of effort into having his record expunged and cleaning up his life, so he was understandably upset about the arrest.

The Police Report

According to the official police report about Lalo's arrest, California Highway Patrol Officer Rick Pérez and his partner, Mike Witherspoon, members of a special Highway Patrol DUI Task Force, were traveling east on Interstate 10 near Holt Boulevard at approximately sixty-five miles per hour when they spotted a silver Toyota Camry approximately a hundred feet ahead of them in the number 5 lane. According to Pérez, the roadway turns slightly to the left at this point, and the officer observed the Toyota suddenly veer to the right, letting the front passenger-side tire cross approximately one foot over the solid white line that separates the number 5 lane from the right shoulder. The Toyota then moved back into the lane. Approximately ten seconds later, the car suddenly veered to the right once again, and the passenger tires crossed over the white line approximately one foot onto the shoulder. As the vehicle approached Alta Vista, the Toyota crossed the white line for the third time, veering to the left this time, into the number 4 lane. The vehicle's speed during the time was between sixty and seventy miles per hour.

Officer Pérez immediately accelerated and positioned himself approximately forty feet behind the Toyota, activating his emergency lights with alternating headlights. His partner ordered the vehicle to exit the freeway at Kellogg Drive. The Toyota slowed down to approximately fifty miles per hour and exited the freeway, promptly pulling over to the right shoulder and stopping, as directed. As the officers approached the Toyota—Pérez on the driver's side and his partner on the passenger side—the driver's door opened. Pérez ordered the driver to close the door and remain in the vehicle. The driver complied.

The officer described the driver's dress as "good and clean." The driver was wearing a gray shirt, black pants, and a white jacket and was described in the police report as "cooperative," though his eyes were "watery" and his speech "slow." Pérez added that as he approached the Toyota, he smelled a "moderate" odor of an alcoholic beverage. The driver of the vehicle produced a valid driver's license, which identified him as residing in the city of Pomona.

The officer informed the driver that he was stopped because he was weaving from left to right and drifted out of his lane several times. The driver immediately began to explain that he was tired. When asked how much alcohol he had consumed, he said that he had "taken several drinks from one beer earlier in the evening."

According to the police report, the officer requested that the driver "answer several pre-field sobriety test questions and perform several pre-field sobriety tests due to the odor of alcohol emitting from his breath and his admission of alcohol consumption." The officer then asked the driver to exit his vehicle and perform several field sobriety tests, which he failed to complete satisfactorily, as he was described as having "exhibited poor balance, coordination, and the inability to follow simple instructions." Based on these tests, Pérez "formed the opinion that he was under the influence of alcohol and unable to safely operate a motor vehicle."

Preliminary Alcohol Screening (PAS) Device

Mr. López was read the PAS device admonition and he declined to take the test. According to the police report, he stated, "I don't want to blow in the machine and have it go crazy!" Officer Pérez stated, "After his completion of the field sobriety tests, it is my determination that Mr. López failed to satisfactorily perform these tests as I had explained and demonstrated."

At the conclusion of the field sobriety tests, Officer Pérez arrested the defendant. He then said that he read the defendant an implied-consent form and that the defendant had refused to submit to a breath or blood test as is required by law. The defendant was taken to the City of Industry Sheriffs' Station, where Officer Pérez recommended that he be charged with driving under the influence.

Lalo's Story

When I first met with Lalo for coffee, he told me he was very worried, not only because he had been arrested but also because he had missed his first court date earlier in December and he found out that the judge had issued an arrest warrant for him. He asked me to go with him to court because he was afraid the judge would put him in jail for his failure to appear. He showed me the notice to appear and it was difficult to read the date. I could understand why he did not want to appear before the judge without a lawyer.

Lalo recounted what happened on the night of his arrest. He had been working very late on a joint grant application with a graduate student colleague from Yale. They had been working on the application all week and he had not gotten much sleep. On the night in question, he and the colleague, Rosa Linda Gutiérrez, had dinner. They had shared a salad and a beer. Lalo said he was not under the influence and did not understand why he was arrested. He added that Rosa Linda could testify as to how much he drank that night. There were two cops: a Chicano who was very aggressive and a very affable, young White male. Lalo said he could not believe it because he was convinced the White guy would have let him go, but the Chicano "really had a 'hard on' for me." The White cop was "really cool." Lalo said that he was stalling, giving Lalo more time so that he would not be arrested. On the way to the station, the White cop had stopped several cars and wanted to go and stop to eat but the Chicano cop insisted on going to the station first. Lalo said that he had indeed refused to take the PAS test, which is an optional preliminary alcohol screening that is less reliable than a regular blood-alcohol test. The White cop had told him not to worry, that he would have a chance to take the regular blood-alcohol test at the station, but when the cops took him to the station, no one administered that test, so Lalo never got a chance to take it. Lalo added that he was scared because when he was first stopped, the cops had approached his vehicle with their hands on their weapons.

The Judge

My client and I first appeared before the Honorable Gordon Levine on January 4. I apologized on behalf of my client for his previous failure to appear and explained to the judge that Lalo had done so because he had not received timely notice of the charges; in fact, the notice had arrived after the first scheduled court appearance. I apologized to the court once again on behalf of my client, guaranteed that Mr. López would appear at future court proceedings, and requested that the court recall the warrant.

Judge Levine has only been on the bench for about a year. He had attended Boalt Law School in Berkeley and was on law review. He started out working in the DA's office in Los Angeles and had been in private practice for a short period of time before the governor appointed him to the bench. About 95 percent of all judges in California are appointed, and the vast majority (approximately 85 percent) are pro–law enforcement and prosecution, according to my friend, ex-student, and mentor Juan Guerra (a very successful private defense attorney). The judge ordered the warrant recalled and we set the arraignment in three weeks. I had told the court that we wanted to continue the arraignment because we had not had a chance to examine the relevant discovery, which consists largely of the police report and a probable-cause report that was submitted by the arresting officer to the Department of Motor Vehicles. Judge Levine appeared to be fairly young, perhaps in his mid-forties; he wore glasses and was not particularly tall or short. He was pleasant enough, a bit aggressive perhaps, but efficient, and he seemed very concerned that cases move along in a timely manner. I learned only later that he was an ex-DA and decidedly favored the prosecution.

I also had the opportunity to meet with the district attorney, a thirty-something Korean American male, to see what the state's offer would be. The offer was a standard one for a first-time DUI—a fine of about $1,600, including the penalty assessment; attendance at a year-long drunk driving class; and a three-year summary probation during which the offender could not violate any law. I tried to see if we could get a dry reckless-driving offer, but the DA would not budge.

At the next hearing, we had a new district attorney, a pleasant young White woman who appeared to be about thirty years of age named Katie Albright. Albright had graduated from the University of Illinois School of Law and had been a district attorney in Chicago for several years before becoming an assistant DA in Los Angeles. She was friendly and engaging and reiterated the initial prosecution offer, which she said was "standard" for a first-time DUI. She also warned that because this was a refusal, if the defendant was convicted, by statute he would be required to do some jail time.

Over the next few weeks, I sought additional discovery and the case was continued. The discovery motion, dated February 26, stated:

The Defense respectfully makes the following informal discovery request of the People:

1. Any photographs, videos, and or audio recordings pertaining to stop and arrest of defendant Lalo López on 10/29.
2. Telephone log for Roving CHP DUI Task Force Unit for Officer Mike Witherspoon (ID#00000) and Officer R. Pérez (ID#00001) for 10/28 to 10/29.
3. Any notes written by Officer M. Witherspoon and/or R. Pérez relative to arrest of defendant Lalo López on 10/29/200?.
4. The names, addresses, and telephone numbers of all persons the prosecution intends to call as witnesses at trial.
5. Any exculpatory evidence.
6. All relevant real evidence seized or obtained as part of the investigation of the offense charged.

Alfredo Mirandé
Attorney for defendant, Lalo López

At the next hearing, Prosecutor Albright complied with the request and provided the discovery. The judge set the trial for April. Our strategy from the start, frankly, was to delay the trial until classes had ended in the first week of June, so that both my client and I would be free of our academic responsibilities and could focus on the trial. Lalo had told me that his doctoral qualifying exams were scheduled for the beginning of June and that he wanted me to continue the case so that he could study for his exams. I had told the judge that our witness had gone back east to continue her studies and would not be available until June. He denied our request for a continuance and scheduled the trial for April 9, with a trial-readiness conference (TRC) set for April 6. On that date, we received a one-month continuance and the trial was scheduled for May 7, with the TRC set for May 4. The judge warned that there would be no more continuances and that the trial would start as scheduled, with or without our defense witness. Now it was clear that the judge was pro-prosecution.

The Trial

Voir Dire

The trial started on the afternoon of May 10 with jury selection. The selection of a jury is one of the most important—and at the same time, one of the most misunderstood and unexplored—phases of a trial. During a trial, it is easy to lose sight of the fact that the fate of your client ultimately rests in the hands of the jury, not the judge. Although there is a great deal of folklore surrounding jury selection, or voir dire, in the end it appears to be more of an art than a science. There are no hard and fast rules about selecting a jury. When I pressed my good friend Juan Guerra for some hints on jury selection, he finally told me that for a DUI you wanted relatively young men who were used to having a drink or two after work and who understood how the police treated people, but he was quick to add that ultimately, he would want people on the jury who were more likely to believe someone like me than someone like the cop. I took this to mean that I wanted critical thinkers who challenged authority and who would not automatically believe everything that law enforcement says—and that I wanted to avoid people who were pro-police and believed that the police are infallible.

Jury selection began with the judge asking the bailiff to call the next available jury panel. I was surprised that the jury panel was small, consisting of about forty people. The judge welcomed the panel; introduced the clerk, court reporter, and bailiff; said a little bit about the nature of the case; and then asked the attorneys and the defendant to introduce themselves. The judge then asked whether anyone on the panel knew any of the lawyers, the defendant, or the officers who would be testifying. After the introductions, the clerk read off the names of eighteen prospective jurors, and the jurors were asked to sit sequentially in the jury box seats, which were numbered consecutively from one to eighteen.[1] Going from left to right as you face the jury box, the first row consisted of jurors 1–6; the second row, jurors 7–12; and the third, jurors 13–18. The judge then asked the clerk to swear in the jury.

The judge read off a list of twelve or so background questions, consisting of things like the occupation of the prospective juror and his or her spouse, where the juror lived, his or her marital status, the ages and occupations of any children, whether he or she had friends or family in law enforcement or the legal profession, whether he or she had ever served on a jury—and if so, the type of case and whether the jury reached a verdict—and finally, whether he or she had any religious or moral beliefs that would prevent passing judgment on the defendant. The judge then went through each of the questions with each prospective juror. After the judge finished, he allotted each attorney about fifteen minutes to address and question the jury panel.

I used the voir dire not only as an opportunity to learn more about the prospective jurors but to educate the jury panel and to make them more aware of the constitutional rights of defendants. I started off by asking, "If the judge asked you to deliberate at this point and bring back a verdict, what verdict would you have to give?" The jurors seemed puzzled by the question and were reluctant to respond. Several said that they could not render a verdict. I pressed them for the correct answer, which was to say that they would have to arrive at a verdict of not guilty, if there was no testimony. The judge reminded the panel that this would be the correct outcome, given the presumption of innocence in our system. Another question was, "Under our system of criminal justice, Mr. López has to prove his innocence?" I also asked, "Is the word of a police officer more credible or believable than the word of an ordinary citizen?" Finally, I asked, "Would you consider yourself a leader or a follower?" Interestingly, only one or two persons admitted that they were "followers."

At first, the jurors were reluctant to agree that the word of a police officer was more credible than that of an ordinary citizen, but once one person slowly raised his hand and said boldly, "Yes, I believe that they are more credible!" The statement appeared to have a domino effect, as other jurors started to slowly raise their hands. I jokingly said something about this feeling like an auction, and it did not seem like my comment went over well with the judge and prosecution.

During the voir dire, I also made a special effort to address the Fifth Amendment constitutional right of the defendant to protection against self-incrimination, placing the burden on the prosecution to prove each and every element of its case beyond a reasonable doubt. Finally, I stressed that in order to find a person guilty, the jury would have to have "an abiding conviction" that the prosecution had proved each and every element of its case beyond a reasonable doubt.

I found the voir dire to be an interesting but ultimately scary experience for a number of reasons. First, I was surprised that a large number of people on the panel appeared to have close ties with law enforcement—it was not uncommon for them to have spouses, children, or friends and relatives in law enforcement. Second, I was disappointed that there were a large number of older, conservative people on the panel. Finally, there were only a handful of Latinos and Asians, and no African Americans, on the panel.

After the attorneys finished questioning the eighteen members in the jury box, the judge asked whether the attorneys wanted to challenge anyone "for cause." I should explain that there are two bases for challenging a prospective juror—for cause and in peremptory challenges. If a challenge is for cause, one or more of the attorneys will try to disqualify a prospective juror by claiming some form of bias in favor of the prosecution or defense. For example, in this case, there was one person who had a very close friend who was killed by a drunk driver and she felt that she could not be fair and impartial, so the judge agreed with my request to eliminate her for cause. Although I challenged a couple of other jurors for cause because they had close ties to law enforcement, only one person was removed for cause—the woman whose close friend was killed by a drunk driver.

In peremptory challenges, each attorney is allowed ten free challenges to eliminate a prospective juror without providing a reason or justification. What is interesting is that although you do not need a reason for peremptory challenges, you cannot have a bad reason. Under *Batson* and *Wheeler* in California,[2] for example, you cannot use race or gender to exclude people from a jury, so if a defense attorney sees that the district attorney is using race as a pretext for excluding members of a particular race from a jury panel, the attorney can challenge the exclusion and say that the peremptories are in fact race-based and, therefore, unconstitutional.

Although *Batson* and *Wheeler* made race-based peremptory challenges unconstitutional, they did little to eliminate the use of race as a basis for excluding people from juries. What *Batson/Wheeler* accomplished is to put the pressure on the prosecution to provide a race-neutral explanation for the exclusion. Under a *Batson* claim, once a defendant makes a prima facie case that the challenges were race-based, the burden shifts to the prosecution to articulate a race-neutral explanation for the exclusion. The ultimate burden is on the defendant to show that the exclusion was race-based.

The Supreme Court further weakened the *Batson* standard when it ruled in *Hernández v. New York* (1991)[3] that peremptory challenges can be used to exclude Spanish-speakers from a petit jury if the prosecution has been able to articulate a race-neutral reason for their exclusion. The race-neutral reason in that case was that the prosecution was not convinced that the Spanish speakers would be able to disregard what the witness said and accept the official translation provided by the interpreter.

Race was not really an overt issue in the jury selection for Lalo's case, except for the fact that there were so few Latinos in the jury pool—though the area is predominantly Latino. The judge excused a couple of people, with the concurrence of the attorneys, for "hardship." One person had a pre-planned vacation to Rio de Janeiro, an LA public defender was about to start his vacation, the manager of a major grocery store claimed that the grocery employees were about to strike and that it would create a hardship for him to serve on the jury, and an elderly woman in a wheelchair was released for medical reasons. The prosecution and the defense alternately excluded prospective jurors on the first day. At around 4 p.m., it was clear that we would exhaust all of the members of the jury, so the judge adjourned, sent the jury home for the day, and asked the bailiff to request another jury panel for the next morning.

There were some difficult decisions in picking the jury. In the end, we excluded people based more on their attitude toward law enforcement and the rights of defendants than on race, age, gender, or occupation. The final jury selected consisted of five White men, four White women, one Latino male, one Latina, and an Asian women. In the end, I believe that the White men exercised a considerable influence on the jury. The prototype of the jurors we favored were White men thirty to forty-five years of age in professional or skilled jobs. We disfavored older people and people with strong ties to law enforcement. The foreman of the jury, in fact, was a gregarious young man who appeared to be an Iraq war veteran, who wore a shirt with an American flag on each day of the trial. We picked men who, as I noted, were not opposed to drinking and would not be overly deferential toward law enforcement. In addition, we selected the Chicana and at least two middle-aged White women who appeared sympathetic. We did not have a strong read on the Asian woman, but she appeared to be neutral toward law enforcement. A couple of Asian women and at least one Asian man who were excluded during the voir dire were very much against any kind of drinking and driving and pro-police. I recall one prospective Asian juror in particular who seemed to have difficulty with English and insisted that drinking and driving were against the law. When I pushed her on the point, she said that she could not drink anything and drive. I pointed out that the standard was not based on her tolerance of alcohol, but on that of Mr. López or a typical person.

Opening Statement

After the voir dire, the first major phase of a trial is the opening statement. The opening is important because it gives each side the opportunity to provide an outline of the issues and the evidence that will be presented at the trial. Also, since the prosecution puts on its case in chief first, it is an opportunity for the defense to present a preview of the trial for the jury. Although there is a calculated risk involved, I generally refrain from giving an opening and reserve it for after the prosecution rests. I do not give an opening because I would prefer not to tip off the state to the defense strategy. I also feel that giving an opening provides you with less flexibility and commits you to pursuing a particular course of action. For example, at the beginning of the trial, I did not know whether my client would be testifying. I would have him testify only if it was deemed necessary—and my client would not have to testify if I could successfully impeach the prosecution witnesses. I was hoping my client would not have to testify.

The prosecution gave a brief opening, which closely paralleled the police report. She stated that the jury would hear testimony from two officers who would each state that on the night of October 29, the two officers were traveling east on Interstate 10 when they spotted a silver Toyota Camry that was weaving side to side across the white divider; that the officers stopped the vehicle; that the driver admitted he had been drinking; that Mr. López was given a set of field sobriety tests, which he failed; and that Mr. López refused to submit to a blood or breath test. After the prosecution finished the opening, I informed the judge that the defense was reserving the opening and would not give one at this time.

The Prosecution Case

The prosecution called as its first and main witness the arresting officer, Rick Pérez, a five-year veteran of the California Highway Patrol (CHP) and a member of the CHP DUI Task Force. The direct examination began with him describing his training and experience. Pérez said he had completed a forty-hour DUI training course at the police academy, which included training on the administration of various field sobriety tests, adding that over his five-year DUI Task Force career he had made hundreds of DUI arrests.

Pérez testified that he and his partner, Officer Witherspoon, were traveling west in the number 5 lane near Holt Boulevard when they spotted a silver Camry traveling in the same lane about a hundred feet ahead. He said he and his partner observed the Toyota drifting slightly to the right, and about ten seconds later it drifted again to the right and then back into the number 5 lane. Then, after a few seconds, according to Pérez, the Toyota drifted to the left.

Pérez added that after the Toyota drifted to the left, he immediately put on his overhead and emergency lights and accelerated to within forty feet of the Toyota. His partner then used the microphone and ordered the defendant to exit at Kellogg Drive. The driver of the Toyota immediately slowed to about fifty-five miles per hour and exited the freeway as instructed.

Once off the freeway, Pérez said, Officer Witherspoon used the microphone once again to order the driver to pull over to the shoulder and stop the vehicle. The driver complied. Pérez said that as he and his partner approached the vehicle, he could smell an "odor of an alcoholic beverage emitting from the vehicle," and he could see that the driver's eyes were "watery." The driver reportedly admitted that he had taken "several drinks." Because of the driver's admission to drinking and because of the smell of an alcoholic beverage and the fact that the driver's eyes were "watery," Pérez said he asked him to take several field sobriety tests and concluded that he was unable to satisfactorily perform the tests.

Officer Pérez then went into great detail in describing the field sobriety test results, telling the court how he had explained and demonstrated each test to the defendant. He began with the "one-leg stand" test, noting that the test measures a person's balance and that people under the influence generally have an impaired balance. One thing that I noticed is that he talked about how he "generally administered" the tests and not what he had done with my client in this particular case. When I pressed him as to what he had done in this particular case, the cop tried to have it both ways, saying first that this is what he did generally and then saying he said that this is what he did in this particular case because he always does the same thing. Pérez then testified that he told Mr. López to stand with his feet together and his hands at his sides and then to raise one foot six inches off the ground and then to look at his foot, all the while maintaining his hands at his sides and counting to ten. He was further told that if he stopped, he was to start once again and continue the count where he left off. Pérez said that in performing the test, Mr. López began counting but that he immediately raised his arms about eight inches for balance. He then dropped his foot and started counting again from one, instead of continuing with seven, which is where he had left off. He counted and made it to six once again and then began counting at one, defying the instructions. Pérez said he then asked López if he was done, and he said "yes."

The Romberg balance test is designed to test the ability of the person to follow simple instructions. Pérez said he explained the test and told Mr. López to stand with his feet together, hands at his sides, and to tilt his head backwards and count to measure thirty seconds, stopping the count at thirty. As in the police report, Pérez noted that the defendant had "estimated 30 seconds in 40 seconds" and added that a person's "internal clock" is "slower" when he or she is under the influence. He also added that he noticed that while Mr. López was performing the test, his eyelids were "fluttering," and this was consistent with a person being under the influence of alcohol.

The last field sobriety test was the "finger count." In this test, the subject is generally asked to hold out his hand with the palm out and to touch the thumb alternately to each finger from one to four. Officer Pérez demonstrated the test as he described it, alternately touching his thumb to each finger, starting with the index finger and ending with his pinkie. He said the defendant told him he understood the test but he only completed one-and-a-half tests, while three tests were requested. The test was said to measure short-term memory and "divided attention." Pérez described the defendant's performance as "consistent with a person who is under the influence." Pérez said the defendant was placed under arrest based on his weaving, the odor of alcoholic beverages emitting from him, and his performance on the field sobriety tests.

Officer Pérez then proceeded to describe how the defendant had refused to take the PAS test. I could tell from the sequence of the questions that the prosecution intended to introduce the prejudicial statement in the police report that he "did not want to blow into that thing and have it go crazy!" so I was waiting to raise a timely objection. As the prosecutor was about to ask whether Mr. López had said anything as he refused to take the PAS test, I loudly objected. The judge looked surprised but immediately ordered the witness not to answer, and he called the attorneys and the court reporter to a sidebar discussion in his chambers. I was surprised and initially impressed that the judge appeared to take a strong stand and admonished the prosecutor that she could not introduce the statement without first laying a foundation. He said that the case law was clear that since you have a right to refuse, it is contradictory to introduce a statement made in connection with the refusal to impeach the person. The prosecutor argued that it was being offered not for the truth of the matter but to show the defendant's mental state and to show that he was "hiding something." The judge said that he would not admit the statement unless the prosecution brought him cases the next morning before court that supported her position.

The prosecution brought in copies of two cases the next morning, but they were not really on point. I was, therefore, surprised that after the noon recess, the judge ruled that he would allow the statement in but that he would add a jury instruction that would admonish the jury to give the statement only whatever importance, if any, they felt it merited.

Officer Pérez testified that he then told the defendant that under the implied-consent law he was required to take a blood or alcohol test. Pérez then read the chemical-test admonition form in court and said that he had read it verbatim to the defendant. At the end of the form, it says that one has a choice on whether or not to take a breath test; Pérez said the defendant had answered "no" when asked if he would do it. He was then allegedly asked whether he would take a blood test, and he answered "no." Mr. López was then transmitted to a local jail facility and booked.

Cross-Examination

My strategy in the cross-examination was twofold: (1) to highlight all of the things that my client had done right during the DUI stop, and (2) to point to contradictions in the cop's testimony. One of the things that I noticed, for example, was that on the stand, Pérez consistently added things to embellish his testimony that were not in the police report.

Before going into the cross-examination, I should say a little bit about the nature of my law practice, which as you know is far from conventional. Because I have done all of my law practice as a solo practitioner, I have not had any formal mentorship as a lawyer. Whether working as a public defender or a prosecutor or in private practice, early on in most attorneys' careers they have some sort of formal or informal mentoring and training. Although I have not had any formal mentoring or mentors, over the past few years I have consulted with several attorneys. As noted, one of the persons I have consulted with many times is Juan Guerra, a very successful private defense attorney who was my former undergraduate student long before I went to law school. Especially on the eve of a trial, I would often consult with Juan, and he generally provided me with sound coaching and advice.

One of the things I learned from Juan is that the most important thing to do right at the onset of the cross-examination is to "marry" the cop to the police report. I began by asking Officer Pérez about the police report. I asked whether he had prepared a police report, what a police report contained, and most importantly, why the report was important. The idea was to bring out that the report is very important because it is done immediately after the incident, when the facts are fresh in the officer's mind. Since the police make many stops and arrests in the course of a year, it is essential that they record their observations as soon as possible while their recollection of the incident is new in their minds. The report is especially crucial because the only persons who were present during the incident were the officers and the accused. Despite its importance, the police report is hearsay and cannot be introduced as evidence.

Still, it becomes the basis for determining whether criminal charges will or will not be brought against the accused.

After getting Officer Pérez to testify about the importance of the police report and to give an assurance of the report's accuracy, I then asked him whether he had had an opportunity to review the report, and he admitted that he had. In fact, Pérez and his partner had been in court the previous Friday, Monday, and Tuesday, and I had personally observed Pérez carefully studying the report as he waited in the hallway. I asked him to confirm that while waiting for the trial to start, he had had ample opportunity to review his report and to discuss it with his partner. Prior to the start of the trial on Tuesday, Pérez and Witherspoon had been sitting in the jury box in chairs 5 and 6, and it was clear that they were discussing and comparing notes on the report. I finally "married" Pérez to the report by asking whether there was anything that he wanted to add or to take out of the report, and he replied, emphatically, "No." I then asked him whether he "stood behind the report" and he gave me a firm, defiant "yes."

The next step in the cross-examination was to go through the police report point by point and to get Officer Pérez to acknowledge all of the things that my client had done right. He reluctantly admitted that my client was not speeding, that he immediately complied with the officer's directive to exit the freeway on Kellogg Drive, that he slowed his vehicle to fifty-five miles per hour, that he exited the freeway without incident, and that he pulled over to the shoulder and parked his vehicle. Pérez also admitted not only that Mr. López produced his driver's license without fumbling with his wallet but that he had handed the officer his license without being asked to produce it. He admitted that my client was extremely cooperative and polite and that he knew where he was, where he had come from and where he was going. He knew that he was at Cal Poly Pomona and that he was in Pomona and that he was on his way home. Pérez also admitted, as he had noted in the police report, that Mr. López was dressed neatly and was wearing black pants, a gray shirt, and a white jacket. Finally, the cop admitted that my client answered all of the officers' questions clearly and did not have any problem understanding the questions, that the officers did not have any problems understanding his answers, and that Officer Pérez would have noted it in the report if he had noticed problems with the defendant understanding.

I also attempted to downplay the so-called "signs" of driving under the influence. Officer Pérez noted that Mr. López's speech was slow, but he acknowledged that some people speak more slowly than others and that he did not know whether Mr. López was speaking more slowly than he normally did. The officer also admitted that the first thing that Mr. López said to him was that he was tired and that being tired might also make one's eyes "watery" and impair one's performance on the field sobriety tests.

Pérez reluctantly acknowledged that he had noted in the police report that the smell of alcohol was "moderate," not strong. In short, I went slowly through the entire sequence of events from the observed driving to the stop, the pre-field-sobriety-test questions, and the background information to establish that Mr. López had driven perfectly after allegedly weaving across the white line; had followed all directives in slowing down, exiting the freeway, and pulling over to the curb; and had no trouble following or understanding directions, showing awareness of his environment and surroundings.

I was fortunate to have Lalo as a client because he is intelligent and observant, took notes on the testimony, and helped me to isolate contradictions and inconsistencies in Pérez's testimony. In fact, there were so many contradictions that Lalo would get frustrated with me sometimes because he felt that I might have omitted or skipped over an inconsistency. The cross-examination turned out to be long and tedious. I noted how the judge was very busy with his normal calendar, and so we were typically in session only about three or four hours per day. On a typical day, the judge would hear his calendar until about 10:30 or 11 a.m., and we would convene for an hour or ninety minutes in the morning. We would then recess until about 1:30 p.m., or more often 2, and we would be in session until around 4 or 4:30. This made for a long cross-examination that appeared to be even more prolonged than it was because of the interruptions and delays.

I noticed during the direct examination that the cop would take every opportunity to continually embellish the record so that it would work against Lalo. For example, on the stand, Pérez testified that Lalo's vehicle had weaved across the white divider approximately twelve to eighteen inches, whereas in the police report he had said it was only approximately twelve inches. When I pointed to the inconsistency, he stated that he did not recall what he had stated in the police report, so I asked him whether he wanted to look at his report to refresh his recollection. He then looked at the report and acknowledged that this was not what he had put in the report. I then asked him, each time his testimony deviated from the report, "Mr. Pérez, you are not trying to embellish your report, are you?" and he would answer, "No."

Another example of how the arresting officer embellished the record was when he testified that he had smelled alcohol on my client throughout the evening, including not only during the initial stop but also during the pre-field-sobriety-test questions, during the field sobriety tests, and after the arrest on the drive to the police station. This was not in the police report.

A Bag Full of Tricks

On the eve of the trial, I had consulted with Juan Guerra to see whether he felt it would be a good idea to use some sort of audio-visual aids during the trial. He said that it depended on what I wanted to use and why. I told Juan that I wanted to Google and download a map of the freeway section where Lalo's vehicle had allegedly weaved across the solid white lines separating the lanes. I mentioned that the police officer had said in the police report that the freeway angles slightly to the left at the point where Lalo allegedly weaved to the right and that the map of the freeway showed that the freeway was straight and did not angle to the left. Pérez was obviously trying to suggest that the reason Lalo weaved to the right was because the road angles slightly to the left. I also told him that I wanted to take some photographs of the place where the stop occurred and the field sobriety tests were performed. Juan said, "Sure." He felt it would be fine to introduce these exhibits.

During the direct examination, the district attorney had asked the cop to sketch a freehand drawing of the freeway section where he first spotted Mr. López's vehicle. I was somewhat embarrassed for the cop because he drew a rather crude map by hand with the relevant exits and noted that the distances in his drawing where not intended to be to scale. I could not believe that the DA's office did not have the resources to Google the freeway section and produce a real map. Predictably, the cop drew a bend in the freeway at the point where he said in the report that it "angled slightly to the left," as if he were the only one who could notice the angle.

I had some problems downloading a blown-up a copy of the freeway. The Kinko's in Riverside said it could not blow up the map because it was copyrighted, so I finally found a place near the court that would download it. We also obtained a couple of photographs of the scene to show that the asphalt surface was bumpy and sloped down, and that it was not "a smooth asphalt surface," as was noted in the police report.

We finally obtained enlarged copies of the freeway map and the scene of the stop. My client and I were worried because we learned the blown-up photos would not be ready until the last minute, so we picked up the photos and map during the noon recess near the conclusion of the direct examination of the cop. I came back after lunch with a huge Kinko's bag, which contained photographs of the freeway and three enlarged photographs of the location of the stop and field sobriety tests.

The cross-examination started immediately after the noon recess. After the preliminary questions, which as I said were designed to "marry" the cop to the police report, I produced a copy of the enlarged map of the freeway and placed it on the large easel between the witness stand and the jury box. The officer's freehand drawing of the freeway was on butcher paper on the easel, so I placed our map over that hand-drawn map. I asked the officer to identify the map. The judge interrupted me and took judicial notice of the fact that this appeared to be a downloaded and enlarged copy of a Google map of the Interstate 10 freeway between Holt and Kellogg boulevards.

I noted that the arresting officer had testified that the road veers slightly to the left, and I asked him to point to where it was on the map that the road veers to the left. He responded that the veer is slight and is not readily obvious to the naked eye. Another inconsistency in the testimony is that the cop had noted in the police report and testified in open court that as the Toyota was approaching Via Verde, Pérez had accelerated and pulled to within forty feet of the silver Toyota, activating his overhead and emergency lights. The inconsistency was that there are approximately two miles between Via Verde and the Kellogg Exit, so there was no explanation for why the driver of the Toyota had not pulled off the freeway prior to Kellogg. The officer would have had the jury believe that the patrol car followed the Toyota for approximately two miles with its emergency lights on and that the Toyota had failed to slow down or pull over to the right until the car got to Kellogg. If this had happened, surely it would have been noted in the police report. From the police report, it was clear that the officer had activated his emergency lights and directed the driver of the Toyota to exit the freeway immediately before the Kellogg Exit. It was significant, and what came out during the cross-examination was that Lalo had in fact driven the

Toyota perfectly and without incident for approximately two miles after he was said to have been observed veering to the left into the number 4 lane before Via Verde.

Later on in the cross-examination, I also introduced two of the photographs that were taken at the scene of the stop and the field sobriety tests. One was taken from the roadway and was facing in the direction of the campus and showed that the road veers slightly downward and is rather bumpy. Unfortunately, when I showed the officer the photograph, he said that the Toyota had pulled to the curb prior to this point, implying that the rough and choppy road surface in the photograph was not the surface on which the tests were performed. When I brought out the second photograph of the scene, the cop said that he did not recognize the area where the photograph was taken, even though it was an area adjacent to the other photograph.

For the remainder of the trial, I would carry the large shopping bag with the photographs of the map and the scene wherever I went. When I came into court in the morning, I would discreetly and quietly place the bag under the defense table, and whenever we took a break or had recess, I was careful to take the bag with me wherever. During the first part of the cross-examination, the prosecutor complained to the judge, outside the presence of the jury, that she had not been provided with copies of the map and photographs as stipulated under the code of civil procedure. She said that she also wanted to see what was in the bag that the defense counsel had put under the table. The judge admonished me and told me that I had a duty to provide timely copies of the entire discovery to opposing counsel. I told the judge that I had provided the copies immediately after I received them, which was during the noon recess the prior day. I told him, moreover, that the map of the freeway and the photographs of the scene were readily available to all persons and part of the public domain. In other words, I noted that while one is supposed to provide copies of evidence in one's possession that the other party does not have access to, the prosecution *did* have access to my map on the Web and could have had access to photographs of the scene as well.

Later, the young prosecutor would complain to other prosecutors about my "bag of tricks," but there was nothing devious, unfair, or unethical about introducing a map of the freeway or photographs of the location where the stop and field sobriety tests were conducted.

The Defense Case

The first witness for the defense was Rosa Linda Gutiérrez. As I mentioned earlier, Rosa Linda was a graduate student at Yale University; she was focused on labor economics and was doing her dissertation on immigrant labor in Los Angeles. She had met Lalo at an immigration conference in Seattle in June of the previous year, and they found they had common research interests around immigrant labor and immigrant rights. She had spent an extended period of time in Los Angeles doing research for her dissertation. Because of their common interests, they had stayed in touch and were working on a couple of articles and a research grant together. Lalo had provided her with feedback on her dissertation and on some articles.

In fact, Lalo had shared that one of the reasons he was so tired that night is that he and Rosa Linda had been together the night before he was arrested working on a joint research grant that had been submitted electronically. Rosa Linda was an ideal witness because she was young, highly educated, and extremely articulate. A couple of months before the trial, I had provided the prosecution with her date of birth, social security number, and the following witness statement:

Defense Witness Rosa Linda Gutiérrez

Ms. Rosa Linda Gutiérrez (birthday, October 1, 1977)

Ms. Rosa Linda Gutiérrez, a graduate doctoral student at Yale University, will testify that she was with Mr. Lalo López earlier in the evening on the night of his arrest, on or about October 28 or 29. Her testimony will be that she and Mr. López had been working on a research proposal together during the previous week, that she was with him that evening, that they had dinner together, and that they shared one beer. She will further testify she was with Mr. López up until he drove home and was talking to him on her cell phone when the CHP officers stopped him on the evening of October 28. Her testimony, based on her observations and experience, was that Lalo López was not under the influence on the evening in question.

After the prosecution rested, the clerk called Ms. Rosa Linda Gutiérrez to the stand at approximately 3 p.m. on Monday afternoon. I should note that the judge had complained on several occasions about the length of my cross-examination. He had promised the jury that the trial would end by Thursday, May 17, at the latest, and he was beginning to worry that the trial would not end in time.

Rosa Linda Gutiérrez looked radiant. She wore a very pretty, flowery blouse and a black skirt, and her answers were crisp and to the point. The prosecution had indicated in the pre-trial that she would object to any extensive discussion of the witness' academic background. In fact, during the voir dire she inserted a question about whether people were more credible simply because they were more educated. It was clear that the high level of education of the defendant and the witness was a sensitive and intimidating point for the prosecution.

I made it a point to not stress Ms. Gutiérrez's education. In preparing her to testify, I told her that I would ask her how she met Lalo and she should relate that they were both graduate students with research interests in common. I told her to mention the fact that she was a graduate student at Yale matter-of-factly, like it was not a big deal or as if everyone went to fancy schools like Yale.

Gutiérrez said they were research associates and had become friends. She recalled how they had been working on a research proposal and that she had been with Lalo at the university the previous night working on the proposal until approximately 12:15 a.m., and the next time she saw him was at around 8:30 p.m. the next evening. They had gone out to celebrate the completion of the grant proposal. They went to eat dinner at a TGI Friday's near the shopping mall by her house and had shared a large salad. She testified that Lalo had ordered a beer and she had taken a few sips from his beer.

At the end of the testimony, I asked Gutiérrez whether she had grown close to Lalo and she answered, "Yes." I then asked her whether she would lie for Lalo, and she looked me squarely in the eye and said, "No!" There were several things that were critical about Gutiérrez's testimony. First and foremost, it showed she had been with Lalo just before the DUI and knew how much he had to drink. Second, she had impeached the cop's testimony because Pérez had said that Lalo had taken several drinks. Finally, Gutiérrez testified she was talking to Lalo on his cell phone when he was stopped, so she would be able to help establish a timeline for the events that occurred.

Gutiérrez made everyone laugh when she was critical of Lalo's cell phone, saying that his phone was faulty and that he had been having trouble with the charger recently. In fact, she said, the two kept getting disconnected because his battery was low and this was frustrating to her. Fortunately, she had a copy of her phone bill, which she brought with her.

The prosecution had objected to the introduction of the telephone bill when we came back from the noon recess at 1:30 p.m. She objected because I had not provided her with a copy of the telephone record until the last minute and because the cell-phone company did not authenticate it as a business record. I responded that I had not had a copy of the telephone bill until that morning and that I did not want to introduce the telephone bill as evidence. I simply wanted to use it so that Gutiérrez could refresh her recollection. Fortunately, the judge allowed the use of the telephone bill for this purpose.

Gutiérrez testified that she and Lalo had spoken for about a minute at 11:17 p.m. and for two minutes at 11:19 p.m., and that at 11:24 p.m. they had a conversation that lasted eight minutes, with another conversation following from 11:32 p.m. to 11:34 p.m. She said that in the middle of the last call, he said, "Oh, I think I am being pulled over, I have to go." She tried unsuccessfully to call again at 12:06 a.m. and 12:13 a.m. At 12:15 a.m., an officer answered and told her that Mr. López had been arrested.

The beauty of Gutiérrez's testimony was that she was able to say that she was talking to him at the precise time that he was pulled over and that he was tired but not under the influence. She was also able to corroborate the timeline. The 11:32 p.m. call would have been around the time that Lalo was attempting to connect his charger into the cigarette lighter. This provides an alternate explanation for the so-called weaving. The 11:32–34 p.m. time also corroborated the cop's approximation of the time of the stop. During cross-examination, I had gotten the officer to admit that there were many reasons why a person might weave other than being under the influence. In fact, talking on a cell phone would be a common explanation.

During cross-examination, the prosecutor tried unsuccessfully to discredit and rattle the witness. She asked the witness who had driven to the restaurant, and Gutiérrez said that she drove because Lalo had driven all the way from Riverside to her house in Los Angeles and that this only seemed fair. The prosecution also asked about the extensive number of phone calls to Lalo. This opened up the door for me to address the phone calls in the week before the incident and to bring up that they had spoken a number of times per day on each of the days preceding the night of the arrest. Finally, the cross-examination focused on the intimacy of the relationship. Rosa Linda admitted that it had evolved from a professional relationship to a "dating" relationship. She also admitted that she had stayed with Lalo during her latest visit to LA, but stated this in a very matter-of-fact way and did not get flustered.

In the end, I was incredibly happy and relieved by her testimony. She answered clearly and directly and seemed not only extremely bright and alert but very credible. Juan had told me that I might not have to put my client on the stand because if she was effective, she could testify to 85 to 90 percent of the things he would have testified to. After Gutiérrez's testimony, I decided not to put Lalo on the stand, and the defense rested.

Closing Argument

We did not know until the last minute whether Lalo would be testifying, because that would all depend on whether we needed him or not. From the onset, Lalo had wanted to testify and assumed that he would. Like many clients, he was anxious to tell his side of the story. Throughout Pérez's testimony, one could see the frustration on Lalo's face as the cop lied or distorted what had happened. For example, Lalo had told me repeatedly that Pérez's partner Witherspoon was really "cool," and that it was Pérez who was "a real dick." Lalo said that Witherspoon had assured him that he could take the drug/alcohol test of his choice at the station. Lalo added that it was clear that Witherspoon was "trying to help me out and would have let me go."

Lalo was looking forward to Witherspoon's testimony and was sure that it would contradict Pérez. The little bit of contact that I had with Witherspoon confirmed Lalo's assessment. He was a six-foot man with a receding hairline and a soft, friendly smile, lacking the hard edge of most police officers. However, over the past few days, Witherspoon had been in the courthouse and I had the opportunity to observe him in the hallways and in the courtroom. I remembered the day that Pérez and Witherspoon were talking in the jury box. Each one had a copy of the police report, and they were making reference to various parts of the report and smiling and nodding knowingly. They seemed like two college students—more specifically, frat boys—cramming for an exam.

I was hoping that Witherspoon would not testify because, whether he was an obliging guy or not, I knew he was a police officer and that he would not contradict his partner on the stand. They were both cops and did belong to a *kind* of fraternity, after all. In the end, the prosecutor set the stage for Witherspoon to not testify during the re-direct of Pérez. She got Pérez to testify that Witherspoon was simply serving the secondary role of backup for security reasons and that he was not really that involved in the stop, interrogation, or conducting the field sobriety tests. The prosecution, therefore, rested after Pérez's testimony. I was a little bit surprised that the DA opted to rest, but in the end I believe that she had decided not to take the risk that Witherspoon might contradict Pérez's testimony and provide me with more ammunition.

The closing argument is a very important part of the trial because it provides one with an opportunity to bring together all the loose ends in the trial. I also like it because it allows one to argue, and although lawyers don't testify or present evidence, most judges will give one quite a bit of latitude in interpreting the facts.

The prosecutor's closing basically summarized Pérez's testimony on direct. She said that in order to gain a conviction under the applicable DUI statute, a prosecutor must prove all elements of the crime. Those elements are located in the California Jury Instruction for Criminal Cases (CALJIC) § 16.830, and are as follows:

1. A person drove a vehicle, and
2. At the time, the driver was under the influence of any alcoholic beverage or any drug or under the combined influence of any alcoholic beverage and drug.

In Lalo's case, the prosecution also had to prove the special allegation that he refused to take a blood-alcohol test, as is required under California's implied-consent law, after being advised of the requirement and consequences.

"Under the influence" is further defined in CALJIC § 16.831, which states, "A person is under the influence of an alcoholic beverage or under the influence of a drug or under the combined influence of an alcoholic beverage and a drug when as a result of drinking such alcoholic beverage and using a drug his/her physical or mental abilities are impaired to such a degree that he/she no longer has the ability to drive a vehicle with the caution characteristic of a sober person of ordinary prudence under the same or similar circumstances."

Prosecutor Albright concluded that she had proved beyond a reasonable doubt that on the evening in question, the accused was operating a motor vehicle, that he was under the influence, and that he refused to submit to a blood-alcohol test after being advised of the requirement to take it and the consequences of not taking it. Officer Pérez testified that Mr. López's automobile was weaving, that he was unable to follow "simple instructions," and that he failed to adequately perform the field sobriety tests. The officer also testified that he smelled alcohol throughout the evening and that Mr. López's speech was slowed and that he had watery eyes.

There were two themes or catch phrases that I tried to develop in the closing. One was, "What are they trying to hide? What is it that they don't want you to see?" The other was, "Don't let this young woman [the prosecutor] tell you that. . ." I started by explaining how in our system, the DA gets "two bites of the apple" because he or she gets to open the closing and then also has an opportunity to respond or rebut the defense closing. I told the jury, "This may seem unfair—I know there was a time when I was younger that I thought it was unfair. But it is not unfair. You want to know why it is not unfair? It is not unfair because we [the defense] don't have the burden of proof—she has the burden of proof." I said this while pointing at the prosecutor, who was sitting a few feet in front of me and slightly to my right, with her back to me. "She has the burden of proving each and every element beyond a reasonable doubt. It's a heavy burden. So it's fair!"

I then moved on to discuss the division of labor in the court, explaining the purpose of the closing. I told the jury that the judge interpreted the law, witnesses who testified under oath presented evidence, and the "trier of fact" under our system of justice was not the judge or the attorneys but the jury. Lawyers do not testify or present evidence. Because lawyers argue, what you get in the closing is merely argument—a lawyer's interpretation of the facts. I concluded by saying that there was only one defendant in this case. "The only person facing criminal charges with criminal consequences here is the young man sitting at the defense table," I said, pointing at Lalo.

I then took the opportunity to lambast the prosecution. I began by saying that I had no idea what the resources of the district attorney's office are, but, "Do not let them tell you that they did not have the resources to go online and download a map of the incident location. Do not let them tell you that they do not have the resources to get a picture of the scene. They have the resources! Why didn't they bring in a map or photos of the scene? What are they trying to hide? What do they not want you to see?"

When I had shown the cop a picture of the scene, he said it was not the scene—that in fact the arrest took place behind a sign at the entrance to the campus. "Why didn't they bring in pictures of the scene?" I asked in the closing arguments. "What are they trying to hide?" I added, "They do not want you to see the fact that my client drove perfectly for more than two miles from Via Verde until he was asked to pull over to the curb and stop. They do not want you to see that he obeyed all commands, that he produced his license, that he knew where he lived, that he answered all twenty-two pre-field-sobriety-test questions and that he was cooperative. They do not want you to see that he was tired and was on his cell phone when he was stopped. They do not want you to see that he had less than one beer to drink and had not gotten much sleep the previous week. What they want you to see are all of the things that he did wrong during the stop and none of the things that he did right." I pointed out that the officer had written down "two drinks" and "several drinks" in the police report, suggesting that Lalo had had two beers, rather than several sips from one beer, as Ms. Gutiérrez testified.

"Do not let her [the prosecution] tell you that PAS refusal or the alleged comment made in connection with the refusal is evidence of 'a guilty mind,'" I told the jury. "The cop told Mr. López clearly that he did not have to take the PAS. He told him it was a 'preliminary alcohol screening' device to help the officer assess whether he was under the influence. By law, you cannot use the PAS refusal as evidence against the defendant because he has a right to refuse. Officer Pérez told Lalo López that he didn't have to take the PAS; now he is trying to use the statement that he supposedly made in refusing to take it against him."

I told the jury, "Let's assume Mr. López made the statement. Let's take the bull by the horns. Why would he make the statement? One possibility is that he did not trust the machine. Another possibility is that he knew that he had done well on the field sobriety tests. He knew he only had one beer. Finally, he knew he did not have to take it and that the police did not have enough evidence to arrest him.

"Do not let the prosecution tell you that the cop is a neutral or objective party," I told the jury. "He has a job. He works under a DUI grant and, as with any job, he is evaluated based on his job performance. You heard his testimony. He got paid overtime the night that Lalo López was arrested. He worked an eighteen-hour shift that day. He has a vested interest in catching and arresting drunk drivers. His job performance is dependent on making DUI arrests and getting convictions."

I continued, "Don't let her tell you that this is a minor case, that it is not 'the crime of the century.' Don't let her tell you it is not important. It *is* important!!! When this is over, all of us are going to walk away. We are going to go home. But it is important for the man sitting over there." I pointed to the defense table. "It is important because he is the only person facing criminal charges with criminal consequences."

My friend Juan had warned me that referring to "criminal consequences" is walking on the edge, but that some judges will let you get away with it and even if they do not, you have already said it. Sometimes I have used this phrase and the DA has stood up and loudly objected, because you are not supposed to mention punishment for an offense because the only person that is concerned with punishment is the judge, not the jury.

I concluded by talking about challenging the field sobriety tests and recapping the timeline of events during and after the arrest. From the testimony, it is clear that Lalo López did everything right up until he performed the field sobriety tests. And when I asked Pérez to explain the scientific theory behind the Romberg balance test, he said that the test was not scientific and that in fact, only two of the three tests were scientifically valid. He had administered these tests not because they were scientific but because he had administered them many times in the past and it was easy to administer them.

Lalo López said that he had had less than one beer, and nobody questioned the fact that he had no more than one beer. The DA did not question it. The arresting officer did not question it. And everyone knows that the rule of thumb for a person of average height and build is one beer per hour. If you drink one beer per hour, you will not be under the influence. In fact, the cop stated that Lalo "was a large man." Officer Pérez testified that he "smelled liquor" on Mr. López throughout the evening, but he did not put that in his police report and he surely would have put it in the report if it was important.

The timeline in this case is very important, and it supports Ms. Gutiérrez's testimony as well as what Mr. López told the police. Officer Pérez stated that he first spotted the silver Camry around 11:30 p.m. and he estimated the time of the stop at about 11:32 p.m. Ms. Gutiérrez, in turn, testified that she called Lalo at 11:32 p.m. and that the call ended at 11:34 p.m. The time of the last call, 11:32–11:34 p.m., and her testimony that Lalo was having trouble with his cell phone because the battery was going dead, is consistent with the cop's description of following the silver Camry between 11:32 and 11:34 p.m. and his statement that the vehicle was weaving. There is no evidence that he was, in fact, weaving, but if he was weaving, the cell-phone call would explain why.

During the closing, I pointed out that in the opening, the DA had promised two witnesses but only produced one. I asked rhetorically (following my theme, "What are they trying to hide?"), "Why did they not produce the other officer who might corroborate or contradict Pérez's testimony?" I said, "Don't let the prosecution ask you why Mr. López did not testify. He did not testify because under our system of justice he does not have to testify. It is not his burden. It is the prosecution's burden, and remember that you cannot draw any inference of guilt or innocence from the fact that he did not testify."

Dr. Jekyll and Mr. Hyde

A theme that I stressed throughout the closing was the inconsistency in the officer's testimony regarding Lalo's behavior. In the police report and throughout the trial, Pérez had stressed that the defendant was extremely cooperative. For example, he slowed down to fifty-five miles per hour and exited the freeway, pulled over to the side and parked at the curb, attempted to exit the vehicle to meet the police officers, had his license ready when the police approached the driver's window, and answered all questions. In fact, Pérez had testified that Lalo López was so cooperative that after he was arrested, the officers parked his car in the campus parking lot so that he could go back the next day to pick it up. They also had him sit in the front of the police vehicle with Officer Witherspoon while they transported him to the station. The testimony asserting this was consistent with Lalo's statement to me that Witherspoon was a "really cool" guy and that he had assured him that Lalo could take the blood test at the police station. Lalo also said that Witherspoon had seemed to be stalling for time when he wanted to eat before they took Lalo to the station, and when he stopped a couple of cars en route to the police station.

One of the highlights of the closing was when, in describing Lalo's behavior, I exclaimed, "He's like Dr. Jekyll and Mr. Hyde! One minute, he is polite, soft-spoken, and cooperative, the next minute he explodes and refuses to take any test and yells out, 'I do not want to blow into that machine and have it go all crazy!' I ask you, how credible is that? And how credible is it that after he refused to take any test, the cops would provide valet service and park his car for him? I am sorry, ladies and gentlemen, but the testimony does not pass the smell test."

Jury Deliberation

On Wednesday, May 16, at approximately 2:30 p.m., the case went to the jury. After the jury left the courtroom, the judge told us that he would check in on them around 4:30 p.m. and that we could stick around if we wanted to, but that we should not go too far just in case the jury came back quickly. Lalo and I decided to wait and we went to the cafeteria to get some water. The cafeteria was closing, so we sat out on the benches in the hallway of the courthouse and talked about the case. We went over every single detail, especially the humorous parts of the case.

It was strange, because over just the past couple of days I had felt as though I had really bonded with Lalo. I had known Lalo for about six years. But although he had taken several classes from me and we had talked a lot outside of class, it was only now that I felt like I had really gotten to know him. I shared with Lalo, as we sat in the courtroom hallway, that I could not predict the outcome of his case but that I felt like we had put up a really good fight. This was important because I did not think that the judge would be vindictive. Even though one has a right to a jury trial, some judges are known to punish defendants for exercising that right, especially if they get upset at the defense attorney, but they are not supposed to be punitive unless the defendant has perjured himself or herself on the stand.

Anyone who tells you that they do not get nervous or apprehensive when they are awaiting a verdict is probably lying. This was not a death penalty case, but it was important, especially to my client. I could certainly tell that he was nervous about the verdict. But I told him I felt we had done just everything we could have. I felt that the high point of the defense case was the testimony of our star witness, Rosa Linda Gutiérrez. She was great and extremely credible.

Another highlight was the closing, in which I felt we had been successful in pointing to the many contradictions in the cop's testimony—successful in connecting all the dots. Still, it was hard to read the jury. None of the members smiled or looked at us throughout the trial, although most were very attentive. The judge told the jury not to have contact with the lawyers, and they took this to heart. We had a very prolonged cross-examination, and there was a good chance that they might have gotten turned off by my detailed questioning of the cop. Had we been beating a dead horse? The jury was also fairly conservative. The pickings had been slim at the beginning, and the few obviously pro-defense people who were originally present had been excused via peremptory challenges. Did the remaining jurors wonder why Lalo had not testified? Would they hold it against him, even though they had been instructed not to?

What about Rosa Linda's testimony? Did the jury believe her, or would they think she was lying to protect her boyfriend? During the cross-examination, the prosecutor had asked whether the relationship was more than a "friendship." Rosa Linda had looked the DA straight in the eye when she said it had started as a professional relationship and then became a friendship before it had recently evolved into a dating relationship. I know that I am biased, but I really felt that Rosa Linda was an amazing witness. In her attractive white, flowery blouse, she seemed almost to harbor a halo. I thought she did about as well as could be expected, and the fact that she did not skirt or deny the fact that she and Lalo were involved in a personal romantic relationship made her that much more credible. This was a modern-day, nontraditional Chicana who was smart, honest, and credible. She also conveyed a strong sense of modest self-confidence and independence, especially when she said that she drove to the restaurant because he had driven all the way out from Riverside, and when she talked about their common research interests.

Lalo and I were understandably apprehensive after the trial, but waiting is usually a good sign for the defense. When you get a really quick verdict, it is likely to be a conviction rather than an acquittal. It is usually a "slam dunk" for the prosecution, but seldom for the defense. The longer a jury is out, the more likely it is that the defense has succeeded in raising "reasonable doubt"—so if the jury is out for some time, it is some sort of a moral victory at least, even if the ultimate verdict is guilty.[4]

We went back to the courtroom around 4:20 p.m. and the judge was sitting on the bench bantering with the bailiff, the public defender, and some other attorneys, who were waiting for their clients to arrive so they could enter their pleas or be sentenced. The atmosphere was light, and one of the public defenders, a woman, was cracking some pretty funny lawyer-type jokes. She had a good sense of humor, so we were able to take our minds off the jury for a few minutes. At about ten minutes to 5 p.m., the judge told us that he was going to dismiss the jury for the day but that we should be on call in case the jury reached a verdict. I assured the judge that we could be in court within forty-five minutes of being called, and I left several telephone numbers with the clerk.

The next day was Thursday and I taught on Tuesday and Thursday, so I figured if the jury stayed, I would have to miss class again. I hated to miss another class, but I had prepared a quiz and one of the graduate students was ready to administer it. I had just started to prepare for class when the telephone rang at exactly 10 a.m. It was the call I had been both expecting and dreading. It was the clerk of the court, who said in a calm, clear cheerful voice, "We have a verdict." I said, "Thank you, we will be there before 11 a.m." I called Lalo immediately and told him I would meet him in ten minutes outside of his apartment.

The thirty- to thirty-five-minute drive seemed longer than that. We talked about a lot of things, but mostly about the case and the possible verdict. The more we talked, the more pessimistic we became. We arrived at the court at about ten minutes before eleven and went immediately into the courtroom. The judge was in the middle of doing his calendar, so we waited for about five or ten minutes for him to take a break and ask the bailiff to call in the jury. We had seen the jury when we came in. They had been sitting on the benches and standing in the hallway outside the courtroom. The jurors seemed happy, smiling, and relaxed, but none of them looked at us or smiled. This was not a good sign.

When the jury came in, we noticed that the number-one juror seat was empty. The other jurors said juror 1 had to go get the jury ballots. It turned out that, just as we predicted, juror 1 had been elected jury foreman. He was the gregarious guy who wore the American flag shirts and was always smiling and cracking jokes. The judge asked the foreman whether he had the ballots, and Lalo shook his head and turned to me and said dejectedly, "They got me!" Why? "Because he said 'ballots,' so they must have found me guilty on the refusal."

We waited for the worst as the jury foreman handed the ballot to the bailiff and the bailiff, in turn, handed it to the clerk. The clerk read the verdict: Not guilty! We could not believe what we heard. I turned and looked at Lalo and he was shaking his head and softly crying. I put my hand on his shoulder in a comforting way, and said, "Congratulations!"

Reflections

Now that the case has ended and I have had a chance to reflect, I want to briefly discuss some of the ethical issues that arise when you are representing one of your students or anyone that you teach or supervise. As with most of my clients, I did Lalo's case pro bono. I do not think that the ethical problems stemmed from the fact that I did the case pro bono, however, as much as from the fact that I was involved in a supervisory position with him, which created a potential conflict of interest. At the start of the quarter, Lalo had asked me whether he could be a "reader" for my class. It was a large class of about one hundred students, but since it did not have a discussion section or a teaching assistant to hold the discussion, I certainly needed and welcomed his help. Instead of a teaching assistant, then, the class acquired a "reader"—a graduate student who can help with miscellaneous tasks like reading papers, recording grades, and taking attendance. Readers are paid by the hour and only make about twelve dollars per student enrolled in the class, so the money is a lot less than a teaching assistant would get, but it is also less work, since you don't have to hold weekly discussion sections or hold office hours with students.

Although Lalo had been my student in several graduate classes, I had never had him as a teacher's assistant or as a reader. Under normal circumstances, I would have welcomed him as a teaching assistant or reader to help me out with the class. The problem was that I planned to use the reader not to read but to do things like administering quizzes and showing videos, especially if I had to miss class because of the pending trial. I mentioned this to Lalo early on, but it did not seem to faze him and he still wanted to be my reader, so I reluctantly agreed to let him.

It was not really a problem until the trial started because I was able to schedule the court appearances at times when I was not teaching and when Lalo was available, usually a Monday or Wednesday morning. I could also appear #977(a) for Lalo. But it became a problem once the trial started because I could no longer use Lalo to cover my class, since he also had to be in court. I knew that the situation was beyond his control and my control and that there was nothing we could do about this, but it made me realize that my initial reluctance to have him as a reader was well justified.

A related problem, which we laughed about after the trial, was that because we run in a small circle, we ended up independently asking the same person, Sergio—a fellow graduate student—to fill in for each of us. Sergio was a teacher's assistant with Lalo in a large introductory class of about five hundred students. I had asked Sergio to cover my class and administer a quiz for me on one of the days I was in trial. I told him I had a case, but I never told him or anyone else anything about the case or the fact that I was representing Lalo, in order to protect his privacy. Well, it turned out that Lalo had also not told anyone about the case, but that he had also asked Sergio to cover his discussion section for the large introductory class on the same day. I spoke with Sergio after the trial ended, and he said he had started to figure out what was going on because we were both asking him to cover for us on the same days and because Lalo seemed like he was "acting weird and was all stressed out about something."

The next issue is a bit more delicate and complicated. I noticed that shortly after Lalo agreed to be my reader, he started trying to carefully delimit the things that he would and would not do in the class. I should say in his defense that Lalo is very busy, perhaps overextended, so this was not that surprising or unexpected because he had a lot on his plate. He told me that he would be taking his doctoral qualifying examinations at the end of the quarter, so he would not want to spend a lot of time doing the final grading during the week of finals. I had explained from the onset that I did not really use readers to read, grade, or prepare exams, but only to record the quizzes, keep track of attendance, and occasionally show videos. I explained at the beginning of the quarter that if Lalo helped me with these functions, he would not have to do any grading or make up any quizzes or exam questions for the class. I would make up all of the quizzes and exams. All he had to do, specifically, was run the exams on the Scantron machine, record the weekly quiz scores, help me take attendance, administer the midterm and final exam, and provide input on student participation in the class.

Because Lalo was a teacher's assistant in another class, he had a discussion section on Tuesday at 1 p.m., so he had to leave after about twenty minutes of my class and could only really help with attendance on Thursdays. He also asked whether I had someone in my office who could record the attendance. I told him I could find someone, so each time he took attendance, he would give me the attendance sheet and I would have it recorded. I would take care of the attendance sheet on

Tuesdays and would have one of my office staff record the attendance. Lalo also gave me sporadic comments on student participation, but he did not keep extra copies of the class seating chart and I do not think he would have written any comments unless on a given day I gave him a copy of the seating chart and reminded him to do it. I am not sure how to say this, but after a while, I frankly started to feel like I was assisting him—rather than the other way around.

Lawyers are expected to be zealous advocates for their clients, and I am certainly a zealous advocate for mine. Even though I do most of my cases pro bono or charge very little, I take my responsibilities as a lawyer very seriously and feel like I always go the extra mile for my clients. I think what I found frustrating in this case was that I did not feel like Lalo was also going the extra mile for me as a reader in the class. He did a good job of recording the grades in a timely manner, but after each quiz or the midterm, he would give me the Scantron sheets, so students were instructed to go to me if there was an error or problem with the quiz score (which was posted on i-Learn, an electronic program that allows students to check grades and comment on classes online). This created a lot of work for me because students were consistently reporting on real or perceived errors or inconsistencies in the grading. Just before the final exam date, Lalo also informed me that he was starting to teach another class in Los Angeles and would not be available on the date of the final examination, so I had to administer the final without him.

I believe that I frankly started resenting the fact that Lalo seemed to take a somewhat minimalist attitude toward his duties in my class. Although this was never verbalized, I expected him, in other words, to reciprocate the effort I was putting into being his lawyer, and in retrospect, this seems unfair on my part.

With the benefit of hindsight, I think that it was wrong for me to have had Lalo working for me during the trial, not so much because he was unavailable to help me out with the class on the days we had court but because it created a potential conflict of interest for me in the sense that I was his attorney *and* his professor and faculty supervisor. There was a conflict between the attorney/client relationship and the supervisor/student and professor/reader roles. Fortunately, it affected my relationship with him as a reader more than as a client because it wasn't until the trial had concluded that I really became aware of the problem and realized that he was not reciprocating my efforts.

Do not think that I am being negative about Lalo—he was a great client, a very good student, and a warm person, and we genuinely bonded not only as attorney and client but as fellow Chicanos. Unfortunately, I think that the work I did for him as an attorney started to color my perception of him as my student, and this was unfair, unfortunate, and perhaps—as I've said—just plain wrong.

I attended a fancy law school and took a lot of classes on public interest law and was part of the progressive lawyering for social change curriculum in law school. I remember how, in one of my clinical law school classes that focused on working with subordinated communities, we talked about the ways we would react if a client did not do something that she or he had agreed to do, and whether it would make any difference if it was a paying client or not. The case I remember in particular was hypothetical and concerned the story of a certain "Mrs. G";[5] it was based on an article written by Lucie White about a single Black welfare mother in North Carolina who had five teenage daughters. Mrs. G had been in an automobile accident and had received a six-hundred-dollar settlement as compensation for the accident. When the welfare authorities became aware of the payment, they proceeded to deduct the amount from her welfare check.

After all, according to the welfare regulations, she was required to report the settlement as "income" and to have it deducted from her stipend. After conferring with each other, the client and White—a poverty lawyer in a conservative and traditional small North Carolina community with a rigid racial caste system— agreed that during the hearing, Mrs. G would testify that she had used the money for basic necessities (like groceries, and school clothes and sanitary napkins for her teenage daughters).

During the hearing, Mrs. G shocked White when she inexplicably took the stand and proceeded to present a very different story from the one they agreed on. On the stand, Mrs. G—normally a very quiet, shy, and reserved woman—became increasingly self-righteous as she proclaimed that she had used the money to purchase not necessities but "Sunday shoes" that her girls could wear to church. Although Mrs. G gave eloquent and compelling testimony and she prevailed in the trial, the attorney was miffed and upset with her client.

In the hypothetical case in class, my professor started by asking, "Would you get upset if a client doesn't do what you agreed on or expected? If so, would it matter whether the client was a paying client or not? In other words, would you get more upset with a nonpaying client?"

Although Lalo never had the opportunity to testify and I felt that he was an ideal client in working cooperatively with me, doing everything that I asked, and helping me to defend him effectively, I was disappointed in his performance in assisting me in the class. As I think I've made clear, I think I was disappointed because I felt I had gone all out for Lalo as an attorney and I expected for him to reciprocate when he worked with me as a reader.

As I reflected on this, I started thinking not only about Mrs. G but about Paulo Freire's teachings on the *Pedagogy of the Oppressed*.[6] Freire was not a lawyer but an educator who worked with peasants in Brazil and articulated a theory of oppression and liberation. He felt that liberation would come through the oppressed and not from their oppressors, because only the power that comes from the oppressed would be sufficiently strong to free both themselves and their oppressors from their relationship.

Now, I am not saying that in our interactions Lalo was oppressed or that I was the oppressor in the traditional sense of the word, but we *were* involved in a power relationship in which I as the professor and faculty supervisor had the formal power, and in this sense, you could say that I represented the "oppressor" and he the oppressed. Freire talks about "false generosity" and warns that we should be leery of the false generosity that comes from the oppressor because it is a generosity that ultimately does not seek to liberate but to perpetuate oppression.

Wrongful Termination

9

Age Discrimination

Big John

Queridísimo Alfredo,

I am sorry to hear that you have been sick and that your health was interfering with your courses and your practice. Fortunately, my health has been great and I have really been able to dedicate myself to work and to my new poetry project. When I finish, I will be sure to send you a copy. I have to tell you, I attended a music event last weekend that you would have loved. I went with my South American friends to listen to two bands: a vallenato band from Colombia and a boleros trio that played only music covers from Los Panchos. When you visit the Bay, I will make sure to take you to a great event.

    Congratulations on your daughter's marriage! You will have to tell me all about it when you return from Oaxaca. Your last case about Lalo was illuminating, as usually one sees what the client expects of the attorney but rarely does one see what the attorney expects of the client. I do agree that this case presented a conflict of interest, but what surprises me is that I would have expected Lalo to not only reciprocate your efforts but to have exceeded them. As you described, it seemed that you were doing more work in the courtroom *and* in the classroom than he was. I find myself in a similar situation with the clients from Milagro. I want to be a rebellious nonregnant lawyer, but sometimes I cannot help but feel frustrated by clients' lack of effort. I find it difficult to not feel as if my work is not being appreciated. How would you advise me to deal with these personal feelings? Rascuache lawyers have feelings, too!

Atentamente,
Fermina

Amiga,

This is a very special field report. I hope to respond to your letter and write something about the class tomorrow, but first I want to give you the news on a friend who passed away last Thursday from a massive stroke. I learned about it Saturday and was not able to make the memorial service on Sunday. I sent a message by e-mail to his wife to give her my *peseme* (condolences) so it could be read at the memorial, including the poem I'll share with you below. I am imparting to you my experience with John because in addition to being a good friend, John ended up being my client, so it relates to my class because I am teaching law and subordination again this year, the class that focuses on "rebellious lawyering." John was a really special person. He was one of a kind, who seemed somehow bigger than life.

When John's wife, Sandra, invited me to say something about John at the memorial, I didn't know what to say or where to begin, so I wanted to write something about John because I always find it easier to express myself in writing. One could fill a library with stories about him. Each of us has a rich collection of stories or anecdotes about "Big John"—stories that I am sure we will use to remember him and that we will no doubt embellish with time. I may have a somewhat unique perspective on John because I got to see different sides of him. I knew him first as a colleague, then as a friend and occasional tennis partner, and finally as a client.

John and I were colleagues many years ago, long before I thought about law school, as we were both teaching sociology at the same university. His warmth, intelligence, and charisma immediately drew me to him and we quickly became friends. We played tennis once or twice a week. We would play in the evening and then go to some local bar to celebrate and to talk. You take almost any city—Los Angeles, San Francisco, Chicago, or Riverside—and John could tell you where the real classic bars were, places where interesting people hung out. I guess you could call him a poor man's connoisseur of interesting bars.

This proved to be problematic, because we would go out drinking and stay out until the wee hours when the bars closed. We finally arrived at what seemed like a simple and logical solution to the problem. We would go out to play earlier in the afternoon before it was dark, so that we could get to the bars early and would not stay out as late. Unfortunately, we soon learned that regardless of how early we started playing, we always ended up staying up until the bars closed. John was not a very good tennis player, by the way, but he played with a lot of flare and intensity.

John grew up in Chicago in a large, competitive Irish family and a tough working-class neighborhood. His dad worked in the steel mills in East Chicago and was a tough, no-nonsense kind of guy. John's background was urban and working class. He attended Catholic schools, was an altar boy, and always excelled as a student, but despite his intelligence and accomplishments, he was always a guy who was much more comfortable at the neighborhood bar than at the university. His father was a union man, and after John got out of academia, he served as a representative for his local union and was very active in union politics.

I wanted to keep this brief, so I tried to think of a few words that would describe John. You had to know John, to be with him, to experience him, in order to understand him. I don't really have the words to describe John fully because he really defied description, but some of the words that come immediately to mind when I think about John are:

Smart
Warm
Engaging
Hospitable
Passionate, and most of all,
Caring.

John was one of the smartest, best informed, most engaging and charming persons I have ever met. He was certainly smarter than most of us, and infinitely smarter, better informed, and more perceptive than the people who surrounded him at work. This proved to be problematic when he first tried his hand at teaching, and also later when he left academia and went to work as a statistician for the city of Los Angeles. His intelligence and competence caused problems because a lot of those who surrounded him, particularly at work, were intimidated and threatened by him.

John was also incredibly hospitable and a wonderful host. It is appropriate, then, that we celebrate John's life with a smile and that we party and savor life, because John certainly knew how to party, and he lived every day of his life with tremendous gusto and intensity, celebrating each day as though it would be his last.

When I represented John in his wrongful-termination suit recently, I saw another side of him. He was serious, intense, dedicated, and surprisingly demanding—yes, very demanding. John was a wonderful client in the sense that he was smart and well informed about law. He was, in the very best sense of the term, a very good "lay lawyer" and an incredibly knowledgeable client. He read about the law and kept abreast of current cases. John understood law on a superficial level, but he was frustrated by it. I guess he was naïve because he knew and understood how law *should* work, not how it does work. This frustrated the hell out of him.

The Mission

John and I were only colleagues for two years. He was a visiting assistant professor at the university and his position was not renewed, despite the fact that he was a very talented and charismatic teacher and was doing interesting research on community empowerment and development. He graduated from Harvard with a PhD in sociology with honors and was far more talented than most of his colleagues, but he was not political in the sense that he did not know how to play the academic game and to kiss up to the people with power in the department and the university. He also had great parties with very interesting people. After his appointment was not renewed, John got fed up with academia, so he took a job in Los Angeles. Most academics go where the job is, but John was different. He and Sandra had apparently always wanted to live and work in Los Angeles, so he moved to LA and started looking for work. He eventually got a job working for the city as a research analyst and statistician, in charge of compiling statistics for the city. Sandra got a job as a social worker and was counseling the elderly. John worked for a number of years for the Los Angeles transit system and continued to publish articles and present papers at conferences on transportation safety and issues like the relative safety of school buses.

Although John was increasingly cynical about academia and had long abandoned pursuing a university teaching career, we kept in touch on and off over the years and remained friends. We had not been in contact with one another in recent years until one day, I got a call from John. He was on his way to the San Bernardino Mountains with his thirteen-year-old daughter, Angie. Angie would be attending a summer mock-trial competition for gifted junior high students. John was staying at Riverside's historic Mission Inn and wondered whether we could get together for dinner.

We had a very enjoyable dinner in the beautiful outdoor Mission Inn patio and reminisced about the past and the good old days when we had been colleagues and fellow tennis partners. At first, John said that everything was fine at work and that he was still working for the city of Los Angeles and that he had been transferred to another department, but he eventually confided that everything was not fine after all. In fact, he had been having a lot of problems at work and was forced into early retirement after some twenty-one years on the job. He was told officially that he had to either resign or retire for budgetary reasons, but this was clearly a pretext. He said that his supervisor had a lot less education than he had and was threatened by John. The supervisor didn't know what to do with him, so he harassed him and wrote him up for petty things and eventually forced him to retire. Since he was the oldest one in the department and all the people who were forced to retire were older employees, he felt this was clearly an open-and-shut case of age discrimination.

I was immediately impressed with John's understanding of the law. I had always known he was very bright, but I was surprised to learn that he had spent a lot of time in the law library. In our talks, I related that I had taken on a couple of cases of employment discrimination. John was surprised but encouraged by the fact that I had done wrongful-termination and employment-discrimination cases. About a week later, as he passed through Riverside again en route to Los Angeles, he called and asked to have lunch. During lunch, he asked me whether I would be willing to take on his case. I told him that I had a number of other cases that were taking a lot of my time, especially a disability-discrimination case, so I was reluctant to take on new cases.

John assured me that his case would not take much time and that the city would settle once I filed the lawsuit. I reluctantly agreed to take the case with the expectation that it would settle quickly.

The Complaint

I filed the complaint in state court on or about March 4, naming the city, the head of personnel, and John's supervisor, as well as the head of his unit and the public utilities commission, as defendants. About a week after I filed the complaint, I received a telephone call from a Frank Rasmussen, who identified himself as a Los Angeles city attorney who was representing the city on the case. He impressed me as superficially polite but ultimately arrogant, pompous, and condescending. Rasmussen remarked that he did not know whether I had "much experience in civil practice," but that he had been in private civil practice for seventeen years before joining the Los Angeles city attorney's office. Perhaps because of my "limited experience" in the civil area, he implied, I might not know or appreciate the fact that under the law, managers had immunity and could not be sued as individual defendants. He also "informed" me that I couldn't bring tort claims against the defendants and that one of the defendants, the head of personnel, was on maternity leave and could not be sued as a defendant.

Over the next few months, I would learn not only that the city was not eager to settle but that the city attorney would use every ploy possible to prolong the case. He began with a series of legal maneuvers that were designed essentially to paper me to death. Rasmussen was right about one thing, and that was that my experience in the civil arena was limited. I had done mostly criminal cases and some family law and only a handful of civil cases. As noted, he proceeded to attempt to protect the two top-level managers, arguing that the head of personnel, Elizabeth ("Betty") Morgan, had not been actively involved in the decision to effectively terminate Big John by forcing him to retire. He also claimed she was not at work and had not been personally served because she was on maternity leave and we didn't have a home address for her. As for the head of the Los Angeles public utilities commission (LAPUC), Robert Kaplan, Rasmussen argued that he, too, had not been directly involved in supervising John or in the decision to terminate him.

One of the first things I did was to attempt to "meet and confer" with Rasmussen, hoping that we could resolve the matter quickly and arrive at a settlement, as John had suggested. I soon discovered that Rasmussen was not interested in settling the case. I think his strategy, as noted, was to paper me to death with the hope that it would prove costly to my client and that we would abandon the case. What he didn't realize, though, is that Big John wasn't paying me anything. We never signed a retainer agreement, but John assured me that I would make a "large sum" once the case settled that would make it "worth my while." I thought that he would offer to reimburse me for some of my out-of-pocket costs and travel expenses, but he never did. The only thing that he paid for, in fact, was the initial filing fee and the fees for two of the motions I filed.

I filed the complaint in the Superior Court of Los Angeles. The named defendants were the city of Los Angeles, Robert Kaplan (head of LAPUC), James Ellis (Big John's immediate supervisor), Rodney McKain (assistant head of human resources), Elizabeth Morgan (head of personnel), and "Does 1–100, Inclusive." Although this was basically an age-discrimination claim, the complaint was for damages (wrongful termination) and included the following causes of action: (1) breach of contract; (2) breach of covenant of good faith/fair dealing; (3) age discrimination; (4) promissory estoppel; (5) wrongful termination in violation of public policy; and (6) fraud and deceit, which was dropped in the amended complaint.

Fighting Removal to Federal Court

Under the federal rules of civil procedure, when a plaintiff brings a cause of action that involves both federal and state claims, defendants have the right to "remove" the case to federal court. This was clearly a state claim based on California law and filed in the California superior court, but in the cause of action for age discrimination, I listed both the state statute (Gov. Code § 12940[a]) and the federal age-discrimination statute (ADEA [29 U.S.C.A. § 623]). In retrospect, I see that this was a tactical mistake because it gave Rasmussen an opening. Shortly after I filed the complaint, the defendants sought immediate removal of the case to the U.S. District Court for the Central District of California. I had never handled a case in federal court, and my only experience with the federal rules of civil procedure had been when I took a civil procedure class in my first year of law school and clerked for a federal judge in the summer. Fortunately, the California rules of civil procedure are modeled after the federal rules, but I still had to do a mini-cram course on removal under the federal rules.

On April 14, the defendants filed a request for removal in the U.S. District Court for the Central District of California. Such requests are generally granted automatically, since it is assumed that defendants have a right to pick the forum in which they want to defend the charges against them. On April 17, I filed the first amended complaint, dropping the fraud and deceit causes of action and reference to the federal age-discrimination statute and at the same time including a notice of opposition to the notice of request for removal filed by the defendants in the U.S. District Court for the Central District of California. I also filed a request for immediate summary remand and presented the following facts in support of the request:

(a) A civil action bearing the above-caption was filed in the Superior Court of California, in and for the City and County of Los Angeles, Action No. 05-439205 on or about March 4, and is pending therein; and

(b) The complaint alleged state claims for breach of contract, breach of covenant of good faith/fair dealing, promissory estoppel, fraud and deceit, and age discrimination pursuant to Gov. Code § 12940 et. seq.

(c) Plaintiff made reference to violation of ADEA (29 U.S.C.A. § 623), but the complaint was and is based on California causes of action for breach of contract, wrongful termination, and age discrimination pursuant to Gov. Code § 12940(a) et. seq.

(d) Plaintiff subsequently filed a first amended complaint, which is attached as Exhibit A, and which contains no federal causes of action.

(e) The District Court, therefore, lacks subject matter jurisdiction, and should make an order for summary remand under Title 28, Sect. 1446, (c) (4).

(f) And per Title 28, Sect, 1446, (c) (4), the U.S. District Court in which a notice of remand is filed "shall examine the notice promptly," and "if it clearly appears on the face of the notice and any exhibits annexed thereto that removal should not be permitted, the court shall make an order for summary remand."

WHEREFORE, plaintiff prays that under 28 U.S.C. § 1446, et seq., the United States District Court, Central District of California, shall make an order for summary remand of the case to the Superior Court of the state of California, Los Angeles, for all further proceedings.

Alfredo Mirandé
Attorney for plaintiff, John C. Ryan

The District Court issued an order denying the plaintiff's request for immediate summary remand, noting that if the plaintiff wished to file a motion to remand, he must notice the motion on the normal thirty-five-day calendar pursuant to Civil Local Rule 7-2. The District Court ruling added that the defendants' motion to dismiss was rendered moot by the filing of an amended complaint by the plaintiff. The defendants filed another motion to dismiss, which was set for hearing on June 2, and the plaintiff filed a properly noticed motion to remand, set for hearing on June 9. The District Court subsequently granted the plaintiff's motion to remand, deferred ruling on the motion to dismiss, vacating the June 2 and June 9 hearings, and remanded the case to the Superior Court of California, Los Angeles County.

I felt it was important that the case was successfully remanded to the Superior Court. It was important because it is generally agreed the California Fair Employment Act (FEHA) extends greater protection to plaintiffs than its federal counterparts, Title VII of the Civil Rights Act and the ADEA (29 U.S.C.A. § 623). Another reason for opposing removal is that federal juries are generally more conservative and less generous in the awards they grant successful plaintiffs. Finally, I figured that the fact that the defendants were anxious to have the case removed to federal court was sufficient justification for requesting the remand. I recall how once when I was in child dependency court proceedings, all the lawyers on the case and the judge agreed on a course of action. My good friend and informal mentor, Juan Guerra, advised me once that if you go into court and all the other parties are for something, if you are not sure of the law, you should oppose it on principle because if all of them are in agreement, it cannot help you.

The Demurrer

Defendants then refiled verbatim the same motion that had been filed in the federal court as a motion to dismiss, labeling it a "demurrer" to the plaintiff's first amended complaint in the state court. In the demurrer, the defendants claimed that the first, second, and fourth causes of action "failed" because the plaintiff's employment was by statute and not by contract, and that the claim for wrongful termination in violation of public policy should be dismissed because it somehow "replicates" his FEHA claim for age discrimination.

In the opposition, I argued that the demurrer to the first, second, and fourth causes of action should be denied. The plaintiff's employment was held by contract, not statute, as the defendants claimed. And the motion to dismiss the plaintiff's cause of action for wrongful termination in violation of public policy should be denied because the plaintiff had stated a tort claim for wrongful termination, which is independent of his age-discrimination claim under the FEHA.

Unfortunately, the judge ruled favorably on the defendants' motion to dismiss the breach of contract, as well as the related breach of covenant of good-faith and fair-dealing claims, arguing that there is a body of case law affirming that public employment is held by statute, not contract. However, the judge denied the defendants' motion to dismiss the cause of action for wrongful termination in violation of public policy, and this was an important victory for us.

Discovery

Both federal courts and California courts have broad discovery rules, which require that the parties share relevant information that is in their possession. Defendants began discovery by issuing a detailed request for documents and response to interrogatories. Since conducting depositions is an expensive process, interrogatories are a simple and inexpensive way to obtain relevant information from another party by asking them written questions that they have to answer under penalty of perjury, without having to spend a lot of money on depositions. They also provide extremely useful background information for the deposition. There are two types of interrogatories, form and special. Form interrogatories are standardized questions in various areas of law (wrongful eviction, employment discrimination, breach of contract), whereas special interrogatories are designed to meet the needs of the specific case.

Big John took the interrogatories very seriously and provided almost all of the requested documents and supplementary documents, and he meticulously answered all of the special interrogatories. The documents provided are too extensive to list in their entirety, but they included copies of John's educational history; diplomas received; academic transcripts; awards; employment history and qualifications; curriculum vitae; record of employment and memorializing of terms of employment with CLA; documents reflecting salary, benefits, and other compensation; relevant employee handbooks in various units reflecting salary, benefits, and other compensation; salary levels for various occupational classes occupied; documents supporting claim of age discrimination; commendations and certificates of appreciation; communication between the plaintiff and the United States Equal Employment Opportunity Commission (EEOC); documents pertaining to the city of Los Angeles' (CLA's) offer of early retirement and the plaintiff's response to the offer; documents relative to complaints of discrimination and harassment made to the defendants; charges of discrimination filed with the department of Fair Employment and Housing (FEHA); documents submitted and received from the EEOC and/or FEHA; documents showing city rules and policies, correspondence between the defendants and plaintiff; conversations/communications with coworkers; conversations and communications with other persons; personal notes and a chronology of events; documents concerning emotional/mental illness; a warning label for a prescription for fluoxetine; documents pertaining to present and future economic damages; medical expenses related to injuries incurred and treatment for nominal depression and anxiety; the source and total amount of annual income since termination; documents supporting termination as "pretextual"; a "release from probation" letter from McKain; a document regarding replacement after termination; documents related to seeking and finding employment after employment was terminated; and documents as to eligibility for retirement and retirement benefits.

Despite this enormous list, there were some documents that John could not produce. For example, in response to a request for performance evaluations, he noted that they would be in his employment file. He also noted that he had not attempted to calculate his noneconomic damages, that he kept no scrapbook or photo album relative to the complaint, and that he was still searching his files concerning any documents relative to eligibility for retirement. Finally, he noted that he was searching his files for documents supporting the allegation of age-based harassment. In July, we made our own request for documents, which in many ways paralleled the request for documents made by defendants—which John had promptly and dutifully complied with.

On July 11, I sent the first amended request for production of documents and special interrogatories to the defendants. Incredibly, the request for production of documents yielded no documents, and the answers to the special interrogatories were vague, evasive, and completely unresponsive. Normally, discovery requests are formal and made on pleading paper, but they are not filed with the court. The parties are expected to cooperate without involving the court directly. After many unsuccessful attempts to obtain discovery, on December 12, I filed a formal motion to compel discovery, arguing that defendants had failed to make a good-faith response to the plaintiff's special interrogatories and request for documents.

From the responses to the plaintiff's first set of special interrogatories to Robert Kaplan (exhibit A), James Ellis (exhibit B), and "most knowledgeable person" (the person most qualified to answer the questions, exhibit C), it was clear that the defendants had not responded to the interrogatories in good faith. For example, in response to special interrogatory 1, addressed respectively to defendants Kaplan (exhibit A), the head of LAPUC; and defendant Ellis (exhibit B), John's supervisor; as to "each position held by the defendants," each defendant gave the following response: "Defendants object to this request on the grounds that it is overbroad and burdensome and is neither relevant to the issues in dispute nor calculated to lead to the discovery of admissible evidence. Defendants further object to this request on the grounds that it is calculated to harass defendant." Defendants Ellis and Kaplan were the plaintiff's supervisors, and the plaintiff had alleged that they were not qualified to supervise him. The interrogatory was not vague, was certainly relevant, and was in no way calculated to harass the defendants.

Interrogatory 3 similarly asked respondents Ellis and Kaplan for "a list of any complaints made against defendants by an employee of the city of Los Angeles." Once again, the defendants objected, using the same "boiler plate" grounds that "it is overbroad and burdensome and is neither relevant nor calculated to lead to the discovery of admissible evidence. Defendants further object to this request on the grounds that it invades defendants' legitimate privacy interests and the privacy interests of third parties." Although the interrogatory asks for "a list of all complaints," not just those involving age discrimination, against the defendant, each of the defendants responded as follows: "Without waiving these objections, defendant responds that no LPUC employees other than plaintiff have made any complaints of age discrimination against him."

The defendants' response to the plaintiff's first request for production of the documents made of defendants Kaplan (exhibit D), Ellis (exhibit E), McKain (exhibit F), Morgan (exhibit G), and "most knowledgeable person" (exhibit H) were equally vague, evasive, incomplete, without merit, and too general. Moreover, this request for production of documents also yielded no actual documents.

I noted in the motion that since July 5, the plaintiff's attorney had made several efforts to meet and confer with Rasmussen, the attorney for the defendants, but had been unsuccessful in resolving these issues or in obtaining responses to the special interrogatories or the request for the production of documents. "Having no alternative," the motion said, "plaintiff is seeking an order compelling further response to the special interrogatories and request for documents, and for monetary sanctions against defendants and their attorney, Frank Rasmussen."

"You're Fired!"

I saw John in October when he completed his deposition. John had sent me an e-mail message, and I was very busy and had not had an opportunity to respond, so on December 10, I sent him an e-mail updating him on the case and apologizing for not responding sooner, with the subject line "Catch-up."

> John:
>
> Sorry for not responding to you. I had a trial that lasted about a week. On top of that, I had eight qualifying [graduate] exams, have to read final papers, and am dealing with all kinds of stuff as Chair of Ethnic Studies. I went ahead and filed the motion to compel discovery and set it for March 10. I set it that far off because I would also like to do a summary judgment motion on or about that date.
>
> You received a letter from the court reporting services. You have 30 days to review your Depo. The address is 41 Spring St. (213) 982-5051, and the reporter is Rachel Bach. This is another Rasmussen trick. Normally, he would have agreed to have the original sent to us and we would not have to pay for a copy. He is making you go in, or forcing us to pay. I think it would probably be 400–500 dollars. Do you want to buy it? I have all of the Exhibits, which will be attached [to the deposition]. You can call and see how much the Depo would cost us. It would be nice to have it for the SJ motion, although we could use the Exhibits, since our SJ Motion will be based on the fact that they have not put forth evidence to deny your prima facie case. Anyway, please call her to see how much the Depo will cost.
>
> Alfredo

On Friday, December 16, I received the following cryptic response:

> Alfredo:
>
> I am planning to proceed "Pro Se."[1] From what I've gathered, Rasmussen realizes that he doesn't have much of a case and is only

doing what he is doing to make it difficult. I think he is motivated more by trying to beat you than to win the case. I believe that if he and I were to sit down we could probably arrive at a settlement in short order. I will impress upon him that it is in everyone's interest to settle quickly. I doubt that it even needs to go as far as a settlement conference with the judge, but if it does the judge will jump at the opportunity to have it settled according to what I am proposing.

I don't really need what we originally asked for in the request for the production of documents since I spoke earlier in the week with a personnel analyst who told me that I was the only one effectively laid off. He's going to supply me with some documents if he can find them. In any event, there is prima facie evidence for age discrimination with respect to both disparate treatment and disparate impact.[2] I've been researching the law and have no doubt that I will prevail.

John

Later that evening, John apparently had a change of heart and he sent the following message:

Alfredo:

Although I still have some concerns and misgivings, I've been thinking it may be better to proceed as we have and avoid any delays that would come from my filing a motion to go pro se. I would not like Rasmussen to think there is any difficulty between us and use it as a wedge issue. Even more, I would like him to continue his understanding of my knowledge of city politics and employment law so that he doesn't feel comfortable in the continuing of his tricks. What I am proposing—and it needs to be examined to make sure it is procedurally correct—is for you to e-mail him, saying that it would be a good idea, for reasons of expediency and so as to not continue to clog up the court system, for he and I to meet in an attempt to arrive at some sort of settlement. From my understanding, the courts always look favorably upon any attempt to settle as early as possible and, since this would avoid his motion for a summary judgment and our—successful—rebuttal of it, it would seem that this is the most appropriate course of action. Let me know what you think, since I want to move on this over the next week or so.

John

The next morning, I promptly prepared and signed a substitution-of-attorney form and mailed it to John. In the next day or so, I had a chance to think and to reflect on what had transpired and knew that there was no way that I could continue to represent John. I also knew that it was inappropriate for the opposing counsel (Rasmussen) to meet with a represented party without that party's attorney being present. John clearly wanted to "have his cake, and eat it, too." He wanted me to continue to represent him, while he met and negotiated with Rasmussen. On Sunday, I sent him the following e-mail explaining my position:

> John:
>
> I signed the substitution-of-attorney form and mailed it to you on Saturday. Please sign and return. You said you wanted to represent yourself and I took you at your word. Once I receive the signed form, I will file it with the court, and with Rasmussen. I will send a fax to Rasmussen, telling him that you will be representing yourself. If you like, you can tell Rasmussen that I did not have the time that this case requires because of my other duties, or whatever else you like, but I don't think you need to tell him anything. You have an absolute right to replace your attorney and, as you well know, you don't have to explain it to anyone.
>
> It happens all of the time.
>
> I want to wish you the best of luck on the case. I will get your file materials together and mail them to you as soon as possible. I think you know that I have spent countless hours on the case, more hours than I should have. I would not want to continue under any circumstances. In fact, I have a duty to inform Rasmussen that you are representing yourself.
>
> Alfredo

We had some problem in getting the substitution-of-attorney form properly signed and authenticated, but once it was completed I filed the form with the court on January 17 and gave notice to Rasmussen that John was proceeding in pro per and substituting for Alfredo Mirandé as his own attorney. In the ensuing months, I was busy with school and my other cases, so I didn't have much contact with John. The early settlement that John had expected did not materialize, however. Six months later, I received the following e-mail message:

Alfredo:

I had the settlement conference today and it didn't go well. I think that lawyers on the panel, being lawyers, don't have much regard for pro se plaintiffs. They suggested caving in to Rasmussen since they thought his motion for summary judgment would prevail. I am not sure about that since it certainly doesn't constitute uncontestable facts. I'm thinking about moving forward but am not sure I have the energy any longer. I don't want to concede but don't want to lose later on either.

John

I knew that the city was not going to settle the case and was not surprised by the message. I did not know what to say, so I did not say anything. On July 6, I received a telephone message from a clerk at the court, informing me that they needed a fax of plaintiff's motion to continue for the judge's review. It was clear that the court did not realize that John was representing himself, so I faxed a quick message to John. The message and his reply are listed below.

John:

I received a phone message this morning from Carla in Dept. 210. They need a copy of your reply to the motion to continue, which is set for hearing tomorrow. They need it for the judge's review. The fax is (213) 555-3545, attention "Carla."

Alfredo

Alfredo:

Many thanks for the heads up. I am faxing over a copy even though I hand delivered an endorsed copy on Monday. I really wonder about the competence of the clerical staff there.

John

On August 30, John was granted leave to amend the complaint to add a cause of action for retaliation, but in the end the city would prevail on its summary judgment motion as to all causes of action. In fact, on December 13, almost exactly one year to the day after John had decided to proceed in pro per, the court granted the defendants' demurrer to the complaint and ordered that the following judgment be entered in the case: "It is adjudged that plaintiff Ryan, John, take nothing from defendants..." On December 29, John filed a notice of appeal and request for transcript. John passed away on February 24, and on April 18, an order dismissing the appeal was entered, as the plaintiff was requested by the Court of Appeal to file an opening brief, and he did not file.

Reflections

Fermina, as I tried to think of an appropriate conclusion to this chapter of my life, it was difficult to find the words to explain how I felt. First, I wanted to say that I couldn't write about John without confronting the enormity and finality of death and the tragedy not only of Big John's case but also of his life and untimely death. Second, because I was very fond of Big John, I hesitate to say anything that might appear to be critical or negative toward him. My mother used to say that one shouldn't speak badly of the deceased. She was, therefore, always reluctant to talk about my dad after he passed away, especially to talk critically of him. As you know, my parents both liked to play cards and their favorite song was "Cartas marcadas," a really old song whose title translates as "Stacked Deck of Cards." I could not think of a more appropriate song, since their life was certainly tragic and conflicted, and in a very real sense, things were "stacked against them." They were two intelligent, charming people who were simply incompatible.

As I reflected on my feelings about Big John and my unexpected "firing" as his attorney, I was reminded of Renato Rosaldo's brilliant essay "Grief and a Headhunter's Rage," a fascinating analysis of bereavement among the Ilongot, an isolated group of about 3,500 people who live about 90 miles northeast of Manila and who are best known for their pursuit of ritualized headhunting. Rosaldo discusses the cultural force of emotions and how much of our understanding in anthropology and other social sciences is based on cognitive, rather than affective, understandings of the other.[3] So as not to trivialize Big John's death, let me say at the outset that although he was a dear friend and I felt his death deeply, my sense of loss was in no way comparable to the loss one experiences or the rage one feels in response to the inexplicable death of a close family member, such as a child, parent, sibling, or spouse.

Renato relates how he and his wife Michele had lived and conducted ethnographic field research among the Ilongot for thirty months over a period spanning fourteen years, and how he was supposedly an "expert" on the Ilongots, having written several articles and a book about them. However, it was not until Michele's untimely death during an anthropological expedition that he began to question and seriously re-examine his previous understanding of Ilongot ritualized headhunting. Renato and Michele had started field research among the Ifugaos in northern Luzon, Philippines. As Michele walked along a trail with two Ifugao companions, she lost her footing, fell down a sixty-five-foot precipice into a swollen river, and drowned.

Rosaldo had previously dismissed the one-line statements of older Ilongots, who told him that they took heads to "throw away the grief" that they felt during bereavement, as just too simple or pithy to be true. He sought more elaborate and complex explanations for ritualized headhunting and unsuccessfully looked to exchange theory and other social science theories for plausible explanations. It wasn't until he suffered the inexplicable death of his wife that he began to experience and really grasp the uncontrollable rage that his Ilongot respondents had previously described so vividly and simply to him. "Only after being repositioned through a devastating loss of my own could I better grasp that [the] Ilongot mean precisely what they say when they describe the anger in bereavement as the source of their desire to cut off human heads."[4]

The relevance of Rosaldo's essay here is that he had to "reposition" himself emotionally as both subject and object in writing and reflecting on the headhunters. He notes that using personal experience can function as an effective vehicle "for making the quality and intensity of rage in Ilongot grief more accessible to readers than certain modes of composition," but in doing so, one runs the risk of being dismissed as being in an act of mourning or of discovering the rage in bereavement for the first time. Rosaldo notes that his essay is an act of bereavement or mourning and a lot more. It is at once "an act of mourning, a personal report, and a critical analysis of anthropological method...."[5] I hope that this chapter is ultimately a similar act of mourning, a personal report, and a critical analysis of the perils involved in nontraditional, ordinary law practice.

As in anthropology and sociology, all too often academic accounts of law and lawyering are presented as detached, objective, neutral, and impersonal descriptions of reality, devoid of feeling and emotion. In the end, my experience as John's lawyer was an intensely personal, emotional experience filled with incredible highs and lows, and in describing my feelings and emotions, like Rosaldo, I must therefore now reposition myself as a subject.

I experienced a wide range of emotions when I first read and then repeatedly reread John's cryptic message informing me that he was proceeding, as he put it, "pro se," and in effect firing me. First and foremost, I felt a strong sense of betrayal. Yes, betrayal. Ironically, I had been reluctant to take on John's case because wrongful-termination and employment-discrimination claims are incredibly costly and time consuming. At the time, I told him that even if I could find the time to represent him, I did not have the money and resources to do it. I lacked the money and resources to depose either the named defendants or the potential witnesses that could help us to make a prima facie case in order to effectively oppose a summary judgment motion, or a demurrer. I had reluctantly agreed to represent John only after he "assured me" that the case would never go to trial and would settle once we filed suit. I spent hundreds of hours and many resources on the case; incurred substantial expense in making copies, doing mailings, and engaging in travel; and was not reimbursed, nor even thanked, by John, for my efforts.

But ultimately the issue was not time, money, or resources. If it had been about time or money, I would have either not taken on the case or I would have insisted on a sizable retainer before taking it. No, in the end, I made the time and put in hundreds of hours on the case. The issue was loyalty and commitment. Loyalty is important to me in my personal life and my law practice. I felt I had been loyal to John. I took his case, worked hard, and stayed on the case, even after it was clear that there would not be a quick and easy settlement. I stayed because I felt a strong sense of loyalty and commitment to John and his cause, not only because I was his lawyer but because I was his friend. I persevered with the case because I did not want to abandon him when he needed me most. When he fired me, I felt betrayed.

I was also disappointed in John because it was clear that he ultimately did not have faith or confidence in me as a lawyer, or even as a person. I felt resentful because I had come to believe that we were a very good team. I respected and valued him as a client, but he obviously did not respect or value me as a lawyer. John ultimately did not trust or believe in me and this was disappointing. It hurt me deeply that he felt that he could do better representing himself. Although I knew and still deeply believe that a client has an absolute right to select and terminate his lawyer at any time, I would be lying if I told you I was not hurt when he fired me.

At the same time that I felt a strong sense of betrayal and disappointment, once the initial shock of being fired wore off, I was filled with an overwhelming sense of relief. It was like a huge burden had suddenly been lifted from my shoulders. I was relieved in more ways than one.

Lo Siento

I had an opportunity to see John in a social setting twice in the last couple of years when he visited with me in Riverside. It was during these visits that I saw another side of him. I saw a warm, caring, and proud father. I saw him when he took his youngest daughter to the mock-trial workshop for gifted children. Though she was only about thirteen at the time, she was very bright and interested in law, drama, and a host of other things. The last time John visited was a few months before he fired me. This time he was with his older, twenty-year-old daughter, Rebecca.

He was returning from a trip to San Diego to see and say goodbye to a good friend, Nick, who was dying of cancer and only had a few days to live. When we had dinner again on the Mission Inn patio after he visited his dying friend, he was very emotional about his last meeting with Nick, and he wasn't someone that often showed his emotions. I think that his meeting with Nick had forced him to confront the inevitability and finality of death. It was kind of like the movie *The Big Chill*, as Nick had apparently invited all of his close friends to visit him in the final days before his death.

We spent a lot of time socializing with John and his daughters on these visits, and it was neat to see this side of John—the warm, indulgent, catering, and proud father. It was funny because John drank quite a bit and it was not uncommon for him to fall asleep in his chair as he was talking to you. It was wonderful to see how warm and caring his daughters were with their dad, especially after he drank in excess. On the eve of John's memorial, I wanted to remember him the way he was the last time I saw him—not only as a very bright, charming, and engaging person but as a warm, loving father. As I started to think about John as a father, I recalled an excerpt that Chicana writer Sandra Cisneros wrote about her father that reminded me a lot of John.

> When my father died last year, a piece of my heart died with him.
>
> My father, that supreme sentimental fool, loved my brothers and me to excess in a kind of over-the-top, rococo fever, all arabesque and sugar spirals, as sappy and charming as the romantic Mexican boleros he loved to sing. Dame un poquito de tu amor siquiera, dame

un poquito de tu amor nomas ["Give me a little bit of your love, give me just a little of your love."] . . . Music from my time, father would say proudly, and I could almost smell the gardenias and Tres Flores hair oil. Before my father died, it was simple cordiality that prompted me to say, "I'm sorry," when comforting the bereaved. But with my father's death, I am initiated into the family of humanity, I am connected to all deaths and to their survivors, "Lo siento," which translates as both "I am sorry" and "I feel it" all at once. Lo siento. Since his death, I feel life more intensely.[6]

Lo siento.

Tu amigo,
Alfredo Mirandé

❖ 10 ❖

Toward a Theory of Rascuache Lawyering

Querido amigo,

I was very saddened to hear about the death of your friend, Big John. I understand that you shared a very special relationship with him and I appreciate your sincerity in talking about him. Thank you for painting such a vivid picture of John and honoring him in your work.

 I can see how frustrating it must be to know how law should work but be surprised at how law *does* work, and to feel that there is not much that you can do about the disparity. We discussed earlier how your practice is so intimate and personal, and this case clearly shows this. After all, lawyers are people, and to get "fired" by a client will certainly make one feel personally hurt, let alone to be "fired" by someone who is a lifelong friend. Do you think that the bonds created between a rascuache lawyer and a client present limitations on practice? Or do you think that these bonds make way for more sincere and zealous advocacy? Please share your thoughts.

 I hope to visit Southern California soon and am looking forward to meeting with you over tea and *cena*. I would have preferred sharing a tequila, but I know that you gave up alcohol and caffeine several years ago. Once again, thank you for sharing the manuscript and your feelings about John.

Lo siento mucho,
Fermina

❖ ❖ ❖ ❖ ❖

Querida Fermina,

Amiga, I want to start this last letter by thanking you for your patience and indulgence in listening to these stories and your wonderful input, suggestions, and questions on individual chapters. I have taken your advice and have decided to write a conclusion that attempts to bring together a lot of the loose ends in the various chapters. I would like to close by taking this opportunity to identify and discuss common themes and issues that arose during the course of this project and to begin to address some important questions raised not only in your last letter but in the course of our correspondence. I should begin by offering a disclaimer in noting that one cannot necessarily generalize from my experience and apply it to other cases, because my law practice has been truly unique and has of course been colored by the fact that I was a part-time, pro bono attorney. Also, I was only able to examine here a limited number of the many cases that I have handled. However, I am confident that the cases that I opted to include are representative of the whole practice. The fact that I have been a part-time, pro bono attorney has undoubtedly shaped the nature of my practice and experience. I have provided legal representation for many people who normally would not have had access to law or to lawyers, people who would not have been represented by a lawyer. Another unique aspect of my practice is that I have focused on ordinary people with ordinary legal problems, rather than on high-profile, sensationalized cases.

I found that one of the problems with being a pro bono attorney, ironically, is time and time management. The fact that I did not typically charge an hourly rate for my services or require a retainer before working on a case meant, unfortunately, that there was literally no limit on the amount of time that I could spend on a case. Normally, the limit would have been set by the client's ability to pay, or in the case of a public defender, by the size of the caseload. For most private attorneys, the more time you spend on a case the more money you make. In my case, however, there was no relationship between how much a client paid and the number of hours that I put into a case. This meant that I probably ended up spending much more time on my cases than I needed to spend. The problem was exacerbated by the fact that I already had a full-time job. As I developed a client base, I found myself putting more and more time into my cases and less and less time into my regular job, which revolved around teaching and research. The only way to justify this, obviously, was to recognize that in the end, my law practice was also my research, and that what I learned in my practice made me a far better and more effective scholar and teacher. However, as my caseload grew out of control early on in my practice, I eventually had to step back and start to severely limit the number of cases I would take.

A second problem with being a pro bono attorney is that I was literally available to my clients at any time. Because I used my home telephone number as my office phone and my home address as a business address, clients and opposing counsel could and did contact me at all hours of the day or night, including weekends and holidays. The only way to control this was by screening my calls and selectively responding to clients as needed. Ironically, because I could not afford to hire a paralegal, clerical staff, or a receptionist, unlike most lawyers I did not have an intermediary who could shield me and protect me from clients. I recall one of my more endearing and persistent clients who called me at 7 a.m. on Christmas Day asking whether it would be fine for him to come over to deliver a Christmas gift for me.

Another problem with being a pro bono attorney, sadly, is that clients are more likely to devalue or to take one's services for granted because they are not paying for them. In retrospect, I believe it would have been good for me to charge people a nominal fee, even if it was fifteen or twenty dollars per consultation. I remember one client in particular. When I would ask if he wanted me to file this motion or that motion, he would almost always opt to have me file the motion. I think that if I had charged a nominal fee, there would have been some "cost" to the client for undertaking the various legal maneuvers and strategies. This may have made the person think twice before proceeding on a course of action because the client would have been more invested in the case.

In a sense, then, being a pro bono attorney made it more difficult for me to practice rebellious or nonregnant lawyering, which ultimately seeks to empower clients and to end the dependent and hierarchical relationship that typically exists between lawyers and their clients. I found, ironically, that pro bono practice may make clients more dependent rather than less dependent on the attorney, although one could certainly require that clients be involved in certain aspects of their own defense in order to empower them and demystify law practice.

On a positive note, as I look back on my practice experience, one of the things that stands out and that I take a lot of pride in is the development of personal bonds I have with clients. It is hard to describe or to explain the unique nature of my relationship with clients. The one thing I can say is that I have not had a traditional attorney/client relationship with them. I think that, in the end, in most cases I have been successful in engendering relationships that were characterized by mutual admiration and respect. I sought to treat my clients with dignity and respect, and they generally reciprocated. But my relationship with my clients has extended well beyond the attorney/client relationship, and I was successful in developing and maintaining reciprocal exchange relationships with many, if not most, clients.

I have already noted the examples of Xavier and Rodrigo, who reciprocated for my legal services by painting my house, but there are other examples. Another client whom I defended on a domestic violence charge paid me by installing a back door for me at my home and doing some odd jobs around the house. One of my first clients, Juan Diego, was a local mechanic. In fact, I first met him not long after I returned from law school and started patronizing a small auto repair shop on the east side of town that specialized in import cars and worked on my Fiat sports car. Over time, I developed a friendship with Juan Diego. And once he learned that I was a professor and a lawyer, he started turning to me with a variety of legal and extra-legal problems that involved his neighbors, his work, his family, and himself. I, in turn, began to use Juan Diego more and more as my personal mechanic. Rather than having me bring my cars to the shop, however, Juan Diego started coming to my home and working on them on weekends and evenings. He was the only mechanic in a two-person shop and the owner was paying him not much more than minimum wage and providing no benefits.

Even though I paid Juan Diego for his services, I was paying him a lot less than I would have paid if I had taken the car to the shop. What mattered was that he was making more money by dealing with me directly without a middleman and I was spending less money on car repairs. It was also comforting to know that I always had a mechanic at my disposal. He, in turn, always knew that he had a lawyer at his disposal. In the end, I ended up representing Juan Diego and his immediate family in at least half a dozen cases. I represented two of his sons in criminal proceedings; one was a juvenile case and the other an adult criminal felony case. I also represented Juan Diego and his older brother in a civil breach of contract case after they bought a pickup truck from a disreputable local used car dealership (called Los Amigos) and returned it less than a month after they purchased it. I also represented Juan Diego's nephew in a felony criminal proceeding, and one of the most difficult cases was when I represented Juan Diego in the family court after his wife filed for divorce. I also coached him and served as his interpreter when he was sued in small-claims court.

I had a similar experience with Chico Méndez, a Puerto Rican client whom I represented in a wrongful-termination/disability lawsuit. Ironically, I first met Chico after Juan Diego had left my Fiat sports car in various states of disarray in my driveway. I happened to be talking to one of my Puerto Rican students, Walter, and I told him that I needed a mechanic because several months had elapsed and Juan Diego had never finished the work that he had started on my car. Walter recommended Chico, and he came out to my house to take a look at the car. In the next few weeks, I came to know Chico fairly well. I soon learned that he was a very intelligent man with a seventh-grade education and a very strong work ethic who worked as a manufacturing technician and was being harassed in the workplace by his supervisor. As a result, I began writing demand letters to his employer on his behalf. Chico had an inexplicable illness and excruciating headaches and was suffering from work-related stress and hypertension. He was subsequently diagnosed with fibromyalgia.

After Chico was terminated for excessive absences, I filed a U.S. Title 7 Disability and Race Discrimination lawsuit on his behalf against the company he had worked for. I also represented him in an unlawful-detainer and wrongful-eviction case after he and his family were unlawfully evicted by his landlord, who had refused to make critical repairs on the unit, such as a leaky roof and mold in the bathroom. Chico and I subsequently became friends.

I have developed a genuine, close relationship with Chico that I have maintained, and even though I am no longer his lawyer, he is still my mechanic and friend. I went with him, his wife, and two daughters to Puerto Rico and stayed at his mother's house. My daughter also visited Puerto Rico and stayed with Chico's family. In a sense, the warmth and hospitality that my daughter and I experienced from Chico's immediate and extended family was an indirect way of reciprocating for the help that I had given him. We do not go out together, but he has invited me to a friend's house to watch boxing on pay-per-view. I have also had him and his family over to my house for dinner and have been a dinner guest at his home. Today, Chico is one of my close friends.

In retrospect, I think that my best clients have not been those who paid me directly for my services but those with whom I was able to enter into a long-term relationship that entailed an exchange of legal services for other services, like car repair, yard work, or carpentry work. Another client, a gardener, reciprocated by fixing my sprinkler system. In the end, I believe such relationships proved to be mutually satisfactory and empowering for clients because clients were able to pay me for my services by plying their trade and also to feel like we were both helping and respecting each other.

Another unique characteristic of my practice, as I have mentioned, is that I have never advertised or actively sought out clients. I obtained clients via personal referrals and word of mouth and I often represented friends and family members of other people that I had previously represented. It is interesting to see how client networks develop and how an attorney's reputation is shaped by the services and good works that he or she has rendered to clients. I therefore often found myself representing close relatives and friends and neighbors of current or ex-clients. A prominent example was Lalo. I represented Lalo not only on the DUI case but on a series of family and child-support matters that he had to deal with. I also represented Lalo's father in a very difficult and drawn-out case when his parents divorced after some forty years of marriage, his sister in a criminal assault case after she had a physical confrontation with a neighbor, and his brother-in-law on a domestic violence charge. I used to joke with Lalo and tell him that he actually needed a full-time attorney.

Another problem that I encountered as a part-time attorney was in billing my clients. With the benefit of hindsight, as noted, I believe that it was a mistake for me not to require retainers and enter into contractual relations with my clients. Unfortunately, I never focused on the compensation end of my practice and did not worry about getting paid for my services until after the case was over. This worked out well in most cases, like with Xavier, Rodrigo, Juan Diego, and Chico, but there were problems with a few clients. In the end, the problems were not really about the money but about misunderstandings and hurt feelings.

I frankly resented the fact, for example, that Big John never offered to reimburse me for my expenses because he *could have* afforded to do so. Early on, we talked about compensation and agreed informally that I would receive ten to 15 percent of the settlement.[1] What we did not agree on, however, was who would pay for my expenses prior to the settlement. At the time, I did not feel it was necessary to draw up a contract because of the fact that John and I were friends. But with the benefit of hindsight, I now see that it was important for us to have had a contract precisely because we *were* friends. I was not expecting to be fully reimbursed. I was expecting for John to say something like, "Here are a couple hundred dollars to help out with some of your expenses," or to offer to help defray the costs in some other way. Here, again, I should say that it was not ultimately about the money but about the fact that I felt that John was exploiting me.

I should comment on the fact that a number of my clients or would-be clients, such as Benny and Lalo, were or had at one point been somehow affiliated with the university. Once I started helping people and representing them in court, it did not take long for people to come to me with legal questions and problems, especially since they knew that I could help them and it wouldn't cost them much. Sometimes I would simply provide information, give a free consultation, or refer people to other attorneys. However, I also ended up representing a number of university faculty and staff, as well as current or former students. I generally, however, avoided representing students who were enrolled in my classes.

Ethical Issues

A number of ethical issues have arisen in the course of my practice. I have already alluded to the potential conflicts of interest inherent in representing someone who I was also involved with in a supervisory position in a different setting. Lalo, you will recall, was my client and at the same time my student and reader, so perhaps it was a mistake for me to have had him as a client. On the other hand, he really was a wonderful client and I think we worked very well as attorney and client. He was mature and had a lot of experience and insight into the legal and judicial system, and I learned a lot from him. I am not sure I said this before, but I think he helped me a great deal through all phases of the trial, especially in picking the jury and cross-examining the cop. The mistake was not in having him as my client, because he was a great client, but in simultaneously employing him as a reader. I can't stress that enough.

A second ethical issue is more complicated and arose with my co-counsel Clemente. You will recall that in the case of the twins, he represented the cousin, Junior, and I represented one of the twins, Marcos. I remember talking to La Güera, Junior's mom, during one of the court breaks and commenting on the cost of gas because we were making so many appearances and had to commute to court on a regular basis. She mentioned that she and her mom were sending a monthly check to Clemente and asked whether he was giving me any of the money. Clemente had asked me to work on the case, and he paid me very little.

As I recall, he only paid me about four hundred or five hundred dollars, and I worked on the case for nearly two years.

Over and above the money, however, I believe that there was a potential conflict because even though Clemente and I were representing different clients, we were in fact working as partners, as a team. The problem as I saw it was that because I generally represented the less culpable of the defendants, it seemed that my clients were often pressured to accept a plea offer that was relatively more favorable to his client than to mine. My client was always the one that did not "pull the trigger." This was not as true in the case of the twins, but it was true in a couple of other cases. In fact, as I think about it, even in the case of the twins my client clearly was the least culpable of the boys. Although it was never clear who actually did the shooting (Mario, Junior, or a third unknown person who was not charged), what *was* clear was that my client was sitting in the back seat and was clearly not the shooter.

I have previously mentioned the case of the woman who was accused of embezzlement in which her husband (my client) pled guilty to a misdemeanor. I had a good-faith belief that the man had absolutely no direct or indirect knowledge of the fact that his wife was embezzling money from her employer, and yet he was pressured to plead guilty to a minor charge, as part of a package deal that was extremely favorable to his wife. He did not actually do jail time, but he had to pay a fine and go out on weekends to clean up freeways. In exchange, his wife, who admitted that she had embezzled, had to repay the money and be under house arrest, wearing an ankle bracelet.

We had another case where two brothers were accused of running a "chop shop," receiving and selling stolen auto parts. The brothers accepted a plea bargain in which the older brother had to go to state prison and the younger one, my client, pled to a misdemeanor with no jail time. The ethical dilemma, again, was that although my client was involved in the business, I do not think that he was involved in the "chop shop" operation. Still, he, too, was pressured by the prosecution (and indirectly by Clemente) to plead guilty to a misdemeanor in order to help out his older brother, since they were offered a package deal.

One of the most difficult cases that I had and one that raised important ethical dilemmas was a case in which I represented my son. There is an old saying in law that "a lawyer who represents himself has a fool for a client." Perhaps a lawyer who represents his son or any close family member is an even bigger fool than one who represents himself. You will recall that my son is a member of a reggae/ska band. The band was on a tour of northern California about four years ago and had just performed in Merced. It was St. Patrick's Day and their day off, so several of the band members went downtown to relax, play pool, and have some drinks at a local bar, the Main Street Bar.

My son, Alejandro ("Mano"),[2] had been watching some people playing pool when he was abruptly and inexplicably ordered to leave the bar by one of the bouncers, who told him he had to exit immediately. The bouncer did not explain why my son was ejected from the bar but was adamant that he leave. Mano was understandably upset, but he complied and went outside and then across the street from the bar to wait for his friends to exit the bar.

When his friends and fellow band members came out of the bar, they began to ague with the bouncer who had ejected Mano for no apparent reason. In the ensuing argument, one of the bouncers grabbed one of the band members who was arguing with him and started choking him. My son came running across the street, yelling for him to stop choking his friend. Mano was subsequently tackled from behind by a huge bouncer, who sat on him and severely fractured my son's leg. A few days after the incident, I wrote the following demand letter to the manager of the Main Street Bar:

> I am an attorney who has been retained by Alejandro X. Mirandé, who was injured at the Main Street Bar around midnight on March 18. Alejandro had left the bar and was across the street waiting for his friends when he observed one of the Main Street bouncers choking one of his friends, Tom Patterson. He then rushed across the street, yelling and imploring the bouncer to stop choking Patterson.
>
> Alejandro sustained a severe fracture of his left ankle and a severely bruised neck when he was tackled from behind, choked, and subdued by one of the other Main Street Bar bouncers. He was in extreme pain and pled with the bouncer to let him go, but the bouncer sat on him until the police arrived. Alejandro was taken to the emergency room by the police. He was not arrested or charged with any crime.

The case was settled before it went to trial and my son received a modest sum that paid for his medical bills and some of his pain and suffering, but in retrospect I have serious misgivings about having represented him. I recall that shortly after the incident took place, I was contemplating suing the bar after they ignored my repeated attempts to contact them by telephone and did not respond to my demand letters. I consulted with Walter, an ex-student, client, and friend, on whether it would be a good idea for me to represent my son. Perhaps it is a Latino thing, but Walter strongly encouraged me to represent my son. He felt that I could argue the case more persuasively and with more conviction because my client was my son.

However, after having represented my son for several months and on the eve of trial, an experienced local attorney strongly advised me against representing my son. He said that whatever the value of Mano's case and damages might be—and from what I had told him it seemed like it could have been substantial—the value would be diminished, regardless of the merits, simply by the fact that my client was being represented by his father. What this experienced attorney was saying was not that I could not do a competent job or be a zealous advocate for my son. On the contrary, he knew me well enough to know that I would be a zealous advocate and would represent Mano well. The point was that no matter how worthy the case was or how well I represented my son, the case would be devalued by the fact that the client was being represented by his father. In other words, the attorney was saying that the judge and jury would see less value in the case or assume that it was less worthy because I, the plaintiff's father, was also his attorney.

As I look back on the case, I wonder whether the fact that the demand letters were obviously written by a lawyer with the same last name, and a name that is very uncommon, might have played a role in the case not settling quickly. What is ironic is that we never wanted to sue. We simply wanted to be reimbursed for the medical bills and other expenses that my son incurred as a result of his injury, and I know that the insurance company that paid for the settlement spent a lot of money on attorney's fees in defending the case.

Without going into the details of the case, I know that during the discovery phase of the case the opposing counsel did a good job of indirectly exploiting the fact that my client was my son. For example, because Mano had recently graduated from college and was working full time for the band but not making much money and because his income was below the poverty threshold, he qualified for waiver of a number of court fees and costs. Opposing counsel attempted to raise these issues not so much directly with the court as in correspondence with me, the attorney. Anyway, I am now convinced that it may ultimately be a mistake to represent close family members or good friends, not only because of the obvious conflict-of-interest issues but because it might devalue the merits of the case.

Toward a Theory of Rascuache Lawyering

Fermina, as a prelude to discussing rascuache lawyering, I wanted to address an important issue that you raised in your last letter when you asked me to distinguish between rebellious lawyering and rascuache lawyering. You also said that you did not understand how I could be a pro bono attorney who never really made any money as a lawyer. Your questions have caused me to pause and to reflect not only on rebellious lawyering and rascuache lawyering, but also on the notion of pro bono legal work.

In the preceding pages, I have consistently referred to myself as a "pro bono" attorney, but I now feel compelled to question whether I really have been a pro bono attorney. I should mention as an aside that I did not start out with the intention of being a pro bono attorney. The truth is that I never gave primacy to financial matters and often found myself getting involved in cases without first settling on a fee. I would generally give clients a rough idea of the cost, but it was always on a sliding scale and much less than fees charged by other attorneys, and even then I did a really bad job of collecting for my services. The problem, if it was a problem, is that I seldom got any money up front and I think this was a serious mistake. As I mentioned earlier, I now believe that I should have charged for my services (even if it was a modest amount), that I should have signed formal retainer agreements, and that I definitely should have gotten paid some money up front, since one is far less likely to get it once a case has been completed.

Amiga, you have raised a very important point that may be at the core of the distinction between a pro bono attorney and a rascuache lawyer. According to the *American Legal Dictionary*, pro bono refers to "being, involving, or doing professional and especially legal work donated especially for the public good," and it is used as an adjective when you refer to pro bono work. The point simply is that when one talks about pro bono work, one implies that the bulk of the attorney's time is not pro bono, the assumption being that pro bono work takes up a small part of an attorney's total time. The concept of pro bono, then, is only relevant for those who normally make their living as lawyers and then donate a segment of their time for the public good, not for people like me or the Brown Buffalo, who never or seldom charge for their services. You will recall that Oscar "Zeta" Acosta said that he "never charged a client a penny" for his services.

My work was not pro bono because I never really charged much for my legal services, so in a sense *all* of it was pro bono or, more accurately and ironically, none of it was pro bono. Another way of looking at this is to see paid legal representation and pro bono legal services as binary and mutually defining concepts, so that you cannot have one without the other. The idea of pro bono legal work makes sense only in a world where attorneys normally charge for legal services and presumably the bulk of their professional work has to be for pay.

Although rascuache lawyering shares much in common with Gerald P. López's idea of rebellious or nonregnant lawyering, there are also important distinctions between the two. One difference, as noted, is that while rebellious lawyering seeks to end the hierarchical relationship that has traditionally existed between lawyers and clients, rascuache lawyering is based on reciprocal relationships of self-help and mutual aid and seeks not so much to end as to equalize these relationships.

Rascuache lawyering recognizes that while lawyers have expertise in the law, they lack expertise in other areas. The unequal relationship that exists between lawyers and clients is obviated by the fact that rascuache lawyering recognizes and values the expertise of the client. I believe that the exchange relations that I was able to develop with clients worked well because in the end, they served not only as a vehicle for clients to pay for the legal services they obtained by plying their trade, but as a way for clients to provide valuable services that I needed. For example, I believe that clients like Juan Diego, Xavier, Rodrigo, and Chico were empowered because they were able to demonstrate that they had valued talents and unique skills and were able to use these skills in exchange for legal services. What is interesting about this reciprocal exchange is that the attorney is at once a service provider and a client. By recognizing and valuing the unique skill and abilities of clients, rascuache lawyering values human capital and human labor, demystifies law and lawyers, and creates a reciprocal exchange of services between lawyers and clients.

My ultimate goal in this book has perhaps been ambitious. The goal, you will recall, was to somehow link Delgado's rich fictional *Chronicles of Rodrigo*, Acosta's autobiographical Chicano movement narratives, and López's fictional vision of progressive law practice. In pursuing this goal, I related my experiences as a part-time attorney in Southern California and presented case studies based on actual cases and real people. A related goal was to use storytelling to further inform our understanding of critical race theory and law practice. Finally, I sought to build on López's idea of rebellious lawyering and to develop a tentative theory of rascuache law practice.

Rascuache (also spelled *rasquache*) means: old, broken, or dilapidated. Art critic Tomás Ybarra Frausto "posited the theory of Chicano rascuache art which meant that Chicanos/as used whatever objects they could find [recycled] and made art from them such as garden planters from old tires, vases from jars."[3] There was a rascuache dimension to my practice because I did not have an office or staff and I met clients at restaurants, coffee shops, donut shops, or at the county law library. I also did not have the resources to depose witnesses or defendants in civil suits or to subscribe to Westlaw, LexisNexis, or other services that are available to lawyers. As in rascuache art, I shaped my law practice from whatever objects, persons, or resources I could find, serving as my own paralegal and law clerk, utilizing the services of the local county law library and librarians, and using friends or students like Walter to serve subpoenas. In a few instances, I hired students or provided them with internships and academic credit for doing legal research. In return, they helped me in conducting necessary research on pending briefs or cases. One of the best examples of rascuache lawyering was the "bag of tricks" I was said to employ during Lalo's DUI trial.

Although having limited human capital and limited resources put me at a disadvantage as a lawyer, I think that the fact that I have been a part-time rascuache lawyer may have worked to level the playing field and sometimes worked to my advantage in the sense that opposing counsel often tended to underestimate me and my ability to effectively represent clients. I certainly believe that this was the case in Lalo and Xavier's cases. In neither case did the opposing counsel expect that I would be taking the case to trial, much less prevailing in the trial.

As noted, Oscar "Zeta" Acosta, or the Brown Buffalo, is an important example of Chicano law practice and rascuache lawyering. However, his career as a lawyer was short-lived and limited not only because of his mysterious disappearance but because he never took on a case unless it was ultimately a Chicano movement case. He therefore ignored or shunned cases involving ordinary situations and ordinary people. Acosta appears to have been inadvertently thrust into the midst of the Chicano movement and the Chicano revolt in the late 1960s and early 1970s, for as he notes in *The Revolt of the Cockroach People*, "When I first arrived in Los Angeles in January 1968, I had no intention of practicing law or pitting myself up against anything."[4] He was only anxious to find "the story" and write "the book," and to "split to the lands of peace and quiet where people played volleyball, sucked smoke and chased after cool blonds."[5] A related problem is that because Acosta was a creative writer, it is always difficult to separate fact from fiction in his writing.

In closing, I should mention that perhaps the most important and unique characteristic of rascuache lawyering, as previously noted, is that it focuses not on sensationalized crimes and high-profile clients like Acosta did, but on ordinary people with ordinary legal problems. All too often, books about law and lawyering have focused either on high-profile, bizarre criminal cases, serial killings, celebrity clients like O.J. Simpson, or famous high-profile attorneys. A unique aspect of rascuache lawyering, then, is its concern with everyday legal problems encountered by ordinary people. It is lawyering for and by ordinary people, but it is work that precisely for this reason is so necessary and important.

It is a mistake to equate rascuache lawyering and pro bono legal work. They are not the same. As I reflect back on my practice, I submit that a key difference between pro bono lawyering and rascuache lawyering is that while you ostensibly do not expect anything in return for pro bono work, you do expect something in return in rascuache lawyering because it is built on the principal of reciprocity and mutual self-help. Rascuache lawyering emanates from the Latino cultural expectation of cooperation, reciprocity, and self-help, but it seeks to level the unequal relationship that has traditionally existed between client and lawyer and to create and nurture symbiotic relationships with clients.

Unfortunately, all too often, pro bono legal work has been based on Paulo Freire's notion of false generosity, or on disingenuous attempts to help members of subordinated communities without at the same time working to empower them or to end the structural forces that work to maintain people in an oppressive and subordinate position. We must be able to recognize and to reject false generosity because in the end, "in order to have the continued opportunity to express their generosity, the oppressor must perpetuate injustice as well. An unjust social order is the permanent font of this 'generosity,' which is nourished by death despair and poverty."[6]

One of the important lessons I have learned from my practice is not only to be more attuned to potential conflicts of interest but to be sure that lawyers become more self-conscious and aware of what they expect in return when they take on a case pro bono. The danger is that if we have a hidden agenda in which we expect something in return for our services as lawyers, we run the risk of perpetuating not only false generosity but also injustice and despair and the regnant hierarchies that we are so desperately seeking to transcend.

⁘ ⁘ ⁘

Notes

Introduction

1. Critical race theory is a movement in law that emerged in the 1980s and seeks to have race at the center of legal analysis. It began as a critique of the progressive Critical Legal Studies movement (CLS), which gave primacy to class but tended to ignore race. According to Váldes, Culp, and Harris, "Critical race theorists have not placed their faith in neutral procedures and the substantive doctrines of formal equality; rather, critical race theorists assert that both the procedures and the substance of American law . . . are structured to maintain white privilege." Francisco Váldes, Jerome McCristal Culp, and Angela P. Harris, *Crossroads, Directions, and a New Critical Race Theory* (Philadelphia: Temple University Press, 2002), 1.

2. Váldes, Culp, and Harris, *Crossroads*, 1.

3. Váldes, Culp, and Harris, *Crossroads*, 1.

4. Váldes, Culp, and Harris, *Crossroads*, 1–2.

5. Váldes, Culp, and Harris, *Crossroads*, 2.

6. Francisco Váldes, "Legal Reform and Social Justice: An Introduction to LatCrit Theory, Praxis, and Community," 14 *Griffith Law Review* 148 (2005); E.M. Iglesias and Francisco Váldes, afterword to LatCrit V Symposium, "LatCrit at Five: Institutionalizing a Postsubordination Future," 78 *Denver University Law Review* 4 (2001), 1249–1333; Váldes, "Foreword: Poised at the Cusp; LatCrit Theory, Outsider Jurisprudence and Latina/o Self-Empowerment," 2 *Harvard Latino Law Review* 1 (1997), 1.

7. Derrick Bell, *And We Are Not Saved: The Elusive Quest for Racial Justice* (New York: Basic Books, 1987).

8. Bell, *And We Are Not Saved*, 20.

9. Bell, *And We Are Not Saved*, 6–7.

10. Richard Delgado, *The Rodrigo Chronicles: Conversations About America and Race* (New York: New York University Press, 1996).

11. I have refined this pedagogical tool in teaching a class on law and subordination that included theoretical readings on lay lawyering and advocacy on behalf of subordinated groups, and which requires that students work in a "field placement" with subordinated groups (e.g., the homeless, day laborers,

and at-risk youth). An additional requirement was that students write weekly "field reports" or journals that critically evaluate the class readings, discussions, and field placements. For more detail on how I started writing the Letters, and created my fictional amiga, see Alfredo Mirandé González, "Alfredo's Jungle Cruise: Chronicles About Law, Lawyering, and Love," *Davis Law Review* 33 (1999–2000), 1347–1375.

12. Some works written by non-lawyers, such as Steve Bogira, have looked at ordinary cases. Bogira, a journalist, focused on the cases coming before one judge in Chicago's Cook County Criminal Courthouse, the busiest courthouse in the country. See Steve Bogira, *Courtroom 302: A Year Behind the Scenes in an American Criminal Courthouse* (New York: Vintage, 2006).

13. Gerald P. López, *Rebellious Lawyering: One Chicano's Vision of Progressive Law Practice* (Boulder: Westview Press, 1992).

14. Kevin R. Johnson, "Civil Rights and Immigration: Challenges for the Latino Community in the Twenty-First Century," 8 *Chicano-Latino Law Review*, 42–89.

15. Johnson, "Civil Rights and Immigration," 50.

16. Bill O. Hing, "Coolies, James Yen, and Rebellious Advocacy," *UC Davis Legal Studies Research Paper Series*, Research Paper no. 107 (May 2007), 1-44, 1.

17. Hing, "Coolies," 4.

18. Hing, "Coolies," 3.

19. Hing, "Coolies," 3.

20. Bell, *And We Are Not Saved*; Patricia Williams, "Alchemical Notes: Reconstructing Ideals from Deconstructed Rights," *Harvard Civil Rights–Civil Liberties Law Review* 401 (1987); Richard Delgado, "The Imperial Scholar: Reflections on a Review of Civil Rights Literature," 132 *University of Pennsylvania Law Review* (1984), 561; Angela P. Harris, "Race and Essentialism in Feminist Legal Theory," *Stanford Law Review* 42 (1990), 581; Mari Matsuda, "Looking at the Bottom: Critical Legal Studies and Reparations," *Harvard Civil Rights–Civil Liberties Review* 22, 323; Charles R. Lawrence, III, "Race and Affirmative Action: A Critical Race Perspective," in Kairys, D. (ed.), *The Politics of Law: A Progressive Critique*, 3d ed. (New York: Basic Books, 1998), 312–337; Margaret E. Montoya, "Mascaras, Trenzas, y Greñas: Unmasking the Self While Un/braiding Latina Stories and Legal Discourse," *Chicano-Latino Law Review* 15 (1994), 1–37.

21. Roberto Unger, "The Critical Legal Studies Movement," in Hutchinson, A. C. (ed.), *Critical Legal Studies* (Totowa, NJ: Rowman & Littlefield, 1989), 323–344; Peter Gabel and Jay M. Feinman, "Contract Law as Ideology," in Kairys (ed.), *The Politics of Law*, 3d ed., 497–510; Robert W. Gordon, "Some Critical Theories of Law and Their Critics," in Kairys (ed.), *The Politics of Law*, 3d ed., 641–661.

22. Gordon, "Some Critical Theories," 642.

23. Gordon, "Some Critical Theories," 641.

24. I have opted to capitalize "Color" in "people of Color" because the term refers to a group of people and not to color per se.

25. Harlon Dalton, "The Clouded Prism," 22 *Harvard Civil Rights–Civil Liberties Law Review* 2 (1987), 435–448, 435.

26. Dalton, "The Clouded Prism," 437.

27. Dalton, "The Clouded Prism," 437.

28. Váldes, Culp, and Harris, *Crossroads*, 2.

29. Robert A. Williams, "Foreword," in Delgado, R., *The Rodrigo Chronicles: Conversations About America and Race* (New York: New York University Press, 1996), vi.

30. Williams, "Foreword," xii.

31. López, *Rebellious Lawyering*, 41.

32. López, *Rebellious Lawyering*, 43.

33. Ian F. Haney López, *Racism on Trial: The Chicano Fight for Justice* (Cambridge: Harvard University Press, 2004), 8.

34. Ilan Stavans (ed.), *Oscar "Zeta" Acosta: The Uncollected Works* (Houston: Arte Publico Press, 1996).

35. Stavans (ed.), *Oscar "Zeta" Acosta: The Uncollected Works*, 5.

36. Oscar Zeta Acosta, *The Autobiography of a Brown Buffalo* (New York: Vintage Books, 1972); Acosta, *The Revolt of the Cockroach People* (New York: Vintage Books, 1973).

37. Stavans (ed.), *Oscar "Zeta" Acosta: The Uncollected Works*, 7.

38. Stavans (ed.), *Oscar "Zeta" Acosta: The Uncollected Works*, 14.

39. Stavans (ed.), *Oscar "Zeta" Acosta: The Uncollected Works*, 14.

40. Stavans (ed.), *Oscar "Zeta" Acosta: The Uncollected Works*, 14.

41. Stavans (ed.), *Oscar "Zeta" Acosta: The Uncollected Works*, 14.

42. López, *Rebellious Lawyering*, 8.

43. López, *Rebellious Lawyering*, 8.

44. *Collins Spanish Dictionary*, 7th ed. (New York: HarperCollins, 2003).

45. "Mean, tightfisted" is a usage that I was not familiar with.

46. Stavans, *The Essential Ilan Stavans* (New York: Routledge, 2000), 193.

47. George Ritzer, "Sociology: A Multiple Paradigm Theory." *American Sociologist* 10 (1975), 156–157.

48. Ritzer, "Sociology," 157.

49. Oliver Wendell Holmes, Jr., *The Common Law* (New York: Barnes and Noble, 1881), 1.

50. Alfredo Mirandé, *The Chicano Experience: An Alternative Perspective* (Notre Dame, Indiana: University of Notre Dame Press, 1985).

51. Bell, *And We Are Not Saved*, 18.

52. Bell, *And We Are Not Saved*, 5.

53. Bell, *And We Are Not Saved*, 6.

54. Delgado, *Rodrigo Chronicles*.

55. Delgado, *Rodrigo Chronicles*, xviii.

56. Delgado, *Rodrigo Chronicles*, 1.
57. Delgado, *Rodrigo Chronicles*, 17.
58. Delgado, *Rodrigo Chronicles*, 17.
59. López, *Rebellious Lawyering*, 36–37.
60. López, *Rebellious Lawyering*, 37.
61. In fact, in the film *Fear and Loathing in Las Vegas*, he is depicted as a wild and crazy three-hundred-pound Samoan lawyer.
62. Stavans (ed.), *Oscar "Zeta" Acosta: The Uncollected Works*, xii.
63. Stavans (ed.), *Oscar "Zeta" Acosta: The Uncollected Works*, 14.
64. Stavans (ed.), *Oscar "Zeta" Acosta: The Uncollected Works*, 14.
65. Stavans (ed.), *Oscar "Zeta" Acosta: The Uncollected Works*, 8.
66. Stavans (ed.), *Oscar "Zeta" Acosta: The Uncollected Works*, 10–11.
67. Stavans (ed.), *Oscar "Zeta" Acosta: The Uncollected Works*, 13.
68. Stavans (ed.), *Oscar "Zeta" Acosta: The Uncollected Works*, 8.
69. Acosta, *The Autobiography of a Brown Buffalo*, 22.
70. Acosta, *The Autobiography of a Brown Buffalo*, 36–37.
71. Stavans (ed.), *Oscar "Zeta" Acosta: The Uncollected Works*, 14.

Chapter 1

1. Proposition 21, the Juvenile Crime Initiative—also known as the Gang Violence and Juvenile Prevention Act—was passed in March 2000. This measure makes various changes to laws specifically related to the treatment of juvenile offenders. It targets gang-related offenders who commit violent and serious crimes, with a focus on juvenile offenders who are affiliated with gangs. The changes can be divided into six categories:

1. Prosecution of Juveniles in Adult Court: Requires more juvenile offenders to be tried in adult court.
2. Juvenile Incarceration and Detention: Requires that certain juvenile offenders be held in local or state correctional facilities.
3. Changes in Juvenile Probation: Changes the type of probation available for juvenile offenders.
4. Juvenile Record Confidentiality and Criminal History: Reduces confidentiality protections for juvenile offenders.
5. Gang Provisions: Increases penalties for gang-related crimes and requires convicted gang members to register with local law enforcement agencies.
6. Serious and Violent Felony Offenses: Increases criminal penalties for certain serious and violent offenses.

2. California Codes: Penal Code § 186.20, aroundthecapitol.com, available online at: www.aroundthecapitol.com/code/getcode.html?file=./pen/00001-01000/186.20-186.33 (accessed January 14, 2011).

3. Penal Code § 186.20, www.aroundthecapitol.com/code/getcode.html?file=./pen/00001-01000/186.20-186.33 (accessed January 14, 2011).

4. For a discussion of the Sleepy Lagoon case, see Sleepy Lagoon Defense Committee, "The Sleepy Lagoon Case" (pamphlet), Los Angeles Citizens' Committee for the Defense of Mexican American-Youth (1942); S. Guy Endore, *The Sleepy Lagoon Mystery* (Los Angeles: Unidos Books and Periodicals, 1944); Alfredo Mirandé, *Gringo Justice* (Notre Dame, IN: University of Notre Dame Press, 1987); and Eduardo Pagan, *Murder at the Sleepy Lagoon* (Chapel Hill: University of North Carolina Press, 2003).
5. Endore, *The Sleepy Lagoon Mystery*, 31.
6. Endore, *The Sleepy Lagoon Mystery*, 31.
7. Endore, *The Sleepy Lagoon Mystery*, 32.
8. Interview with the author, December 8, 1986.
9. John Asbury and David Raclin, "Injunction Confronts Gang Violence," *The Press-Enterprise*, August 25, 2007, B-1.
10. Asbury and Raclin, "Injunction Confronts Gang Violence," B-1.

Chapter 2

1. I should note that Alma turned out to be a great research assistant and helped me out a lot with my cases that summer. The following spring, she was admitted to an elite law school and eventually graduated from that school, one of the top law schools in the country.
2. Alma García's journal, in author's possession.
3. Alma García's journal, in author's possession.
4. See *Moore v. Illinois* 434 U.S. 220 (1977).
5. Alma García's journal, in author's possession. The backlog in the court system Alma refers to is a serious problem in California, as is overcrowding in prisons. See note 5, chapter 7 for a discussion of the backlog of cases in Riverside County court.
6. Alma García's journal, in author's possession.
7. Alma García's journal, in author's possession.
8. Alma García's journal, in author's possession.
9. Alma García's journal, in author's possession.
10. Alma García's journal, in author's possession.
11. Alma García's journal, in author's possession.
12. Preliminary hearing transcript (PHT) 22, lines 22–23.
13. PHT 55, lines 21–23.
14. PHT 30, lines 6–7.
15. PHT 62, lines 18–20.
16. PHT 47, lines 16–18.
17. PHT 129, lines 7–10.
18. PHT 79–80, lines 24–27.
19. PHT 68, lines 4–6.
20. PHT 69–70.
21. PHT 111, lines 4–5; PHT 110–12.

22. PHT 71, lines 8–14.
23. PHT 72, lines 8–11.
24. *People v. Hernandez* 90 Cal. App. 3d 309, 155 Cal. Rptr. 1 (1978, 2nd Dist.).
25. PHT 102, lines 12–14.
26. PHT 49, lines 6–12.
27. PHT 96, lines 23–26; PHT 74, lines 14–27.
28. PHT 72, lines 8–9.
29. *Bruton v. United States* 391 U.S. 123, 136, 20 L. Ed. 2d 476, 88 S. Ct. 1620 (1968).
30. "Child Protective Services," California Department of Social Services, available online at: www.dss.cahwnet.gov/cdssweb/pg93.htm (accessed January 14, 2011).
31. Murray Levine, "Do Standards of Proof Affect Decision Making in Child Protective Investigations?" 3 *Law and Human Behavior* 22 (1998).
32. Chief Justice Burger, for example, indicated that the standard used has symbolic value because it indicates the value the society places on the rights at stake. *Addington v. Texas* 421 U.S. 418, 426 (1979). See also *Valmonte v. Bane* 18 F. 3d 992 (2nd Circ. 1994).

Chapter 3

1. Michael Hames-García, "Dr. Gonzo's Carnival: The Testimonial Satires of Oscar Zeta Acosta, Chicano Lawyer," *American Literature* 72.3 (September 2000), 463–93, 467.
2. Hames-García, "Dr. Gonzo's Carnival," 474.
3. Hames-García, "Dr. Gonzo's Carnival," 474.
4. Hames-García, "Dr. Gonzo's Carnival," 474.
5. What Terrazas said was, "Jalisco ha sido cuna del machismo, en especial, el jalisciense ha sido el prototipo del macho mexicano en las películas mexicanas y esa imagen ha dado la vuelta al mundo." Translation by the author. Terrazas, Trinidad, "¿Y las muertas de Jalisco?" *El Occidental*, July 26, 2007, available online at: http://www.oem.com.mx/eloccidental/notas/n359234.htm (accessed January 14, 2011).

Chapter 4

1. *Goss v. López*, 419 U.S. 565 (1975).
2. See, for example, Angela Valenzuela, *Subtracting Schooling* (Albany: State University of New York Press, 1999); Luis C. Moll and Richard Ruiz, "The Schooling of Latino Children," in Marcelo M. Suárez-Orozco and Mariela M. Páez, *Latinos: Remaking America* (Berkeley and Los Angeles: University of California Press, 2002), 364.
3. James Diego Vigil, *A Rainbow of Gangs* (Austin: University of Texas Press, 2002), 41.
4. Vigil, *A Rainbow of Gangs*, 41.

Chapter 5

1. Oscar Zeta Acosta, *The Autobiography of a Brown Buffalo* (New York: Vintage Books, 1972); Acosta, *The Revolt of the Cockroach People* (New York: Vintage Books, 1973).
2. Don Mitchell, "The Annihilation of Space by Law: The Roots and Implications of Anti-Homeless Laws in the United States," 29 *Antipode* 3 (1997), 303–335.
3. *People v. Horiuchi* 114 Cal. App. 415 (1931).
4. *People v. Jordan* 19 Cal. App. 3d 362 (1971).
5. *People v. Superior Court* (Caswell) 46 Cal. 3d 381 (1988).
6. *People v. Heitzman* 886 P. 2d 1229 (1994).
7. *In re Ball* 23 Cal. App. 3d 380, 387, 100 Cal. Rptr. 189 (1972).
8. Duncan Kennedy, "Legal Education as Training for Hierarchy," in Kairys, D. (ed.), *The Politics of Law*, 3d ed. (New York: Basic Books, 1998), 40–61.
9. *Marsh v. Alabama* 326 U.S. 501 (1946).
10. *Amalgamated Food Employees Union Local 590 v. Logan Valley Plaza* 391 U.S. 308 (1968).
11. *Lloyd v. Tanner* 407 U.S. 551 (1972).
12. *Hudgens v. NLRB* 424 U.S. 507 (1976).
13. *Brown v. Board of Education* 347 U.S. 483 (1954).
14. *Plessy v. Ferguson* 163 U.S. 537 (1896).
15. Mitchell Duneier, *Sidewalk* (New York: Farrar, Straus and Giroux, 1999).
16. Duneier, *Sidewalk*, 232.
17. Duneier, *Sidewalk*, 232.
18. Duneier, *Sidewalk*, 235.
19. Duneier, *Sidewalk*, 238.
20. Mitchell, "The Annihilation of Space by Law," 303–335.
21. Mitchell, "The Annihilation of Space by Law," 307.
22. Mitchell, "The Annihilation of Space by Law," 321.
23. Ralph Ellison, *The Invisible Man* (New York: Vintage Books, 1995), 3.
24. It should be noted that many mentally ill persons were released onto the streets beginning in the 1960s. See Christopher Jencks, *The Homeless* (Cambridge: Harvard University Press, 1994).
25. Amir B. Marvasti, *Being Homeless: Textual and Narrative Constructions* (Lanham, MD: Lexington Books, 2003), 10.
26. Albert Deutsch, *The Mentally Ill in America* (New York: Columbia University Press, 1945), 40.
27. Marvasti, *Being Homeless*, 10.
28. Marvasti, *Being Homeless*, 14.
29. Marvasti, *Being Homeless*, 21.
30. Marvasti, *Being Homeless*, 22.
31. Marvasti, *Being Homeless*, 21.
32. Julia Wardhaugh, "The Unaccommodated Woman: Home, Homelessness and Identity," 47 *The Sociological Review* 1(1999), 91.

33. Wardhaugh, "The Unaccommodated Woman," 93.
34. Wardhaugh, "The Unaccommodated Woman," 94.
35. Wardhaugh, "The Unaccommodated Woman," 94.
36. Wardhaugh, "The Unaccommodated Woman," 91.
37. Wardhaugh, "The Unaccommodated Woman," 93.
38. Stephen Wexler, "Practicing Law for Poor People," 79 *The Yale Law Journal* (1970), 1049.
39. Wexler, "Practicing Law," 1050.
40. Mitchell, "The Annihilation of Space by Law," 321.
41. Mitchell, "The Annihilation of Space by Law," 321.
42. Wexler, "Practicing Law," 1053.
43. For an interesting study of LA CAN, see Christine Elizabeth Pettit, "We Ain't Scared of No Mayor": LA's Skid Row Residents Fight for Their Right to the City," PhD dissertation, University of California, Riverside, 2010.

Chapter 6

1. Appearing "#977(a)" is when the lawyer is allowed to represent the client and the client does not need to appear in a misdemeanor case.
2. *Serna v. Superior Court* 40 Cal. 3d. 239, 248, n. 6, 219 Cal. Rptr. 420, 707 P2d 793 (1985); *Ogle v. Superior Court* 4 Cal. App. 4th 1007, 1017, 6 Cal. Rptr. 2d 205 (1992, 5th Dist.); *United States v. MacDonald* 456 U.S. 1, 7, 71 L. Ed. 696, 102 S. Cr. 1497 (1982).
3. *Doggett v. United States* 505 U.S. 647, 653 (1992); *Barker v. Wingo* 407 U.S. 514, 530–531 (1972).
4. *Doggett* 505 U.S. at 647.
5. *Ogle* 4 Cal. App. 4th 1007, 1020; *Barker v. Wingo* 407 U.S. at 532.
6. *Doggett* 505 U.S. at 655, fn. 1; *Stabio v. Superior Court* (1994) 21 Cal. App. 4th, 1488, 1490.
7. *Serna* 40 Ca1. 3d at 239 252–253.
8. *Serna* 40 Ca1. 3d at 530.
9. *Moore v. Arizona* 414 U.S. 25, 26 (1973); *Serna* 40 Ca1. 3d at 239, 252.
10. *Doggett* 505 U.S. at 647, 653.
11. *Barker* 407 U.S. at 531.
12. *Doggett*, 505 U.S. at 655.
13. *Doggett*, 505 U.S. at 655–656.
14. *People v. Almarez* 168 Cal. App. 3d 262, 266 (1985).
15. Because of space limitations, appendix B is not included here.
16. *People v. Ogle* 4 Cal. App. 4th 1007, 1021 (1992).
17. *Barker* 407 U.S. at 514, 515.
18. *Barker* 407 U.S. at 527, footnotes omitted.
19. *People v. Seely* 75 Cal. App. 2d 525, 526 (1946).
20. *Doggett* 505 U.S. at 654.

21. *Doggett* 505 at 655; *Stabio v. Superior Court* 21 Cal. App. 3d 1488, 1491 (1994).
22. *Serna* 40 Cal. 3d at 239, 250.
23. *Crockett v. Superior Court* 14 Cal. 3d 433, 442 (1975).
24. *People v. Hannon* 19 Cal. 3d 588 (1977); *People v. Butler* 36 Cal. App. 4th 455, 466 (1995).
25. *Serna v. Superior Court* 40 Cal. 3d 239, 249–250 (1985); *Scherling v. Superior Court* 22 Cal.3d 493, 504, fn. 8 (1978).
26. *People v. Martínez* 22 C4th 750, 94 CR2d 381 (2000).
27. *Jones v. Superior Court of Los Angeles County* 3 Cal.3d 734 (1970).
28. *People v. Pellegrino* 86 Cal. App. 3d 776 (1978).
29. *People v. Hill* 37 Cal.3e 491, 209 Cal. Rptr. 323 P. 2d 989 (1984).
30. *Ybarra v. Municipal Court* 162 Cal.App.3d 853, 208 Cal. Rptr. 783 (1984).
31. *Ogle* 4 Cal. App. 4th 1007, 1018.
32. Declaration of Alfredo Mirandé.
33. *Barker* 407 U.S. 514 [33 L. Ed. 2d 101, 92 S. Ct. 2182] (1972); *García v. Superior Court* 163 Cal. App. 3d 148, 209 Cal. Rptr. 205 (1984, 4th Dist); *Ibarra v. Municipal Court* 162 Cal. App. 3d 853, 208 Cal. Rptr. 783 (1984, 4th Dist).
34. *Ogle* 4 Cal. App. 4th at 1007, 1017; 6 Cal. Rptr. 2d at 205.
35. *Serna* 40 Cal. 3d at 252–253.
36. *People v. Martínez* 22 C4th 750, 94 CR2d 381 (2000).
37. *Barker* 407 U.S. 5141 33 L. Ed. 2d 101, 92 S. Ct. 2182.
38. Funding for Proposition 36 was withdrawn in 2006, but the jurisdiction in which this incident occurred was still implementing Proposition 36 for misdemeanor offenses.

Chapter 7

1. One of the definitions of "client" in the *Encarta* word dictionary is "a person or organization taking advice from an attorney, accountant, or other professional person."
2. The case went up to the U.S. Supreme Court because the city and Police Association unsuccessfully appealed the judgment, claiming that the lawyer's fees were excessive. Respondents were awarded $33,350 in compensatory and punitive damages. They also sought attorney's fees under the Civil Rights Attorney's Fees Awards Act of 1976, 42 U.S.C. 1988, in the amount of $245,456.25, based on 1,946.75 hours expended by their two attorneys at $125 per hour and 84.5 hours expended by law clerks at $25 per hour. Finding both the hours and rates reasonable, the District Court awarded respondents the requested amount, and the Court of Appeals and the Supreme Court affirmed. Thus, the attorneys were compensated for the hundreds of hours they had invested in successfully litigating the case. See *Riverside v. Rivera* 477 U.S. 561 (1986).
3. Sadly, I have learned that Bud's father has passed away.

4. This is called the six-pack method.

5. As a result, a number of cases—including some felonies—have been dismissed because they were tried prior to the speedy-trial statutory deadline and there were no courtrooms available. The Riverside County district attorney has appealed the dismissals to the California Supreme Court, arguing that rather than being dismissed, the cases should have been assigned by the supervising judge to family law, probate, or some other specialized civil courtroom. See Jim Miller, "Top Court Cool to DA in Rift Over Dismissals," *The Press-Enterprise*, September 8, 2010, A-1. In a 7–0 decision, the California Supreme Court rejected Riverside County District Attorney Rod Pacheco's bid to use specialized courts such as family law, juvenile, and probate to hear criminal cases at risk of being dismissed because of speedy trial guarantees. The decision held that while the statute gives priority to criminal cases over civil cases, it is not absolute. See Richard K. DeAtley, "Riverside County: Not All Courts for Criminal Cases," *The Press-Enterprise*, October 25, 2010, A-1.

6. For a misdemeanor, a case must be brought to trial within thirty days of the defendant's arraignment (forty-five if in custody) unless the person waives time. The time limit is sixty days for a felony.

Chapter 8

1. This is called the six-pack method.

2. *Batson v. Kentucky* 476 U.S. 79 (1986); *People v. Wheeler* 22 Ca1.3d 258 [148 Cal. Rptr. 890] (1978).

3. *Hernández v. New York* 500 U.S. 352 (1991).

4. In fact, my friend and mentor Juan Guerra said that if the jury is out for more than one hour, it is a moral victory for the defense.

5. Lucie E. White, "Subordination, Rhetorical Survival Skills, and Sunday Shoes: Notes on the Hearing of Mrs. G.," 38 *Buffalo Law Review* 1 (1990), 1-58.

6. Paulo Freire, *Pedagogy of the Oppressed* (New York: Herder and Herder, 1970), 28.

Chapter 9

1. *Pro se* is when a person represents himself as in an appeal. *In pro per* (or *in propia persona*) is also used to designate that a person is representing herself or himself in court.

2. Title VII of the Civil Rights Act of 1964 distinguishes between two types of discrimination: disparate treatment and disparate impact. Disparate treatment involves intentional discrimination against an individual; with this type of discrimination, the plaintiff must prove that there was an intent to discriminate by the defendants. In a situation of alleged disparate impact, one is claiming discrimination against a group (e.g., older persons, Hispanics), and the plaintiff simply needs to show a pattern and practice of discrimination—not that the discrimination was intentional.

3. Renato Rosaldo, *Culture and Truth* (Boston: Beacon, 1989), 2.
4. Rosaldo, *Culture and Truth*, 2.
5. Rosaldo, *Culture and Truth*, 11.
6. Sandra Cisneros, "The Genius of Creative Flexibility," *Los Angeles Times*, February 28, 1998, 2.

Chapter 10

1. I should mention that attorneys in cases like this would generally receive, at a minimum, thirty-three to forty percent of a settlement.

2. My son's name is Alejandro, but everyone calls him "Mano." He got the nickname as a child because his older sister Lucía could not say *hermano*, or "brother" in Spanish—she could only say "mano." (Interestingly, "mano" and "mana" are common nicknames for *hermano* and *hermana*, but my daughter arrived at the nickname independently.)

3. María Herrera-Sobek, *Chicano Folklore: A Handbook* (Greenwood Press, 2006), 233.

4. Oscar Zeta Acosta, *Revolt of the Cockroach People* (New York: Vintage Books, 1971), 22.

5. Acosta, *Revolt of the Cockroach People*, 22.

6. Paulo Freire, *Pedagogy of the Oppressed* (New York: Herder and Herder, 1970), 29.

Index

Acosta, Oscar "Zeta": autobiography of, 11; and Biltmore Six, 17; as "Brown Buffalo," 1, 10–11, 22, 74, 106, 240; *The Revolt of the Cockroach People*, 11, 20; as creative writer, 16–17, 20, 74, 241; and cultural nationalism, 16, 75, 240–241; and drugs, 11, 17; and gonzo journalism, 74; as legal aid lawyer, 11, 16; legal system and, 16, 18; and *The San Francisco Examiner*, 11; and High School Blowouts (walkouts), 11, 17; and testimonial satires, 75
Age discrimination, 21, 207, 213–218
Age Discrimination in Employment Act (ADEA), 213–215
Alamo Muffler, 146, 151–154, 157–160, 163, 172
Anti-homeless laws, 116–118, 122
Appearing § 977(a), 127–128, 135, 158, 199
Autopsy, 60–62

Barker v. Wingo (federal speedy trial), 130, 132–135
Batson v. Kentucky, 176
Bell, Derrick, 1, 8, 13–14

Biltmore Six, 17
Breach of contract, 213–214, 216, 231
Breach of covenant, 213–214

California Education Code: due process § 48911, 97, 101; hearing § 48914, 93; notice § 48918, 98, 102; possessing knife/dangerous object § 48900(b), 92, 96
Cartas, 2–4, 8, 223
Casa Blanca, 145
Cazares, Roy, 145
Chicano Movement: and Brown Buffalo, 10–11, 26, 74, 240–241; and Chicano Moratorium, 17; and Corky Gonzalez, 17; and Rubén Salazar, 17
Child abuse, 55–58, 61–71, 73, 77
Child Protective Services (CPS), 57, 66–67, 248n30
Cisneros, Sandra, 226–227
Clients: accessibility to, 125; attorney duty toward, 144; exchange of services with, 231, 233, 239; high profile, 6, 229, 241; networks, 125, 233; and rascuache lawyering, 239; retainer, 230, 233

Closing argument, 82–85, 190–193, 195
Complaint: age discrimination, 211–214, 217–218; breach of contract, 213–214; demurrer to, 110; and discovery, 218; domestic violence, 127–128; indecent exposure, 151; leave to amend, 222; and legal aid, 11; and preliminary hearing, 31, 60; and speedy trial, 133, 136; remand, 215; removal to federal court, 213; sexual harassment, 155
Conflict of interest, 23–24, 201–203, 234, 238, 242
Crenshaw, Geneva, 2, 11, 14
Crenshaw, Kimberlé, 2
Crenshaw, Rodrigo: background of, 2–4; chronicles, 9, 11, 240; and progressive law practice, 240; racial indeterminacy of, 4
CRIT, 9. *See also* Critical Legal Studies
Critical Legal Studies (CLS), 8–9, 240, 243n1
Critical Race Theory (CRT), 1–2, 4, 6, 8–11, 13–14, 240, 243n1; assumptions of, 1–2; definition of, 243n1; and narratives, 2; and practitioners, 2, 8, 11, 242; and rascuache lawyering, 14; and rebellious lawyering, 8, 240
Crusade for Justice, 17
Culp, Jerome McCristal, 1, 243n1
Cultural nationalism, 75

Dalton, Harold, 8–9
Day laborers, 105, 243n11
Debonaires, 145

Delgado, Richard, 1–4, 8–9, 11, 13–15
Demurrer, 110, 112, 121, 215, 222, 225
Dependency court, 57–58, 66–72, 215
Deposition, 216, 219
Disability discrimination, 170, 211, 232
Discovery, 147, 171–173, 186, 216–219, 237
Domestic violence: and attorney confidentiality, 87–88; case, 74–81; and child abuse, 55; complaint, 127–128, 135, 231, 233; and drugs, 138; and false imprisonment, 80, 85; investigator, 82; and male dominance, 75; victim recanting in, 79
Dr. Jekyll and Mr. Hyde behavior, 195–196
Drop-out, 103
Due process: California constitution, 92, 100; and expulsion, 94, 96, 102; and Fourteenth Amendment, 92, 100–101, 132; and speedy trial, 128, 133–134
Durkheim, Emile, 13, 120
Driving under the influence (DUI), 167–169, 175, 178, 181, 191, 193

East Los Angeles, 17
East Los Angeles Riots, 16–17, 168
El Sombrero Nightclub, 4, 21–22, 78, 143
Employment discrimination, 144, 211, 215–217, 225
Equal Employment Opportunity Commission (EEOC), 117, 216–217

Ethical issues, 199, 234–238
Evidentiary standards, 67–68
Exchange relations with clients, 86–87, 125, 137, 231–232, 239

Failure to appear warrant, 113, 127–128, 170–171
Fair Employment and Housing Act (FEHA), 215, 217
False generosity, 203, 240, 242
False imprisonment (California Penal Code § 236), 77, 80, 84–85
Field reports, 3, 115
Field sobriety test (FST), 169–170, 178–180, 183–186, 191–194
For cause jury challenges, 175–176
Fourth Street gang, 28–29, 34–35, 37–41, 43–46, 48, 52
Freire, Paulo, 203, 241

Gabriel, Fermina: background, 2–4; cartas (letters), 21–23, 47–48, 54–55, 66, 73–75, 104–106, 114–115, 138, 143–145, 163–167, 207–208, 223–227
Gang: culture, 168; enhancements, 27, 48, 52; Fourth Street, 23–24, 28–29, 34–53, 55, 58; injunction, 50–52, 156; Proposition 21 (Juvenile Crime Initiative), 246n1; Thirty-eighth Street (Sleepy Lagoon), 28, 34–35, 38; Twenty-second Street, 37–40, 44, 46, 49, 51, 53
González, Corky, 17
Gonzo journalism, 16, 74
Gordon, Robert W., 8
Grand Jury (biases in), 17

Greenfield, Alice, 34. *See also* Sleepy Lagoon

Hames-Garcia, Michael, 75
Harris, Angela, 1, 8, 243n1
Headhunters. *See* Ilongots
Hearsay, 31, 51–52, 60, 63–65, 84, 96, 156, 181
Hernández v. New York, 176
Hing, Bill Ong, 7–8, 13
Holmes, Oliver Wendell, 13
Homeless: advocate, 106–109; criminalization of, 114–119; invisibility of, 118–121; lawyering for, 122–124; placement of, 94, 104–106, 113, 243n11; as social problem, 119–120, 123; and trespassing, 104, 108–111, 116–117, 122–128; women, 120
Homophobia, 4, 9, 75
Hortwitz, Morty, 8, 9
Hudgens v. NLRB, 115

Ilongots, 223–224
Immigrant(s), 54–55, 71–74, 125, 187
Indecent exposure, 147–148, 151, 154, 173
In pro per, 252n1 (ch. 9)
Invisible Man (Ralph Ellison), 122

Johnson, Kevin R., 7
Judge Fricke, 33
Jury deliberation, 85, 196–198

LA CAN, 123, 250n43
La Raza newspaper, 17
LatCrit, 1–2, 4, 6, 9, 13, 243n6
Law and subordination, 104–105, 109, 143, 208

Law practice: community, 6; and Critical Legal Studies (CLS), 8; ethical issues in, 199, 234–238; and Oscar "Zeta" Acosta, 10–12, 233–234, 240–241; and the poor, 122–124; rascuache, 3, 5–6, 12–18, 144, 238–242; rebellious vision of, 6–12, 16, 104–105, 144–145; and storytelling, 9–10

Lawrence, Charles R. ("Chuck"), 8

Lawyering for social change, 5–12, 16, 104–105, 145, 202. *See also* Rebellious lawyering

Leybas, Henry, 34. *See also* Sleepy Lagoon

Lloyd, v. Tanner, 115

Logan Valley, 115

López, Gerald P., 6–7, 10–16, 104, 144–145, 240. *See also* Rebellious lawyering; Lawyering for social change

López, Ian F. Haney, 10

Los Altos (Jalisco), 75, 248n5

Macho (machismo), 75, 78, 261

Mario's Restaurant, 30, 148, 153–157, 163–164

Marsh v. Alabama, 115

Masculinity, 75, 87, 261

Matsuda, Mari, 8

Milagro Clinic, 4, 73–74, 143, 207

Mirandé, Alejandro, 3, 25, 50, 66, 155, 236, 253n2

Montoya, Margaret E., 8

Motion to set aside indictment (§ 995), 62–65

Movimiento Estudiantíl Chicano de Aztlán (MEChA), 107

"Mrs. G," 175, 202–203

Opening statement, 81, 177, 195

Paradigm, 12–14, 16, 255
Penal Code § 273(a), 56
Penal Code § 273d(a), 56–57
Penal Code § 1054, 147
People v. Wheeler, 176
Peremptory jury challenges, 175–176, 197
Pomelli, Ascancio, 7
preliminary alcohol screening (PAS), 170–180, 193
Preliminary hearing: in attempted murder, 30–47; bias, 58–61, 70–72; in child abuse, 60–65; description, 31, 60; due process in, 101; motion to set aside, 62–65; results of, 47–50
Pro bono: distinguished from rascuache, 238–242; law practice, 4, 11, 199–201, 229–230, 261; problems with, 229–231, 242
Promissory estoppel, 213–214
Proposition 21 (California Juvenile Crime Initiative), 246n1
Proposition 36 (California), 139, 168, 251n38
Proposition 115 (California), 31
Pro se, 215, 219

Rascuache, 1, 12–14, 16–17, 21–22, 73–74, 141–144, 163, 207, 228, 238–241
Reasonable doubt, 31–32, 67, 83–85, 175, 192, 197
Rebellious lawyering: class, 208; description, 6–12; and homeless, 123; and police abuse, 143–145; and rascuache lawyering, 13–18,

238–242; vision of, 6–12, 104, 144–145
Regnancy: approach to law, 6, 16, 24, 106; definition of, 6; and false generosity, 242; hierarchies, 230, 242; and rebellious lawyering, 16, 106, 207, 230, 238–239; view of clients, 143–144, 239
Remand, 213–215
Removal, 213–215
Ritzer, George, 13
Rodrigo Chronicles (Delgado), 2, 9–11, 15, 240
Rosaldo, Renato, 223–224

Serna (speedy trial) motion, 128–129, 133–134, 137
Sexism, 1, 9, 22, 74
Shibley, George, 33
Shopping center cases, 114–116
Sixth Amendment, 128–130, 132–133, 136
Skinner, B. F., 13
Six-pack method, 138, 149, 174, 252n4 (ch. 7), 252n1 (ch. 8)
Sleepy Lagoon, 32–34, 247n4 (ch. 1)
Standards of proof, 67–68, 70
Stavans, Ilan, 13
STEP Act (Penal Code § 186.22), 25–27, 44, 48–52
Storyteller (storytelling), 9–10, 12
Subpoena, 17, 70, 80, 158, 160, 240
Sudden Infant Death Syndrome (SIDS), 54
Summary judgment, 166, 219–220, 222, 225

Title VII (Civil Rights Act), 215, 252n2 (ch. 9)
Trespassing, 108–111, 116, 122–128
Thompson, Hunter S., 16, 74

Váldes, Francisco, 1, 243n1
Vigil, James Diego, 103
Voir dire, 173–177, 188

Walkouts (High School Blowouts), 11, 17
Western Plains College of Law, 47, 53, 58
Wexler, Stephen, 122
White, Lucie, 7, 13, 202
White privilege, 9, 243n1
Williams, Patricia, 2
Williams, Robert A., 9
Wrongful termination, 209, 211, 213–216, 225, 232

Xenophobia, 74

Yen, Y.C. James, 7
Youth, 32, 103, 105–106, 254

Zealous advocate: in child abuse, 57–60; for clients, 17–18, 57; DA as, 31; ethical issues, 73–74, 237–238; in expulsion hearing, 100, 103; Oscar Acosta as, 17–18; in rascuache lawyering, 121, 201, 228
Zoot-suit riots, 34. *See also* Sleepy Lagoon

About the Author

A native of Mexico City and the father of three children, Alfredo Mirandé is a professor of sociology and served as the chair of ethnic studies at the University of California, Riverside; he also taught at the Texas Tech University School of Law. He received a BS in social science from Illinois State University; MA and PhD degrees in sociology from the University of Nebraska; and a JD from Stanford University. Mirandé was a National Research Council fellow in ethnic studies at the University of California, Berkeley, and a Rockefeller fellow in sociology at Stanford University.

Mirandé's teaching and research interests are in Chicano sociology; gender and masculinity; constitutional law; civil rights; and the relationships among law, race, class, and gender. He is the author of *The Age of Crisis* (Harper & Row, 1975), *La Chicana: The Mexican American Woman* (co-authored with Evangelina Enríquez, University of Chicago Press, 1979), *The Chicano Experience: An Alternative Perspective* (University of Notre Dame Press, 1985), *Gringo Justice* (University of Notre Dame Press, 1987), *Hombres y Machos: Masculinity and Latino Culture* (Westview Press, 1997), and *The Stanford Law Chronicles: Doin' Time on the Farm* (University of Notre Dame Press, 2005). He has also published numerous journal articles on sociology, law, and ethnic studies.

Mirandé is a full-time teacher and researcher and has a limited, largely pro bono law practice specializing in criminal law and employment discrimination.

www.ingramcontent.com/pod-product-compliance
Lightning Source LLC
Chambersburg PA
CBHW031411290426
44110CB00011B/341